Partnering for Organizational Performance

Partnering for Organizational Performance

Collaboration and Culture in the Global Workplace

Elizabeth K. Briody and
Robert T. Trotter, II

ROWMAN & LITTLEFIELD PUBLISHERS, INC.
Lanham • Boulder • New York • Toronto • Plymouth, UK

ROWMAN & LITTLEFIELD PUBLISHERS, INC.

Published in the United States of America
by Rowman & Littlefield Publishers, Inc.
A wholly owned subsidiary of The Rowman & Littlefield Publishing Group, Inc.
4501 Forbes Boulevard, Suite 200, Lanham, Maryland 20706
www.rowmanlittlefield.com

Estover Road
Plymouth PL6 7PY
United Kingdom

British Library Cataloguing in Publication Information Available

Library of Congress Cataloging-in-Publication Data:

Briody, Elizabeth Kathleen.
  Partnering for organizational performance : collaboration and culture in the global
workplace / Elizabeth K. Briody and Robert T. Trotter, II.
    p. cm.
  Includes bibliographical references.
  ISBN-13: 978-0-7425-6013-0 (cloth : alk. paper)
  ISBN-10: 0-7425-6013-9 (cloth : alk. paper)
  ISBN-13: 978-0-7425-6014-7 (pbk. : alk. paper)
  ISBN-10: 0-7425-6014-7 (pbk. : alk. paper)
  1. Partnership. 2. Interorganizational relations. 3. Strategic alliances (Business) 4.
Globalization—Cultural aspects. I. Trotter, Robert T. II. Title.
  HD69.S8B756 2008
  658'.046—dc22   2007040882

Printed in the United States of America

∞™ The paper used in this publication meets the minimum requirements of American
National Standard for Information Sciences—Permanence of Paper for Printed Library
Materials, ANSI/NISO Z39.48-1992.

This book is dedicated to Marc, Andrew, Kathleen, and Anton,
for their love, good humor, and all those hot fudge sundaes,
and
to Sally, for her support in yet another hyper-focused period of our lives.

Contents

Section 3: Sustaining Partnering Relationships

Section 4: Lessons Learned

Preface

This book is a timely contribution to the challenges that thoughtful leaders in business, academia, and communities are facing. A wide range of partnerships is developing in response to changes in the global environment. The global landscape has shifted in numerous ways. The professional workforce is located in emerging economies as well as in dominant ones. Nations in emerging economies search for models and partnerships that can help them expand their technical and social infrastructures. Corporations readily hire people who live and work many time zones away. An expanding global labor force continues to segment work by country, work that is carried out in some cases by partnering firms, subcontractors, or employees involved in distributed work. The increasing practice of operating 24/7 means that organizations not only provide customer service day and night, they also hand off work from one time zone to the next. Given this global environment, it makes sense that an array of organizational configurations has been created to set and achieve goals.

This book paints a picture of how partnerships function and become effective. It provides an overview of the dynamics and life cycles of partnerships. There are eight case studies, each of which describes the cultural issues within specific partnerships, thereby providing insight into the challenges that organizations and institutions face in making alliances work well. The cases probe and reveal the invisible cultural dynamics that can make or break such alliances.

This book will attract audiences from several professional communities: community leaders who partner with a variety of institutions to achieve a specific outcome; business leaders who develop partnerships as part of their plans for strategic growth; people who work in partnerships within corporations; people who work within smaller institutional entities that partner with larger ones; consulting firms and scholarly practitioners who seek to understand the partnerships of their client firms, as well as their relationships with one another and with client firms; business theorists who seek to understand how partnerships can improve a business' chances of success; anthropologists and other social scientists who view institutional forms and relationships as new "social formations" in which human beings craft new ways of working together; and professors who use case-study materials in business schools and graduate schools.

This book is a rich offering of theory, practice, and case, and is powerful in its sharp focus on partnerships. It provides a coherent and explicit theoretical framework rooted in culture theory, which embraces complexity and identifies multi-layered systems. It provides insights regarding both product and process outcomes of partnerships. It includes a coherent approach to its case studies, which include cases ranging from the Saudi government to corporations, universities, and consulting firms. This book contains explicit descriptions of the mixed-methods approach that not only unveils untapped dimensions of partnerships, but also clarifies how social science methods produce insight behind the veil. It has a set of models and metaphors of structures (e.g., institutional, social network) and dynamics of partnerships that provide a dynamic view of the life cycle of partnerships provides historical contexts in which they operate, and insights of many participants beyond those of leaders, producing lessons learned with practical implications.

Building bridges between business and the academy has become important for a number of reasons. The fast pace of change today has forced many institutional entities to find ways to operate effectively despite economic turbulence. It is difficult to step back and evaluate in depth when there is intense pressure to keep moving forward. While many institutions take the time to focus on lessons learned, those lessons are often derived from the contextual details of specific projects or initiatives. Books such as this one can identify lessons from several cases in several contexts and thereby become a reliable point of reference.

In addition, when it is time to make decisions as to whether an idea or practice is working, the basis for such decisions often rests on expectations under pressure—did we produce what we thought we would produce this year, this quarter, this time? Identifying significant dimensions of complex partnerships will be enhanced by having some of these dimensions in hand.

I spoke recently with a vice president of a large, high-tech organization. She told me about her frustration over a corporate decision to pull back from its global strategy, a strategy that she had helped build. Her company was evaluating the success of its Indian and Eastern European teams using the criteria of how well those teams "acted like us." While there were many managers in the firm who had years of experience working and living in these countries, the insights they gained from their experiences were not included in the higher-level corporate decisions. What information is available to corporate leaders who want to evaluate the success or failure of such partnerships? And, perhaps more significantly, to what extent do those leaders have the opportunity to learn about the dimensions of success that they might incorporate into their decision making? In what situations might such leaders be exposed to leading-edge insight?

Institutions succeed and fail on the basis of shared understandings and practices. Shared approaches and getting everyone to work together are important, if simplified versions of what it takes to succeed. Certain metaphors reveal intent, while others encourage fragility rather than strength. Indeed, the notion of success is often based on two things: having a robust strategy in place and having smart people to execute it. This book reveals what is missing from that equation: the social organization of institutions. These dimensions include elements such as transition (partnerships that end may have been successes, not failures); exchange systems (partnerships operate in the market economy and also within internal systems of reciprocity that shape dynamics and behavior); transformation (the outcomes and processes map onto existing cultural complexities); and integration (the partnering players must find ways to integrate their efforts or they will fail). These dimensions are important for creating sustainable organizations.

The social nature of institutions provides a cultural, iterative, and cognitive context in which smart people can thrive and good strategies can be realized. This volume offers depth and sharp thinking with its frameworks, modeling, cases, and lessons.

Patricia Sachs
Tempe, Arizona; January 2007

Acknowledgments

Many people worked hard to make this book possible. We would like to thank the contributors for their interest in partnership culture, for their willingness to develop appropriate partnership metaphors for their cases, and for their overall enthusiasm. Their efforts have made this an exciting and rewarding endeavor.

We are grateful to the management at General Motors Research and Development (GM R&D) for its strong intellectual and fiscal support of this project. Alan Taub, executive director, championed our research and the applications derived and implemented, as well as the development of the book manuscript. In addition, several former and current GM R&D directors supported our efforts, including Jan Aase, Steve Holland, Gary McDonald, and Patrick Popp. GM R&D funded a contract with Northern Arizona University—enabling Bob Trotter to participate in the research—and supported Elizabeth Briody's time during the research and writing of this book.

Finally, we would like to thank Rosalie Robertson for accepting the book and Alan McClare, executive editor at Rowman & Littlefield Publishers, for all of his advice, help, and active support in moving the book into production. Additional acknowledgments are presented in the various chapters.

Section 1

PARTNERSHIP FRAMEWORKS AND MODELS

1

Framing the Partnership Experience

Elizabeth K. Briody and Robert T. Trotter, II

INTRODUCTION

This book is designed to be an alternative and a counter argument to the overwhelming focus on conflict and dissonance in both the American culture and in international partnerships (cf. Yan and Zeng 1999; Park and Russo 1996).[1] Conflict is certainly an important topic, and conflict theory has contributed substantially to understanding cultural processes. Neither conflict resolution nor the absence of conflict, however, guarantees cooperation or positive relationships. Positive relationships must be actively pursued. Our research strongly supports the idea that partnerships are the glue that holds social systems together in spite of the effect that diversity and differences have on human systems. Collaboration and partnerships are not simply systems that are low in conflict or low in diversity of viewpoint. Many thrive in spite of those factors, and a few prosper because of those factors.

Partnerships are complex cultural entities with fascinating beginnings, life cycles, outcomes, and long-term effects. They emerge, maintain, transform, and transition in response to conditions in the external environment, as well as to conditions internal to the partnership itself. They have a definable life cycle and are typically designed to fulfill a particular mission; their value is commonly assessed in terms of how well they accomplish their goals by producing results that enhance partner interests.

This book focuses on the cultural dimensions of partnerships, an emphasis that only occasionally appears in the vast partnership literature. Partnership studies typically direct attention to particular aspects of partnership functioning such as motives (Shortell et al. 2002), learning (Tsang 1999), and performance (Duysters et al. 1999). We prefer to focus attention on the most salient forces influencing partnering dynamics, structure, and outcomes so that we understand partnership culture holistically.

We propose an examination of partnerships based on a holistic model of how they work, using a multi-method cultural models-and-systems approach. Cultural-models theory provides a framework that allows us to perform a much-needed integration of the disparate elements of partnerships. It is a natural midrange theory outgrowth (Trotter 1997) of both general-systems theory (Laszlo 2001) and cognitive anthropology (D'Andrade 1995). General-systems theory provides a framework for understanding both the structure and dynamics of organizational systems, while cognitive anthropology provides a number of solid theoretical and methodological approaches to uncovering the deep content and cognitive organization of those systems. The resulting cultural models can be exclusively ethnographic in nature, such as the primary approaches used by Kleinman (1980) or by Holland and Quinn (1987) in producing cultural models within the context of medical anthropology. Alternately they can take a strongly probabilistic and quantitative direction such as those utilized by Weller (1998), Weller and Romney (1988), and Romney et al. (1986), as well as by Boster (1986) or D'Andrade and Strauss (1992) in such diverse areas as cultural ecology or psychological anthropology.

We assume that any human group, such as a partnership, is culturally organized, as opposed to ad hoc or chaotic. Partners follow agreed-upon cultural rules (Meerwarth et al. 2005), have a structural organization that can be described as interacting parts of the whole (Sengir et al. 2004), and have a set of dynamic elements consisting of beliefs, values, and behaviors that organize the structure and provide a mental map of how to make the whole system work (Briody et al. 2004). Using this three-part approach, we can describe the core elements of partnerships, as well as the variations in rules, structure, and cognitive aspects that are caused by either the external environment or other cultural processes. We can elicit both consensus and variability within and between cultural models of partnerships. The end result is a model that is sensitive to cross-cultural variability as well as to intracultural change through time.

Our approach targets the day-to-day behaviors of partnership participants, along with their expectations and assumptions about how partnerships should work. We define culture as the assumptions, expectations, beliefs, social structures, and values guiding behavior. The worldviews and actions of partnership participants position us to explore the interface between partnership dynamics and structure (called for by Selsky and Parker 2005) as the partnerships change over time.

A Focus on Culture

The book's focus on cultural processes reflects one of the current gaps in the partnership literature (Wong et al. 2005; Geppert and Clark 2003). Partnerships are the central focus of our explorations and explanations, though we recognize the blending of systems of exchange (e.g., reciprocity, market) in partnering relationships (Trotter and Briody 2006). Our cultural model enables us to highlight the complexity of these collaborations, and, at the same time, simplify this complexity so that the key cultural patterns for the observed behavior and outcomes can be specified. We follow a general culture-theory approach that underscores four historical and current theoretical emphases in the anthropological and other social science literature (cf. Harris 1968; Bernard 2005). The four areas of theory development that are particularly relevant to our partnership cases include evolutionary theory, structural theory, cognitive theory, and symbolic theory. This culture-theory approach has been particularly useful in those areas where there have been recent developments of midrange-theory constructs that can be tested and applied to current issues (Trotter 1997).

Anthropological *evolutionary theory* provides a framework for understanding change through time. It includes midrange theory on creativity, innovation, life cycles, cross-cultural conflict, and the general theory of culture change. *Structural theory* has its roots in a structural-functionalist movement in anthropology, but it has been transformed in modern times to provide an analytical approach to understanding the structures and processes that organize all human systems. Structural theory includes general-systems theory, systems dynamics, role theory, theories of power and hierarchy, organizational theory, and many of the current forms of modeling theory that can be used to understand cultural differences in the ways that people organize critical relationships in their lives.

Cognitive theory allows us to explore how culture is reflected in the ways people organize their thinking, how they create systematic shared categories of culture (i.e., cultural domains), and how they then use those domains to interact with the world around them. The primary midrange theories that can be applied to partnerships include a general cultural-models approach, cultural typologies theory, and cultural-learning theories (e.g., enculturation, acculturation), to name a few. *Cultural symbolic theory* is also prominent in many of the partnership case studies and focuses predominantly on "cultural meanings" and the communication of those meanings within a cultural context. The midrange theories described in this area include cultural values clarification processes (e.g., the meaning of the objects exchanged in a reciprocity system), cultural communication (e.g., language, cross-cultural barriers to communication, ethnocentrism), and, particularly important to the book, the use of metaphors in cultural settings.

Our long-term goal is to address all four of these areas of theory in our elaborated cultural models of partnerships. However, specific case studies (coupled with the space limitations for the book) produce individual cases that are most likely to emphasize one of the four areas of culture theory over the others, while generally acknowledging that the others are important to understanding the holistic characteristics of partnerships as well.

The cases emphasize induction, in part due to the need for a fresh look at partnerships. Despite its obvious benefits (e.g., thick description, conceptual development, theory generation), induction is rarely the orientation of choice by partnership researchers. As a result, the dynamics of partnerships are often "concealed" (Parkhe 1993), presumably because they were never uncovered in the first place. The book's mix of ethnographic methods (e.g., observation, discussion, stories, documentary evidence, experience) is helpful in illustrating the richness and complexity of cross-cultural and cross-organizational interactions (Yan and Zeng 1999), especially since it is complemented by the use of social-network analysis (recommended by Brannen and Salk 2000), historical emphasis and analysis (Mowery 1998), and statistical analyses, which a significant portion of the partnership studies incorporates (e.g., Doz et al. 2000).

The partnership examples in chapter 2 and sections 2 and 3 of this volume are longitudinal studies—a type of research that is not well represented in the partnership literature (Selsky and Parker 2005; Wong et al. 2005). The case studies also include a variety of perspectives from among the partnership participants; by contrast, the bulk of the partnership studies tend to capture only leadership views (e.g., Vangen and Huxham 2003; Yang and Taylor 1999). We also present cases encompassing a wide variety of partnership environments and contexts to get at the underlying principles of partnering.

Defining Partnerships

Definitions of "partnerships" vary widely by discipline and theoretical orientation with no clear and uncontested definition. Partnerships are alternately defined as a "joint working arrangement where partners are otherwise independent bodies cooperating to achieve a common goal" (Dowling et al. 2004, 310), a strategic alliance or "long-term cooperative arrangement between two or more independent firms that engage in business activities for mutual economic gain" (Tsang 1999, 212), and a coalition or "interorganizational, cooperative, and synergistic working alliances whereby individuals are united in a shared purpose and shared decision-making to influence an external institution or target" (Boydell and Volpe 2004, 358). Some researchers have argued that the meaning of the term "partnership" has become "elusive" (Tomlinson 2005, 1169) and therefore problematic for analysis (Cravens and Shipp 1993).

Our solution to this epistemological confusion is to create a definition by constructing a model of partnerships. In general, the key features of virtually all partnership definitions include cooperation, collaboration, and synergy, as well as some agreement on their raison d'être and goals, and an expectation of benefit from their joint work. For the purpose of this book, we use the term "partnership" in the broadest sense to comprehend various types of arrangements (e.g., alliances, networks) in which specific individuals, groups, organizations, and agencies set out to act collectively. Our definition includes both dynamic and structural components and outcomes:

> Collaborative arrangements in which participants enter into relationships (the dynamic component), combine their resources, time, and expertise through the various roles they play (the structural component), and work toward the creation of new knowledge, products, and services (outcomes).

Rising Partnership Interest

In the last twenty-five years, there has been a proliferation of partnerships around the world; these collaborations that cross all sectors (Dowling et al. 2004; Yan and Zeng 1999). Much of the partnership literature focuses on the relationship between two partnering entities (e.g., two firms, one firm with one nonprofit), though there are some examples of multiple organizations partnering across sectors (e.g., Gray 2004; Smith and Beazley 2000; Lowndes and Skelcher 1998).

Some of the current partnership proliferation can be attributed to changes in public policy. At least since the late 1970s, U.S. federal policy has encouraged collaboration among universities, firms, and government labs (Cobb and Rubin 2006; Ham and Mowery 1998), along with privatization of public-service delivery (Brinkerhoff 2002a). Governmental policy initiatives have led to a rise in cross-sectoral collaboration in such locations as the United Kingdom (Turpin 1999) and in Australia (Dowling et al. 2004).

Organizational interests are also at play. Motivations include anticipated benefits of new knowledge (Child and Faulkner 1998); enhancement of effectiveness and efficiency (Brinkerhoff 2002b; Hagedoorn 1993); community involvement to secure resources (Smith and Beazley 2000; Stone 1993); opportunities to reduce barriers to new markets (Dacin and Hitt 1997), access to a partner's technologies (Kogut 1988), gains in financial support (Lee 1996); and a change in perspective on the role of the state, private sector, and society at large in "economic life and social provision" (Johnson and Wilson 2006, 72).

EXPLORING THE CULTURE OF PARTNERSHIPS

Partnerships merit investigation because there is a growing interest in addressing fundamental, basic-research questions and in providing insight into the practical dimensions of partnering.

A question asked by both academics and practitioners concerns the high failure rates associated with partnerships (Gill and Butler 2003). Organizational and cultural differences among the partners largely explain the high failure rates—upwards of sixty percent, with some as high as eighty percent (Duysters et al. 1999; Meschi 1997). Many researchers argue that partnering success is contingent upon the degree of "mutuality" among the partners, including "mutual dependence," commitment to partnership goals, and "value balance," whereby partners derive equal benefit (Vereecke and Muylle 2006; Brinkerhoff 2002a). When these conditions hold, partnerships tend to last (Wong et al. 2005; Austin 2000) and perform (Kanter 1994); when such conditions are not present, partnerships tend to weaken or fail (Cobb and Rubin 2006).

The tendency among many partnership researchers has been to conceptualize and compare partnerships in terms of an ideal set of characteristics. "Trust based" (Bachmann 2001) and collaborative arrangements (Cheadle et al. 2005; Vangen and Huxham 2003) seem to represent the gold standard; anything deviating from it is viewed poorly, without any particularly strong evidence that all variation is harmful. Yet actual partnering practice may or may not approximate the ideal (Johnson and Wilson 2006; Weber et al. 2005), or it may fluctuate between the ideal and some other state (Tomlinson 2005). One solution to this dichotomy has been to map attributes of partnership practice onto some scalar dimensions (Brinkerhoff 2002a). Our preference is to examine the evolving partnership culture from the perspective of the partnership participants whose behavior varies.

Partnering Dynamics

Partnering dynamics is defined as the behavioral dimension of partnership activity. It represents the practices, processes, and strategies employed by the participants, the perceptions they hold of each other and of the work in which they are engaged, and the symbolism generated through the partnering activities.

Partnership researchers have emphasized the need for developing and nurturing relationships (Büchel and Killing 2002; Lorange et al. 1992). Attention has been focused on the element of trust—for example, as a substitute for contractual control (Lui and Ngo 2004), and as an alternative to power in managing a partnering relationship (Tomlinson 2005). Commitment and mutual benefit matter (Stuart 1997; Mowery 1988), as do the presence of cooperative goals (Wong et al. 2005). Partnership symbols, stories, and examples provide important clues about expectations and meaning (Kelly et al. 2004; Vaara 2002).

Cultural investigations illustrate areas of congruence and consensus as well as areas of concern and tension (Briody et al. 2004; Olie 1994). They also highlight the development of common frames of reference for problems and solutions (Gray 2004) and "sense making" in which participants engage (Brannen and Salk 2000), such as decision making, priority setting, and preferences. Exploring these dynamics illustrates the difficulties of working cross-organizationally and cross-culturally, since partners have a dual set of responsibilities—to their own organizations and to their partnership colleagues. Indeed, intraorganizational conflicts may dominate over interorganizational conflicts (Nordin 2006).

Partnership Structure

Understanding partnership culture involves exploring partnership structures. We define *partnership structure* as the arrangement of relationships created to accomplish partnership work. Partnership structure entails some division of labor by role (e.g., by function, skill set) and a status hierarchy (e.g., level of decision-making authority, level of expertise). The functions performed by key players have been documented in social-network theory (Borgatti 2003; Borgatti 2002). A central cluster or core of members has been found to play a critical role in maintaining partnerships (Storck and Hill 2000). Partnership structure also includes personnel (i.e., size, composition), technological, and/or monetary resources.

A temporal dimension of partnership structure is manifested in two ways. First, researchers have identified a partnership life cycle with three to five stages corresponding to the creation, development, and maturation of joint work activity (Child and Faulkner 1998; Ring and Van de Ven 1994). At some point in the partnership's life cycle, there may be a shift in conditions external to the partnership and/or in the circumstances associated with one or more of the partners (Bruce et al. 1995; Parkhe 1991). Environmental changes could lead subsequently to changes in partnership structure (e.g., modification of existing partnership). Our view of structure includes the concept of transition in a partnering relationship, as well as the possibility of future partnership activity.

Partnership Outcomes

We identify two types of partnership outcomes. *Partnership-product outcomes* are the goods, services, and processes generated by partnership participants as they engage in their collaborative work. Products and services represent tangible creations or results of partnering interactions such as "better services or improved health for users" (Dowling et al. 2004, 311), publications and research dollars (Bloedon and Stokes 1994), customer satisfaction (Lambert et al. 1999), and financial performance (Gulati et al. 1994).

Partnership-process outcomes are intangibles measuring how the joint work progresses. They are typically viewed as contributing to the more tangible product outcomes (Dowling et al. 2004; Cravens and Shipp 1993). Examples of process outcomes include "level and quality of community involvement" (Smith and Beazley 2000), the development of trust and cooperation among counterparts (Lui and Ngo 2004; Storck and Hill 2000; Das and Teng 1998), and the creation of an agreed-upon set of ways for working together (Adler 1997). There is a clear need to assess and address both types of outcomes in our exploration of partnerships.

Assessing partnership outcomes can be difficult. Many firms apply standard accounting and measurement systems for evaluating partnerships—measures that are misaligned with partnership goals (Gulati et al. 1994). Because it may take years for partnerships to yield financial results (Dowling et al. 2004), an alternate approach considers the extent to which partnerships achieved their stated objectives—based on participant responses (Cheadle et al. 2005; Yang and Taylor 1999). Subjective evaluations are helpful in providing the partnership with direct, near-term feedback that is customized with respect to partnership goals.

FRAMING PARTNERSHIP INVESTIGATIONS

Our framework for exploring partnership culture is illustrated in figure 1.1. Our Cultural Model of Partnering consists of the effect of the external cultural environment—defined as the economic, political, technological, social, and ideological forces—on the partnership (as seen in the larger arrow on the left). The external cultural environment affects two key inputs (dynamics and structure) and their associated output (outcomes). These three internal part-

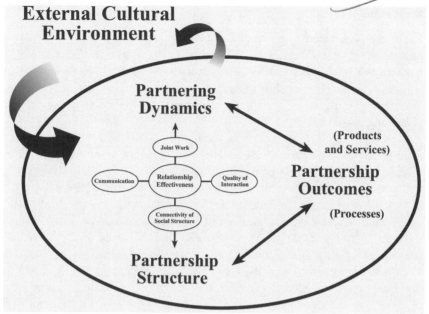

Figure 1.1. A Cultural Model of Partnering

nership elements exhibit a combined countereffect on the external cultural environment (as seen in the smaller arrow at the top of the graphic). We view the relationship between the external cultural environment and the partnership as an open, fluid, and continually evolving system.

Our model focuses attention on the dynamic relationships that link the behavioral aspects of partnering with the structural components. The key dynamic variables include communication, joint work, and quality of interaction, while connectivity of social structure represents partnership structure. We discuss both the relationship dynamics and evolutionary aspects of the model in chapter 2.

MECHANISMS TO CONVEY THE PARTNERSHIP EXPERIENCE

Because of the exploratory nature of inductive work, we have deliberately included a diverse set of partnership types in this volume to explore common partnership patterns. This decision to opt for partnership heterogeneity creates some interesting challenges for producing an integrated work. We knew that we would have to find mechanisms to integrate understanding and coherence across the partnership cases. Toward that end, we settled on two devices: metaphors and a common case study format.

Metaphors

Each case is depicted by a metaphor to characterize and explain its evolving partnership culture. We follow in the tradition of Hall (1959, 1966, 1983), Geertz (1973), Gannon (2001), Gannon and Associates (1994), and others who have used the metaphor to identify values, attitudes, and behaviors of specific cultural groups. Metaphors have not been applied systematically to partnering relationships.

Metaphorical applications have both strengths and weaknesses. One strength is the metaphor's association with different levels of abstraction (Glucksberg 2003) and "openness of meaning" (Cornelissen 2005, 753) so that parallels with partnership culture can be drawn. A metaphor's compactness and its vividness (Ortony 1975) have the potential to express the partnership's essence. Relevant partnership characteristics can be packaged in a memorable image from which discoveries can be made and connections drawn. In that sense, understanding and learning can occur.

Despite the numerous benefits, metaphors have been criticized—most notably because of their imprecision, uncertain and ambiguous meaning, and poor reliability in communication and interpretation (Ramsay 2004). The vagueness of metaphorical boundaries contributes to "confusion" (Ortony 1975, 52). This critique has guided our analysis of partnering metaphors appearing in chapter 11 where we ask what insights about partnership culture can be gained by comparing the metaphors from the individual cases.

Using a Common Case-Study Format

A second device we use is a case study format for all of the cases. It includes the problem focus, the contextual aspects of the partnership that are important in understanding partnership dynamics and structure, a description of how the partnership participants work together, partnership outcomes and accomplishments, and the insights the case offers for theory and application.

Case studies are highly useful when researchers want to understand a particular set of phenomena as a whole. Some researchers emphasize a focus on the local or particular (Stake 1995). Others argue that the case study serves as an explanatory device, addressing how-and-why questions, with the goal of developing theoretical propositions and contributing to the expansion of theory (Yin 2003). Researchers must identify "significant features on which comparison with others in the class can be made," however, and then show that comparison (Denscombe 2003, 36-37). In chapter 11, we derive a set of lessons learned from a cross-case comparison of partnership elements. The lessons learned are constructed so that they can be turned easily into testable propositions.

Each of the cases is strongly informed by ethnographic theory and methods. The field experiences provide opportunities for the researcher to get as close as possible to the "emic" (i.e., insider) understanding of the partnership (Pike 1966). Because the cases include insider understanding analyzed within an "etic" (i.e., social science) framework, we argue that it is possible to gain useful insights from the inside out that are comparable across cases and useful in the generation of lessons learned and testable propositions.

LEARNING FROM THE PARTNERING EXPERIENCE

Learning is an important focus of the organizational literature generally (c.f., Argyris 1999; Senge 1990) and partnership literature specifically (Iles and Yolles 2002). Acquiring knowledge within a partnership context occurs in several ways, including direct participation and conscious attempts to seek and absorb specific kinds of knowledge from one's partner (Huber 1991) and about one's partner (Schuler 2001). Partnering lessons can also be passed on from the experiences of others—lessons that have the potential to modify intended plans or behavior.

Researchers have identified learning characteristics useful for partnership integration and maintenance. For example, some "harmonizing" or "blending" is viewed as essential to developing and sustaining effective working relationships (Adler 1997). The capacity to learn and adapt to changing environmental circumstances—referred to as "organizational fitness" (Beer et al. 2005, 447)—helps partners cope with the future. Partnership "fitness," requires ongoing coordination and cooperation with one's partners in order to reassess environmental turbulence and uncertainty, implement any necessary changes, and then learn from the experience.

Examining partnerships from within offers important opportunities to learn about key cultural processes and human relationships in general—particularly from the perspective of a collaborative approach to cultural understanding. The model, case studies, and lessons learned offer opportunities for those engaged in active partnerships—whether as practitioners or researchers—to understand and compare successful partnership designs. They provide a chance for those just starting out to use the lessons-learned sections of our cases to initiate, maintain, modify, or successfully exit a partnering experience. They also offer those who are interested in partnerships the opportunity to explore various facets of partnership culture.

Partnerships provide a window into American national culture from which we can observe elements of societal change. We emphasize this particular national culture since at least one of the partners from each case is based in the U.S. Consequently we see evidence of American influence in the motivations, expectations, assumptions, and behaviors associated with these cases. In this context, partnerships are not simply collaborative entities designed altruistically for a larger collective good. From the standpoint of American national culture, and perhaps other cultures as well, at least some of the individual partners' goals must be accomplished (Dacin and Hitt 1997). This condition of partner goal satisfaction is consistent with the American concept of success—including mobility based on hard work and the importance of material gain (Hall and Hall 1989; Tocqueville 1990 [1840]). It is also consistent with the cornerstone of American culture— individualism—in which a single partner acts as a collective unit with the intention of accomplishing its specific goals.

At the same time, we see that American culture is undergoing a significant restructuring. The role model of the self-made man (Hall and Hall 1989) seems to be fading into the background as collaborative endeavors become increasingly common within and between community, organizational, and institutional contexts. The shift from the single entity (e.g., university, community group) working independently to complete its goals and objectives to multiple entities working together to accomplish their goals and objectives is transforming the cultural landscape. The way in which this transformation is occurring, the issues associated with it, and its outcomes are reshaping how Americans and others think about work and working relationships.

We also must consider the role of competition within this changing cultural scene. Individual entities such as firms are no longer solely in competition with one another to attract customers or to gain market share. With the advent of partnering, organizations are entering into various kinds of cooperative agreements. These agreements enable the partners to link up with those who have complementary skills, expertise, and the like, thereby positioning themselves to secure benefits that may not have been otherwise possible (Yang and Taylor 1999). Thus, to remain competitive, to achieve one's goals, and to succeed generally, cooperation is increasingly necessary. This book documents these transformations, along with the adaptations required by partnership participants as they break new ground, with new partners and within an increasingly popular organizational form.

NOTE

1. We appreciate the excellent support we received from the GM R&D Library while writing this chapter. Karen Sutton and Laura Nielsen were particularly helpful in acquiring reference materials for us while Heather Simmons and Karen Sutton developed the book's index. We also appreciate Maria DeKimpe's time and effort in combining and formatting all the citations in the References.

2

The Cultural Processes of Partnerships

Robert T. Trotter, II, Gülcin H.Sengir, and Elizabeth K. Briody

INTRODUCTION

This chapter presents an empirically-tested cultural model of collaborative partnerships.[1] Our ethnographic research on partnerships explored several critical foci that are subsequently identified, defined, elaborated, and confirmed in our functional partnership model. Our initial formulation of a collaborative partnership model was stimulated by a request from General Motors (GM) management to identify an ideal cultural model for establishing and maintaining successful research-institution partnerships. Our research on private-sector partnerships indicated that partnership success is largely dependent upon the development and maintenance of strong and productive relationships between the partners (Meerwarth et al. 2005; Meerwarth 2004; Sengir et al. 2004; Trotter et al. 2004).

The broader partnership literature also supports the importance of the quality of relationships on partnership success (Child and Faulkner 1998; Ring and Van de Ven 1994). Subsequently we developed our model by framing data from ethnographic (Trotter and Schensul 1998), social-network, and systems-dynamics modeling techniques (cf. Sengir et al. 2004; Trotter et al. 2004) with cultural or ethnographic theory, including a new exploration of reciprocity within the context of a predominantly market economic system (Trotter and Briody 2006). The resulting model of collaborative partnerships identifies the critical elements that shape the structure, dynamics, meanings, rules, roles, and life cycles of successful partnerships tested within the context of the structure and dynamics of GM's research-institution partnerships, referred to as Collaborative Research Labs (CRLs).

COLLABORATIVE RESEARCH LABORATORIES

In the late 1990s, GM Research and Development (R&D) embarked on a formal strategy for creating collaborative ventures. In these CRLs, researchers from GM R&D were paired with counterparts at a prestigious university. Four partnerships had been established at U.S. universities by 2002 when our research was initiated. The stated purpose of these partnerships was to leverage an important set of talents, skills, knowledge, and research on cutting-edge business and industrial issues. Each partnership was created to yield benefits to both GM and the university—with specific technical goals in mind—and was organized and managed to maximize learning and research output.

Our research group had anecdotal evidence that the CRL partnerships had gotten off to a good start and were accomplishing many of the goals they had set. At the same time, it was clear that the process was being conducted in an ad hoc manner and that very little was known about the partnerships in general or about their collaborative trajectories. One question that arose was whether they had a predictable structure and function, and whether those conditions changed in predicable ways over time. Since GM R&D management was considering extending existing partnerships and forming new ones, our research group was asked to investigate the existing partnerships and to develop an empirically based understanding and set of expectations for evaluating current and future partnerships.

The first lab partnership, GM-Theta University,[2] provided us with a preliminary model of the key stages that labs go through and the partnership transitions that are necessary in the latter part of the partnership cycle. The impetus for this first lab initially came from the university side of the partnership as an extension of existing research relationships between GM and the university.

The second lab relationship, GM-Beta University, provided us with the opportunity to investigate both the early stages of partnerships and gather in-depth data on some of the transitions they faced. GM R&D initiated this second lab by sending an invitation letter to several universities where faculty members were engaged in research projects that had potential applications for GM R&D. The final decision to develop a relationship with a second university was based on three considerations: (1) previous experience that GM researchers had in working with faculty members on GM contract projects, (2) the university's expertise in working on industrial problems, and (3) the types of research projects the faculty members proposed in different technical areas.

This lab instituted a set of scheduled "retreats" as one aspect of the relationship, which was diffused to the other labs. These retreats have kindled significant interest among GM researchers to visit campuses to attend formal presentations and to interact informally with their university counterparts either prior to or following these sessions. This lab also provided valuable information on roles and leadership change.

The negotiations to establish the third collaboration (GM-Iota) produced a key change in the orientation to these labs by relabeling the lab as "collaborative," rather than using the term "Satellite Laboratory," which was an important symbolic change from the original label used to describe the initial two CRLs. One GM leader said, "In the negotiation process, they [the faculty] objected to the phrase 'Satellite Research Labs.' They felt it reflected a sense of them being subservient." An Iota University leader stated:

> Iota negotiators thought that the term "Satellite" had the connotation of incorrectly implying ownership of the lab by GM. The GM negotiators agreed and changed the term "Satellite" to "Collaborative," a change that the Iota negotiators welcomed.

After this terminology change was proposed, all of the labs adopted this new phrasing to describe their GM-sponsored labs.

The final university lab partnership we studied commenced several months after the initiation of the GM-Iota CRL. Lambda University was chosen, in part, because, as one GM R&D researcher put it, "The people at [the university] talked to each other." This obvious communication among faculty members from different areas, as shown in the proposal they submitted as an application for the CRL, was in marked contrast to other institutions that GM considered.

A successful innovation brought into the mix by this university was the establishment of workshops focused on particular technical issues. Researchers from both sides of the partnership found the workshop problems intellectually stimulating and the format engaging. These workshops were opportunities to interact, share expertise, and actively participate in problem solving. They also had the effect of encouraging working relationships among researchers. The combination of collaborative labs allowed us to investigate the range of processes, relationships, and structures that develop in this type of partnership over time.

DATA AND METHODS

Our research on a cultural model of partnerships followed four phases: (1) ethnographic data collection to define and describe the cultural model of partnerships, (2) social network and survey-data collection to elaborate on the relationship dynamics of the partnerships, (3) systems-dynamics modeling (utilizing empirical data available from the partnerships) to test the model we had created, and (4) an in-depth analysis of the role of reciprocity in partnerships. The ethnographic process allowed us to focus on partnership expectations and activities. We identified and explored the conditions applicable to collaborative partnerships, and, as a consequence, identified the key variables for the second phase, the social-network survey.

In the social-network survey, we investigated partnership structure, dynamics, and roles. Both phases followed a comparative empirical-analysis strategy focusing on themes and patterns (Bernard 1998; Schensul and La Compte 1999; Trotter and Schensul 1998), informed by prior ethnographic research on private-sector partnerships (Meerwarth et al. 2005) and GM's global product-program relationships (Briody et al. 2004). The final element from the ethnographic and social-network data collection phase involved the validation of our findings and recommendations (Kirk and Miller 1986). The systems-dynamics model testing completed our exploration of the quantitative data on partnerships.

Ethnographic Data Collection

The ethnographic exploration consisted of collecting interview, focus group, observational, and documentary data and then compiling a descriptive ethnography of the collaborative labs (Sengir et al. 2004; Trotter et al. 2004). We developed open-ended questions for our interviews and focus groups and built rapport with a cross-sectional sample. The ethnographic data provided us with a strong, triangulated, descriptive model of the key conditions, structure, roles, and ideals that contribute to the construction and maintenance of collaborative partnerships.

Social-Network Survey

The ethnographic data subsequently allowed us to design a social-network survey to: (1) identify key relationship variables, concepts, or attributes, that needed to be tested in the survey; (2) include empirical measures of key themes and concepts in the survey; (3) create hypotheses to predict role and relationship links (i.e., how the individuals are connected within the partnership); and (4) provide a mechanism that would confirm distinct stages in the life cycles of partnerships based on their predicted structure and role relationships.

We collected the data through an e-mail-based social-network survey sent to all known participants in the four CRLs. This survey followed a standard social-network format using a focused name generator to identify partnership relationships (Wasserman and Faust 1994). A "key relationship" matrix al-

lowed each respondent to identify the complete list of individuals that they were in contact with as part of the CRL and to evaluate their relationship with each person named. The relationship evaluation included questions in the survey pertaining to joint work, trust, cooperation, conflict, and communication. In fall 2003, we administered a follow-up survey to the same set of CRLs as well as to newly formed CRLs.

Validation

We presented and gathered feedback from GM and its partners in seminars or validation sessions at the various research locations of our study participants to move from an emergent to an empirically validated model. The consensus data from these sessions provided strong validation of the basic model and key elements of the partnership interactions It also provided feedback that the directed recommendations from the research were well targeted and useful from the perspective of both the GM and CRL partners.

Modeling

We used our qualitative and quantitative data as input to an early version of the model. Subsequently we combined the statistical and sociometric analyses from the survey data with network-visualization programs in order to explore the dynamics and evolutionary patterns associated with these partnerships. There were three primary sources of information used in the model conceptualization and model-testing phase of the project. The first consisted of the emergent themes from the ethnographic data, including the key variables subsequently built into the social-network survey. The second comprised a cross-validation check of the partnership and collaboration literatures.

As an example, there were 236,046 citations available in the business literature on the concept of communication, 50,208 on trust, 39,133 on conflict, 36,278 on cooperation, 2,976 on organizational structure, and approximately 1,000 corresponding to our concept of joint work (based on the combination of several categories). There was also substantive literature on the use of social-network analysis in business contexts. The content of selected articles from this search further confirmed the centrality of the components of the emerging model in the creation and maintenance of successful partnerships.

A third input into the conceptualization of the model involved the analyses generated from the social-network survey. The primary network relationship questions included ratings for key interpersonal interactions such as level of communication, importance of communication, level of joint work, importance of joint work, level of trust, level of cooperation, and level of conflict. The fact that the whole range of responses was used by at least some of the respondents indicates that we were measuring conditions that varied both within and across the partnerships, and that could be critically judged by the respondents. Clearly all relationships were not the same, nor were they based solely on a social-desirability condition. In addition, the fact that each respondent varied his/her ratings, rather than simply duplicating the ratings for all individuals named, also indicates that we were tapping into conditions that were variables that were measurable within partnership relationships.

THE CULTURAL COMPONENTS OF PARTNERSHIPS

We followed the general four-part "culture-theory" analysis of partnerships, described in chapter 1. The results, which are described below, provide an elaborate model of collaborative partnerships. The evolutionary aspect of the model is represented by our analysis and description of the partnership life cycle. The data is also analyzed using structural theory (social structure and organization) in the form of network visualization and analysis. The exploration of meaning of both the partnerships and relationships is framed by our use of symbolic theory and theories of cultural meaning. The cognitive aspects of the partnership models provide the opportunity to see how members of the partnerships organize the different elements of the partnership "cultural domain," including types of relationships, roles, partnerships in general, and the structure of our cultural model (cf. Weller and Romney 1988). The systems-dynamics modeling also provides a way of exploring the integrative aspects of the culture. Each of the four theoretical areas informs each part of the model described below, although there is greater or lesser emphasis on one or more of the four theoretical approaches in each specific section.

EVIDENCE FOR A PARTNERSHIP LIFE CYCLE

Partnerships exhibit systematic changes over time. The basic evidence for a common life cycle for these partnerships comes from our ethnographic data, which is informed and triangulated by analysis of the various changes in size and composition, structure, role configurations, and relationship processes in the partnerships compared over time. Partnership cycles are marked by the presence of stages named by the partners themselves. Each stage is linked with particular work and relationship conditions requiring attention by the participants. Partnerships exhibit systematic changes over time.

Some attention in the literature has been directed toward general organizational evolution (Laszlo 2001; Learned 1992), although most of the spotlight has been focused on more static partnership structures and interorganizational theory and practices (Anderson et al.1994; Madhavan et al. 1998). Partnering relationships and activities clearly have a life cycle that can be subdivided (Ring and Van de Ven 1994; Lui and Ngo 2004) with associated markers of transformation from earlier to later forms.

Our basic ethnography of the CRLs suggested that partnerships evolve rather than maintain a static structure and role configuration through time. Therefore we have applied evolutionary (culture change) theories to our data and in the process have created our systems-dynamics partnership model (Sengir et al. 2004). Our model and our empirical data support the premise that partnerships are dynamic, change in size and complexity over time, and follow a stage-based life cycle. The detailed information on how the partnerships (and their cultural processes) are configured at each stage provides critical information to the CRL leadership to help anticipate and solve challenges to the partnerships.

Progressing Through Stages in the Partnership Cycle

All of the CRL partnerships underwent a selection-and-approval process followed by a relationship-development stage, a joint-work stage, a high-productivity stage, and a transition period. The following sections combine our ethnographic data with the social-network survey data to construct visual, verbal, and role-based profiles of the evolutionary stages of these collaborative partnerships. The stage names are based on the actual terms used by CRL participants, combined with summary labels that condense those terms into a validated label.

Initiation Stage

The earliest interactions between GM and potential partners constitute the initiation stage. This stage begins with the identification of a relatively specific research need on the part of GM R&D management, accompanied by fairly extensive knowledge of the prominent universities and/or professors who might be working in a particular technical area or on a closely related set of problems. Once there is sufficient momentum for GM management to justify the establishment of a CRL initiative, a list of potential universities is identified and contacted, often through existing relationships between GM R&D scientists and managers. There is a relatively brief period of informal interaction between key players in GM R&D and the various university key players in order to explore any mutual interests. The field is then narrowed through a combination of lack of interest on the part of some universities and through increased interest, specificity of ideas, and resources from others. The interactions become increasingly formal until a primary candidate is identified.

Courtship Stage

The courtship stage focuses on the negotiation of the specific content and structure of the partnership once a particular university has been selected as a potential CRL partner. It begins with general discussions and ends with a joint identification of thrust areas (i.e., technical areas of work) and the crafting of a formal agreement. A small number of individuals explore common ground in terms of potential joint work, combined with negotiation over key institutional concerns such as intellectual property rights, resources, and commitment of personnel. This stage includes an overriding emphasis on discussing the goals and objectives of the CRL. Key players begin to emerge on each side of the partnership. One participant described those discussions and the subsequent clarification of purpose and structure in this way:

> It took us almost five months to develop the contract . . . Those five months, I think, were very important . . . I couldn't be happier that we spent those five months. They defined what the deliverables were, how we [were] going to approve different projects and propose different projects, what . . . the intellectual property issues that we need to deal with [were], who [would do] what, basically, and also . . . what objectives we [would] be following. That time and planning was very, very helpful to us.

The "assumed" structure for this stage is a ladder configuration, which was seen by GM as the most basic structural starting point for a partnership, following traditional organizational hierarchy. Key individuals from the two partnering organizations are connected up and down their own organizational hierarchy, and are cross-connected between the two organizations at the same organizational level (e.g., director to dean/department chair, researcher to faculty) to form the core of the CRL. However, the courtship stage structure described in our ethnographic data suggests that the ladder does not exist, because there are normally pre-existing relationships among the individuals at different levels in both organizations. These relationshps change the structure into a less hierarchical (and eventually more globular) core. This interconnected structure is more effective for rapidly developing the necessary partnering relationships than the hierarchical ladder configuration.

Start-Up Stage

The start-up stage produces the relationships and structures that hold the overall collaboration on course over time, including good communication, the development of trust, and an increase in the overall quality of relationships. One participant stated, "The people who end up working together need to understand and appreciate each other. They need mutual respect and this is the major element of success for us." The emphasis on relationship development is an important precondition for mutually satisfying joint work. Another participant described the relationship-development process in this way:

> In my area, it has taken these two years to establish a real good, collaborative, collegial relationship. It takes regularly attending [working meetings] to get out of it what we should be getting out of it . . . So, we drive down every few weeks [to Beta University] and we go to the quarterly reviews.

All of our data indicated the need for at least one person to hold the collaboration together and to be an active facilitator in creating a stable and supportive culture in which the new partnering relationships could thrive. One participant commented, "What I've learned is that it's essential to have a committed person at [Theta University] and at GM. The partnership is going to survive or fall on the personal interactions between these two people." Figure 2.1 shows the visual network data for two actual CRL networks during

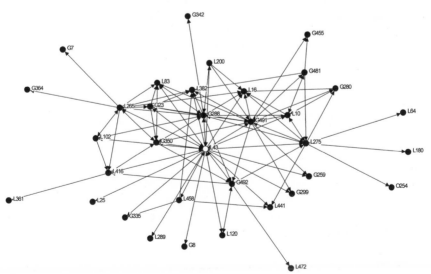

Figure 2.1. Typical (GM-Lambda) Start-Up Structure

start-up. The central individual for the GM-Lambda CRL is depicted as a white dot with numerous connections in the center of the diagrams.[3]

Figure 2.1 also depicts the continuing transformation of the networks into a stable globular core (core-periphery structure) that forms the structural base holding the collaboration together throughout all successive stages of the partnership cycle.

Midterm Stage

The midterm stage of the partnership emphasizes increasing productivity and joint work in addition to maintaining existing positive relationships. One participant commented, "We've established a closer interaction. This is due to the maturity of the program. Now, we are working on stuff. It would have been less helpful to have more [technical] interactions earlier." The midterm stage begins as soon as the core relationships are stable enough to be the foundation for predictable joint-work processes.

During this stage, the thrust areas begin to form. These subgroups appear as increasingly distinct subcomponents within the overall partnership network structure. Figure 2.2 shows the actual structures for a typical midterm stage CRL, including the presence of three thrust areas that are beginning to develop. These thrust areas are represented by clusters of enlarged light dots clustered in different regions of the diagram.

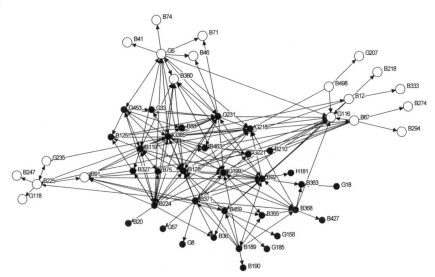

Figure 2.2.   GM-Beta Midterm CRL with Thrust Areas Developing

Mature Stage

In the mature stage, there is continuing need for a core group of key players to keep the collaboration on track in order to meet joint-work goals. One participant commented, "Above the thrust areas . . . there is the integration function. If we do something in one area, we want to know how this will affect other areas and how it will affect how GM does business." However, the major emphasis in the partnership shifts even more heavily to focused joint-work efforts that maintain separation from the core. In its pure hypothetical configuration, the overall structure looks like a boat propeller that provides strong thrust to the partnership. Figure 2.3A provides a hypothetical visualization of this structure, with the core and three thrust areas illustrated by the fan-shaped lobes. These joint work groups are connected by a core global structure to maintain direction and evaluate results, but the major work is going on in the work fans.

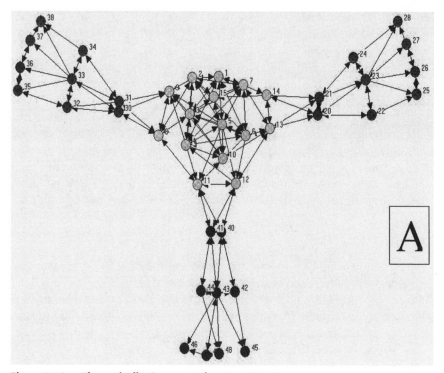

Figure 2.3A.   Theoretically-Constructed Mature Structure

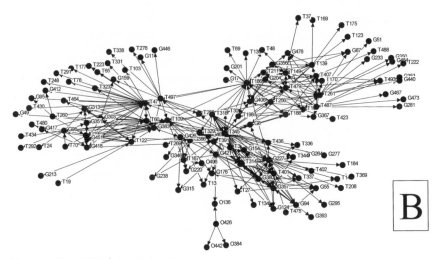

Figure 2.3B.   GM-Theta Mature Structure

While reality is somewhat messier than the ideal, figure 2.3B reveals a core-and-fan structure that is sufficiently close to the ideal to indicate that the hypothetical structure is not only approachable but has appeared in a real-world situation. Figure 2.3B illustrates some additional complexity at the peripheries where there are individuals who are not connected to each other—only to someone in the fan structure—and some additional complexity where there are cross connections between the fans at various levels from core to periphery based on pre-existing or other relationships. A typical example of a CRL participant on the periphery of the network might be a graduate student who is only connected to the thrust area and to the overall network through one person—his/her professor. A typical participant in the middle of one of the fans would be a GM researcher who is connected to multiple people in two or more thrust areas due to mutually defined joint-work efforts.

Transition Stage

The transition stage begins when the social and financial processes that govern both the unilateral and bilateral decisions about the partnership come back into prominence and potentially threaten the relationships and the structures that have been created. Transition issues directly impact partnership dynamics. One or both partners normally become concerned over one or more transition decisions. One CRL participant stated the following:

> We are in the fourth year of the partnership and starting the fifth. The funding runs out in . . . 2002. We have built a mechanism and an infrastructure for this

work. It would be good to know ahead of time if we'll be renewed by GM. We've got students lined up that need the support.

CRL relationships become, at least temporarily, more ambiguous. There can be a relatively high level of distrust, or at least a lowering of the trust, characterizing the partnering relationships during this stage. Communication becomes an increasingly important element in the partnership. Conflict can arise based on both rumor and actual changes. All of these conditions have an impact on both the existing network and on any future network for the partnership.

Several transition options are possible. One option is for the partnership to continue in its original form, as was the case for the GM-Beta CRL when it was renewed. With the continuation option, both the existing joint-work structure and its progress continue largely without interruption. Structurally it is similar to the representation of the mature stage in the first partnership cycle. A second option is for the CRL to be modified. This option allows the CRL to continue but in a reconfigured format. Typically one or more thrust areas are disbanded; alternately, one or more thrust areas may be added. Each of these conditions has an impact on both the core and the joint-work structures of the partnership.

A third option is for the CRL to be split into two or more independent CRLs. This option occurred with the GM-Theta CRL. One of the original three thrust areas was dissolved, and the two remaining ones were allowed to separate and form two new CRLs, causing a need for a new start-up of both structure and relationships combined with continuing relationships. A fourth option is for the entire CRL to be terminated. If the termination process is conducted appropriately, the formal structure of the CRL will disappear, but many of the individual relationships may persist. On the other hand, any of these transitions may have a negative impact on relationships, at least temporarily, causing a need for more relationship development (or repair time) before they work effectively again.

The Emergence and Succession of Key Players

The ethnographic and the survey data emphasize the importance of another element of the structure of partnerships, namely, key individuals without whom the partnerships would have floundered. One participant stated,

> You absolutely have to have people who provide leadership. Leaders are individuals who are aware of what's going on in the program and who are providing leadership to the program, but they are also providing monitoring. They are very, very critical to the success of the program because they are willing to identify

where people are making contributions, and identify and reward those contributions. But they are willing to identify people who are not making contributions [also].

All of the CRLs have at least one, and often several, individuals on each side of the partnership whose primary role is to keep communication lines open, solve problems, and help productive relationships develop. We use the phrase "key players" to indicate individuals who take on critical roles in the formation and maintenance of CRL networks. In many cases, they are individuals in formal positions of leadership, but they also can be individuals who have assumed informal roles that bind the networks together and make the CRLs work. In part of our research, we use the concept of key players to indicate individuals who have formal network characteristics (e.g., centrality, influence) that make them key players in a CRL partnership. Key players hold the collaboration together so that the researchers and technicians can get the joint work done. Both types of individuals (as well as other key players) are critical. When the partnerships are established, individuals volunteer or are appointed on both sides to fill a set of formal roles (e.g., co-director, thrust-area leader). As the partnership work progresses, those formal roles are complemented by a set of informal roles, and certain participants emerge as highly visible and valued by the CRL. These key players ultimately are drawn from the formally designated leaders and from the ranks of interested participants.

From an evolutionary perspective, some of these individuals must be present during the early stages of the CRL life cycle, while some emerge later. Key players learn their roles largely in the process of forming and sustaining the collaboration and in talking with others who are involved in CRLs. It is possible for key individuals to begin in one role and, as the CRL changes, for them to adapt or change their roles and remain key players throughout the life of the partnership. Both our qualitative and survey data demonstrate that there are predictable changes in the overall structure and dynamics of CRL relationships when these changes occur. The following sections provide details on some of these role conditions illustrated by that analysis.

Individuals Who Prevent Fragmentation

Our qualitative data indicate that CRL partnerships depend on a small but steadily growing number of key players throughout the partnership cycle. In the early partnership stages, there are often only one or two critical individuals. Their loss translates into serious fragmentation of the partnership. In later stages, the loss of a single individual is less damaging, though the loss of multiple key players is still problematic. One participant commented, "There's a very natural tendency for two institutions to set up a collaborative project and then have that collaboration naturally fragment or naturally segment."

We were able to test the idea of fragmentation (defined as the removal of a key player from a network when the removal means that either individuals or other subunits in the network are no longer connected to the network as a whole) using a social-network analysis program called Key Player. We defined fragmentation as a measure of the amount of dislocation of individual connections in the network caused by the removal of key players and their connections to others (following Borgatti 2003). We then calculated the degree of fragmentation or natural damage caused by the removal of selected key players from each CRL network. A value closer to one means that the loss of the particular individual has created many small clusters of people that results in a highly fragmented network, and a value toward zero means that most people are still connected within the network. The impact of the loss of key players in our partnerships is presented in table 2.1.

The institutional affiliations of the key players by stage in the partnership cycle are also important. The highest-impact key player in any CRL at any stage is a university key player (designated U1). The removal or loss of that individual causes the greatest fragmentation in the CRL network. As two or more key players are removed from any given CRL, the top two key players tend to represent both the university side and the GM side of the partnership. With the removal of three key players from the network, both sides are inevitably represented. Thus, for the CRLs generally, both sides of the collaboration are critical to their cohesion—increasingly so as the CRLs pass through the various stages of the partnership cycle.

Table 2.1. Fragmentation Caused by Removal of University or GM Key Players*

CRL	Partnership Stage	One Key Player Removed	Two Key Players Removed	Three Key Players Removed
GM-Lambda	Start-Up	0.21 (U-1)	0.40 (U-1, U-2)	0.56 (U-1, U-2, U-3)
GM-Iota	Late Start-Up	0.36 (U-1)	0.48 (U-1, GM-1)	0.58 (U-1, GM-1, GM-2)
GM-Beta	Midterm	0.11 (U-1)	0.21 (U-1, GM-1)	0.23 (U-1, GM-1, U-2)
GM-Theta	Mature	0.14 (U-1)	0.24 (U-1, U-2)	0.33 (U-1, U-2, GM-1)

*KeyPlayer 1.0 (Borgatti 2002a) was used to identify the key players and the levels of fragmentation and reach included in this and other tables.

Individuals Who Act as Bridges

Our network analysis allowed us to identify individuals who act as key players by being bridges (also called cutpoints) to distinct groups in each of the CRL networks. These key players bridge distinct segments or regions of the network. If they are removed, a new bridge must be formed or else contact will be lost or reduced with that part of the network, even though the overall network will probably stay intact. The number of bridges needed in any CRL increases with both the size and complexity of the CRL in each stage. University partner cutpoints are more common throughout the partnership cycle, although the proportion of GM cutpoints increases as the partnerships age. For example, during start-up, Lambda University had four cutpoints while GM had two. By contrast, during the mature stage, Theta University had ten cutpoints while GM had six. Figure 2.4 A and B visually identify these bridges for a start-up stage partnership and a mature-stage partnership.

Individuals with the Ability to Reach all CRL Participants

We identified another key role by conducting a "reach" analysis (using a program called Key Player, Borgatti 2002b). This process allows us to calculate who the minimum individual key players are who can contact everyone in a network directly or though only one intermediary, with minimal overlap in their personal networks. Table 2.2 provides information from our survey data

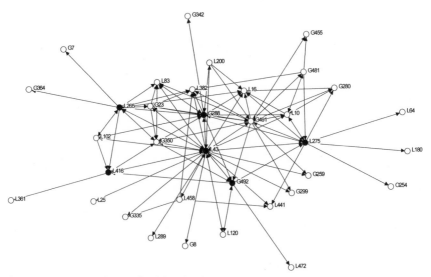

Figure 2.4A.   Cutpoints and Bridges in the GM-Lambda Start-Up CRL

terrific

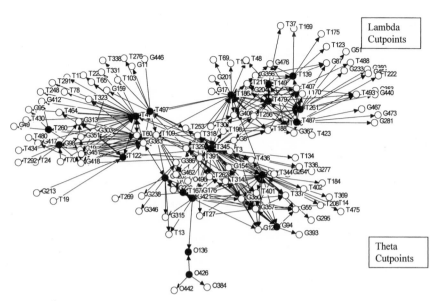

Figure 2.4B. **Cutpoints and Bridges in the GM-Theta Mature CRL**

on the extent of the reach of one, two, or three key players for the CRL networks. Newer networks, such as the GM-Lambda and GM-Iota CRLs, have single individuals (or, at most, pairs of individuals) who can make contact with everyone directly or through only one intermediary. More mature networks, such as the GM-Beta and GM-Theta CRLS, typically utilize three or more people to make all of the links work. The evolution of the networks is evident in that it takes more individuals to reach all parties in the more mature and more complex networks, fewer in the newer ones. These reach findings reinforce the important role of key players throughout all partnership stages.

Table 2.2. **Amount of Reach Accomplished Through University or GM Key Players**

CRL	Partnership Stage	Maximum % Network Reach, One Key Player	Maximum % Network Reach, Two Key Players	Maximum % Network Reach, Three Key Players
GM-Lambda	Start-Up	**100** (U-1)	**100** (U-1, GM-1)	**100** (U-1, GM-1, GM-2)
GM-Iota	Late Start-Up	**89.6** (U-1)	**100** (GM-1, U-1)	**100** (GM-1, U-1, GM-2)
GM-Beta	Midterm	**92.7** (GM-1)	**98.2** (GM-1, U-1)	**100** (U-1, GM-1, GM-2)
GM-Theta	Mature	**89.6** (U-1)	**97.8** (U-1, U-2)	**100** (U-1, GM-1, U-2)

Table 2.2 indicates that the key player with the greatest amount of reach is typically from a university rather than from GM, although the second CRL is an exception to the general rule. The individual who had the most reach in the GM-Beta CRL was from GM, though there was a Beta University participant who had virtually the same amount of reach. The Key Player formula selected the Beta University participant second, but the general rule is not seriously violated by the data. When reach is calculated for two key players rather than one, both university and GM key players emerge, with the exception of the first CRL, which has a complex structure that requires multiple university key players to have the greatest reach.

Even in the most complex stage, however, we find that at least one GM participant is required to achieve 100 percent reach, as can be seen in the entries from table 2.2 that identify 100 percent reach. In all cases, our sociometric analysis demonstrated that with no more than three people, and sometimes fewer, there is redundancy (i.e., overlapping reach) in the network in which two individuals share very similar sets of relationships, even though one has the most reach. This redundancy, combined with the reach found in specific key players, helps protect the network against problems produced by the loss of key individuals.

DESCRIPTION OF THE INITIAL CULTURAL MODEL
OF PARTNERSHIP RELATIONSHIPS

The life cycle conditions of a partnership model need to be complemented by a cultural assessment of several cognitive (meaning, definitional, organizational) elements of the partnerships. Individuals have an important impact on collaborative systems on a person-to-person basis. At the same time, individual effects are shaped and filtered by cultural norms, expectations, roles, and reciprocity rules. We constructed a model of the partnership cultural system using the key relationship conditions that our cultural experts provided but summarized at a system level. The ethnographic data indicated that there are four primary components in a collaborative partnership cultural model: joint work, quality of interactions, connectivity and social structure, and communication (cf. Sengir et al. 2004; Trotter et al. 2004; Trotter and Briody 2006). The overall connections between the four key components of our relationship-dynamics model can be illustrated as an interactive web. Each of the four components, in turn, is a composite of relationship subcomponents that further defines the dynamics of a cultural system. Figure 2.5 is a graphic representation of the relationships-dynamics model and its subcomponents.

The following sections provide details on the key elements of this cultural domain (partnership dynamics), which in turn provide the framework for both understanding and managing the partnerships.

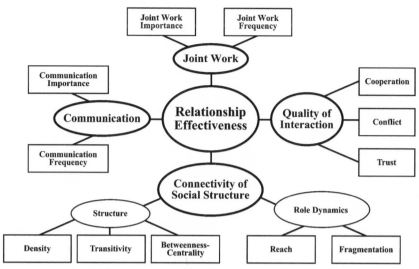

Figure 2.5.   Relationship-Dynamics Model of Partnerships

Joint Work

Joint work, or the process of achieving collaborative goals, is both the raison d'être holding the relationships together and the driving force justifying the establishment of the partnership in the first place. As one leader stated, "The most important ingredient [in a collaborative partnership] is working jointly to keep these guys interested in the program." There were numerous indications in the qualitative data that the time invested in the joint work was critical and sometimes a pressure point on the overall relationship. As one GM research manager expressed, "We should put more effort into it on our side. We set it up and put some effort in, but we aren't engaged as much. That's the danger. You can't get much out of these kinds of things unless you put the time in. Money is no substitute."

Quality of Interaction

The data indicated that there were at least three crucial cultural themes—trust, cooperation, and conflict—that constitute a measure of reciprocity we call "quality of interaction." The components all interact in the model as follows:

Trust

Participants emphasized the importance of building and maintaining their relationships with their partners to enhance trust. One GM researcher stated, "There has to be confidence and trust between the two groups—trust that you'll get results and trust that the relationship will develop into a good one." In fact, trust was the most frequently mentioned feature when quality of interaction was discussed.

Cooperation

The concept of cooperation also emerged frequently in the qualitative data. It appeared both separately and in conjunction with the concept of trust. It therefore became one of the key themes in the data. As one partnership researcher said, "Cooperation must be nurtured." Another stated, "The most important thing is, people have to feel comfortable with each other, because that certainly makes it a lot easier. You need to be able to talk to each other even if you are unhappy, and then you can try to fix it." The general use of the term cooperation, and the emphasis on positive relationships in the qualitative data, caused us to measure perceived person-to-person cooperation levels.

Conflict

The qualitative data generally focused on what was going well within these research institution partnerships. Our study participants, however, provided examples of periodic, temporary, or sporadic conflict. In one example, a GM researcher indicated, "It's a forced relationship. What makes you think you can work with all those people?" On another occasion, one of the research laboratory researchers stated, "Sometimes we have those conflicts with technical directions of what's to be achieved and what's not. Then I think [of] those conflict issues, [and] we just have to have a conference . . . and we try to resolve those issues." Some of the conflict was due to the cultural differences between GM and the research institutions (e.g., issues of intellectual property rights, publication, patents). In other instances, conflict arose from problems associated with either structure (e.g., differences in hierarchies, institutional processes) or individual interactions. Differences between the partners can result in conflict that then affects joint work, communication, and even the structure of the relationship.

Connectivity and Social Structure

We use the phrase "connectivity of social structure" to refer to the configuration of the connections between people and the basic social structure of the model. This structure is needed to maximize the positive components of communication, joint work, and the quality of interaction, while minimizing the competition among these components. One GM researcher explained that his partnership's success was due, in part, to his counterpart's efforts to establish and maintain connections with him and his GM colleagues. He commented, "We've gotten to know each other better. [One of the key players] does an excellent job of keeping us informed and involved, and his faculty involved." Following this lead, we examined two role variables that express the key structural components of the relationship and two structural components of overall network connections: (1) role dynamics expressed as fragmentation and reach, and (2) structural components expressed as network density and transitivity. Other measures will be added over time.

Role Dynamics

The role dynamics portion of the model consists of one positive force (reach) and one negative force (fragmentation) that we measured within the sociometric data.

Fragmentation: The model encompasses the fragmentation data we described above. Fragmentation can be visualized as the creation of individual islands or clusters of relationships with no bridge between them to a larger network component; as such, it acts as a negative force in relationship dynamics. One research manager commented, "There's a very natural tendency for two institutions to set up a collaborative project and then have that collaboration naturally fragment or naturally segment." We were able to visualize and model the impact of fragmentation in the partnerships by removing key players from the overall structure of the partnership in order to determine the impact of that removal on other components in the model.

Reach: The model contains the results of our reach analysis (described above). The partnership-network data indicates that participants have different levels or spreads of reach depending on their abilities and on the size and complexity of the partnership as it changes over time. Individuals who have reach (i.e., the ability to directly or indirectly contact large portions of the network) are a positive force model, as noted by one of our study participants.

He sees his job as director to clearly articulate the long-term goals and to clearly articulate the directions that we want people to go in, but then to not tell people what to do [which might restrict creativity]—to essentially tell them where we want to get and provide the freedom for them to actually get there in the best way they can.

Structure

We used two basic system-level sociometric concepts to describe some of the structure of partnerships: density and transitivity. We are still exploring the impact of these elements on the overall system model. The preliminary conceptualization follows but needs to be tested.

Density: This subcomponent provides a measure for the overall amount of connectedness in a network. The standard way to arrive at this measure is by counting the total number of connections that exist between people in a group and then counting the total number of possible connections. Dividing the existing connections by the potential connections produces a number that identifies the proportion of all existing ties among individuals to all potential ties. The higher the proportion, the denser the network. When the network is dense, it provides more opportunities for alternate routing through the network in case of a failure of one or more links. One GM researcher stated it this way: "The partnership has become much stronger and it's more synergistic and intertwined. We consider it our responsibility that the work is complementary and synergistic." Density potentially translates into a more stable structure for the whole network. It also reduces the problems that occur when someone is removed from the network, thereby resulting in a loss of connections.

Transitivity: This subcomponent is a sociometric measure that identifies the proportion of triples (i.e., three people all connected to each other), compared with the potential total number of these triples. It provides a measure of the connections between the individuals who are connected to a central person rather than a simple measure of all connections. The need for this measure was captured in a quote from a GM participant who praised the ability of one of the research partners to make these kinds of connections between individuals: "During the [joint meetings], he does an excellent job of presenting to us, bringing in others from outside his department, and that has led to some relationships [with those other departments and individuals]." Transitivity is similar to density in that it provides another way of examining the overall connectedness and stability of a network.

Communication

Both interpersonal and systems-wide communications are key components in our relationship-dynamics model. The importance of communication is reflected in numerous statements in the qualitative interviews, succinctly summarized by one of the partnership leaders when he stated, "Communication is the key. We need to know the GM requirements." We have deliberately placed this element fourth in the discussion of the model, however, due to the propensity in American culture to force all interaction into a simple communication (Improve Communication) model.

Our qualitative data indicated that good communication is the most frequently cited ideal component that both parties want in a partnership. Our empirical data indicated, however, that increased and decreased frequency and improved quality of communication had less impact on the other parts of the model (i.e., joint work, quality of interaction) than improvements in the joint work and quality of interaction have on people's perception of the importance and impact of communication. The final rationale for creating this interconnected, four-component cultural model of the relationship-dynamics processes in collaborative partnerships was to allow us to first validate and then test the model with empirical data.

REFINING AND VALIDATING RELATIONSHIP DYNAMICS

We refined and tested our cultural model of relationship effectiveness using systems-dynamics modeling techniques. We hypothesized that each of the four system-level components—quality of interaction, social structure, joint work, and communication—contribute differentially to relationship effectiveness in these collaborative partnerships. Representing relationship effectiveness in a model requires taking into account the varying levels of interactions and feedback. At any particular time, relationship effectiveness is an aggregated outcome of these four components and any subcomponents. In turn, each component affects, and is affected by, the composite relationship effectiveness and the varying levels of the other composite components.

The initial partnerships in our first round of social-network survey data collection were at different stages in their partnership life cycle when we collected the data. We subsequently used the survey data to create an idealized five-year timeline, with each partnership representing an example of a generic partnership at that particular stage of development. We felt reasonably comfortable making this assumption because our qualitative data included life cycle or historical data that suggested that the older partnerships, at one time, experienced the kinds of processes and tensions currently facing the younger partnerships. We also normalized the survey data to accommodate differences in the number of respondents associated with each partnership. We know from the qualitative data that each partnership stage was associated with particular attributes and partnership issues.

Following the administration of the second survey (which clearly validated the original model), we decided to chart the partnership cycle in terms of stages, rather than years, since we found that individual partnerships can be stuck in a stage longer than a year, or they can move through a stage in less than a year. We labeled the progression of stages as follows: courtship, initiation, start-up, midterm, mature, and transition. Our model, however, has no quantitative data on the courtship stage because that stage occurs before a partnership agreement has been reached, and therefore it has very limited quantitative data on the transition stage, which is just occurring.

The initial partnership survey data allowed us to create a baseline trajectory of relationship values for each subcomponent of the model. These baseline curves can be drawn across the stages. When these curves are tied into the systems-dynamics simulation software using correlational data from the survey analysis, they provide an evolutionary model for partnership relationship dynamics. This model can then be used as both a hypothesis-testing and diagnostic tool for understanding the relationships among the key elements of the model. The follow-up survey allowed us to estimate the model parameters more accurately, and it has increased our confidence in the simulations involving dynamics.

Figure 2.6 provides an example of how well the data from the second survey maps onto the baseline survey based on a comparison of joint work frequency. The two curves do not differ significantly even though the composite scores are derived from different partnerships at the same life stage, from data collected at different points in time, and from partnerships that had moved to different stages of the life cycle.

The baseline curves constructed from all of the other elements of the model (e.g., quality of interaction, communication) show the same pattern, which indicates strong stability in the model (Sengir et al. 2004).

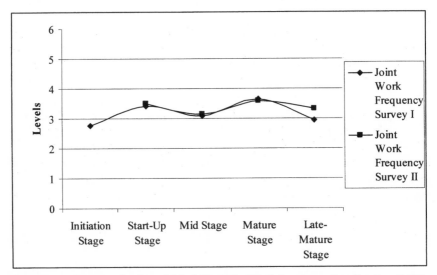

Figure 2.6. An Example of Model Stability: Joint Work Frequency Baseline for all CRLs by Stage and Survey

We conducted a second model-stability comparison using the first and second surveys. Our second stability test was used to determine if partnerships that had moved to a new stage would match the baseline configuration for the original partnership data for that stage. The empirical data from the two surveys shows a very strong correspondence with the baseline for the model relationships, again confirming the stability of the original model. A comparison of all of the other variables by stage for survey one and survey two showed the same correspondence as the example. All of our primary hypotheses on the validity and stability of the baseline constructed for the model and the simulation process are supported by the comparison of our survey 1 and survey 2 data sets on the relationship measures and values embedded in the model.

MODEL-SIMULATION PROCESS

We chose to test our cultural model of partnership relationships using systems-dynamics modeling, since it is a standard way of examining the interactions among the components of a system. In a systems-dynamics framework, each of the components has both positive and negative effects on each part of the system and on the system as a whole. This framework enables an investigation of the nonintuitive dynamics among the key components. A systems-dynamics approach has the potential to represent the emerging behavior of interacting loops (i.e., balancing, reinforcing or draining feedback processes between different parts of the system), the ability to represent nonlinear effects, and the use of continuous-time representation. In addition, by tracing through the feedback loops, we can explore evolutionary processes over time (Sastry 1997). Thus, system dynamics has the potential to lead to new hypotheses, research questions, and extensions of the current model. Our simulations led to an initial proof of concept with respect to the utility of the relationship-effectiveness model (Sengir et al. 2004).

Understanding Interactive Effects Among Model Components

We made further use of our modeling capability by comparing the impact of the interactions of different parts of the system on each other. This allowed us to simulate and investigate the interactions among various components in addition to the conditions present for each component. We converted the basic model into systems-dynamics components, represented as rectangles (or stocks in systems-dynamics terminology), which are stocked by (i.e., accumulate or contain) the survey data that flow into them. Levels in these stocks vary over time based on various direct and indirect forces. Flows represent the actions or activities over

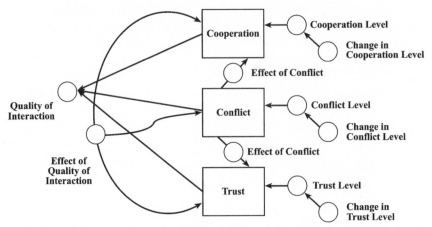

Figure 2.7.   Representing Model Components as Stocks and Flows: An Example for the Relationship Quality of Interaction Quadrant of the Model

time. We can change the levels of stocks via converters (depicted as circles) that represent relationships as mathematical equations. In our example, figure 2.7, trust, conflict, and cooperation are linked (indicated by thin arrows and referred to as connectors in systems-dynamics terminology) to form a composite component in the diagram—in this case, quality of interaction. Quality of interaction is represented as a converter, an element that converts these inputs into an output, which then leads to the other components of the model. These systems-dynamics elements are illustrated in figure 2.7 for the quality of interaction portion of the overall model.

The model also contains feedback loops that represent feedback or causality from increasing and decreasing levels of conflict on cooperation and trust to the other components. Quality of interaction, which represents the interdependent relationships between cooperation, conflict, and trust, in turn affects the levels of the other key components. We represent these cause-and-effect relationships with the loops and converters. Because relationships are neither static nor linear, we illustrate the model as a closed-loop one; dependent and interdependent variables become part of a web of interrelationships.

Simulation Procedure

The full details of the simulation procedure are presented in other publications (cf. Sengir 2004), but in summary, we initialized the stocks in the model with data from the social-network survey to represent different levels of interaction among participants. We then constructed the underlying pattern from the correlations between the key components observed in the statistical inferences in the survey data in order to model the dependencies in the system. Then we varied the levels of stocks one by one while observing the effects on the composite components. We created several theoretical and empirical scenarios to test the utility of the computer simulations. Next we explored cases where one-time jolts represented a step change to simulate significant or dramatic short-term changes in the environment (e.g., sudden decreases in the perceived levels of joint work) that might affect relations.

An Example of Interaction in the Model Components

It struck us that some of the more interesting aspects of the partnering relationship pertained to trust and conflict. We heard repeatedly that without trust, the relationship would not be successful in the long term; indeed, interviewees indicated that trust was a necessary condition for partnership effectiveness. We also knew that this pattern had been reported in the partnership literature (Storck and Hill 2000; Das and Teng 1998). Since each part of our model interacts with other parts, as the levels of conflict rise in a particular partnership, there is likely to be a change in trust, communication, and joint work in that partnership.

Our empirical data identified several persistent and important relationships between trust and conflict. When we examined the relationship between the levels of trust and conflict, we found a negative correlation. Figure 2.8 compares average trust and average conflict over the partnership cycle. The responses of survey participants show a remarkable contrast between trust and conflict in these five partnerships: Trust is very high and conflict is very low as a composite, and trust is largely the mirror image of conflict. The correlation between trust and conflict holds not just at the individual level but at the partner level as well. This pattern confirms much of our qualitative data that these partnerships, as a whole, are working well.

We conducted systems-dynamics simulations of each of the relationships and compared them to the other relationships. When we adjusted the levels of trust up or down (as might happen in a real partnership) there were distinct changes in the levels of communication between partners, changes in the joint-work activities, as well as changes in the quality of interactions, such as improved or worsened levels of cooperation. These changing patterns allowed us to create a number of what-if scenarios for the GM partnerships and consequently led to recommendations for stage-based "best practices" for

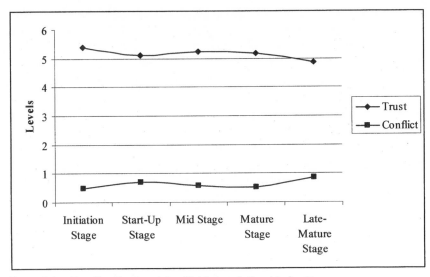

Figure 2.8.   Baseline Trust and Conflict Interrelationship by Stage

both developing and maintaining good quality relationships in partnerships and in diagnosing and fixing problem relationships in those partnerships (cf. Sengir 2004). The impact of each element of the model is not presented here, but the lessons derived from those simulations are (1) the model has empirical validity, and (2) the impact of changing specific kinds of relationships can be both confirmed and predicted from the simulations. The result is that the model can be used as both a diagnostic tool—by adding new data from a new CRL to the mix and comparing it with the model baseline data—and it can be used as a teaching tool to show what impact both new policies and behaviors might have on different components of the system before those conditions are attempted in the actual partnership.

RECIPROCITY

One of the critical issues that our ethnographic theory, systems-dynamics modeling, and social-network analysis confirmed was the importance of reciprocity as one of the primary elements in creating, maintaining, and exiting from the critical relationships that are at the heart of collaborative partnerships. This finding caused us to focus our efforts in elaborating our partnership model by doing a more thorough analysis of the data using the classic concept of reciprocity from economic anthropology.

Reciprocity consists of the cultural expectations, rules, values, and socially accepted behaviors people subscribe to in order to create, maintain, and end important social relationships. It constitutes the cultural economics of relationships. For our analytical framework, we define "reciprocity exchange" in collaborative partnerships as a process of establishing, maintaining, modifying, and exiting social relationships through the exchange of goods and services, including acts of goodwill, between individuals, institutions, or groups.

The need for an expanded theory of economic exchange prominently surfaced as a part of the 1970s' formalist-substantivist debate between anthropologists, other social scientists, and formal economists (Sahlins 1972; Befu 1977; Polanyi 1944), who debated the primacy of market economics over all other forms. The formulation of the concept of reciprocity, and its subsequent modification into its modern form, comes from ethnographic research on gift giving (Mauss 1990 [1923]; Bourdieu 1996), food sharing (Wenzel 1995), general resource distribution (Sahlins 1996; Bruno 2004), and other forms of relationship reinforcement (Axelrod 1984; Nettle and Dunbar 1997).

Originally, three different types of reciprocity (i.e., balanced reciprocity, generalized reciprocity, and negative reciprocity) were identified as the key elements for understanding how reciprocity directly affects relationships within a cultural context (Mauss 1990 [1923], Sahlins 1972). All three continue to be central to understanding the exchange process in relationships between individuals and institutions (McGivergan 1995; Ikkink and Van Tilburg 1999), though there has been a gradual evolution of the general understanding of reciprocity over the past thirty years based on critiques of the concept (cf. Goldman 2001).

Reciprocity is a key theoretical mechanism for understanding the process of maintaining healthy collaborative partnerships. Ethnographic research in various cultures around the world firmly established the presence of extensive exchange systems based on relationships and alliances rather than market exchange and market values. Our research, however, indicated that neither GM nor its partners were sufficiently aware that collaborative partnerships involve two different exchange systems (market exchange and reciprocity, not just market exchange) or that separate cultural rules were associated with each system. We also felt that they might not be aware that partnerships could be put in jeopardy if the expectations, values, and rules of the market exchange system were applied inappropriately and repeatedly to the reciprocity exchange system.

Market exchange and reciprocity require different kinds of knowledge and interventions to ensure that collaborative partnerships are stable and productive. The forces behind market exchange are often values and behaviors (e.g., self-interest, rational assessment of cost and value) that do not take the importance of relationships into account in determining the exchange. By contrast, reciprocity is focused much more exclusively on the cultural models of relationships. A number of authors have pointed out that market systems are not stable or viable without the other forms of exchange balancing the market processes on a cultural level (Anderson et al. 1994; Carr and Landa 1983; Landa 1981).

Evidence of the Importance of Reciprocity in Collaborative Partnerships

There were a number of cultural indicators that the core interactions within all of the CRLs were strongly shaped by reciprocity. Some individuals went so far as to say, "It's all about relationships," while others included relationships in a mix of complicated partnership elements. The following sections provide details about the cultural evidence of the importance of reciprocity in partnerships.

Reciprocity Metaphors

A specific indicator of reciprocity in the CRLs was the presence of a large number of linguistic metaphors that included strong family and kinship images, such as dating (e.g., explaining how the partnerships developed early on), marriage (e.g., what the nature of the relationships were in both good and difficult times), and how people interacted (e.g., like friends, like family). For example, one GM participant prescribed, "You have to be honest with each other. It's like the building of relationships." Our interviews and focus groups contained numerous relationship value phrases such as "trust and mutual respect," "working together," and "being open to suggestions" that are more common in intimate relationships than in market relationships.

The concept of sharing is particularly important in the data, with the idea of voluntary sharing being a much stronger relationship builder than any exchange based on buying or selling knowledge. One example of this type of sharing was described by one of the university researchers: "It's a two-way thing. We share with GM what we get from the research from other sources of funding . . . so they get the value of that research as well as the research that they fund."

Rules Identifying the Importance of Reciprocity

A second indicator that reciprocity was integral to the CRL partnerships appeared in the informally stated rules about how partnerships work best. The majority of these partnership rules focused on establishing, maintaining, or improving relationships. These rules did not concern the market value of what was desired or the importance of market-value-based exchanges. For example, one university CRL leader stated, "GM has to trust that we can deliver. They must have patience and trust us." Another commented, "If you want truly spectacular results, if you want breakthroughs rather than just step-by-step science or pedestrian kinds of science, you cannot tell people [researchers) what to do."

Many of the rules described how often the participants should interact, the types of formal and informal interactions that were desirable, and what the balance between work and relationship activities should be (e.g., meals for relationship building, informal time for brainstorming). One of the GM leaders summarized the importance of relationship building by saying, "At [one university], we spent a lot of time during the first two years getting it off the ground. We had no technical results until the third year. We had to find out if we could work together. We had to find out how we would work together."

Time Spent on Relationships

Another indicator of the centrality of reciprocity in these partnerships was the extent of time that CRL leaders devoted to developing, maintaining, and/or improving relationships independent of directly engaging in the collaborative work. CRL leaders spend time coordinating partnership interactions so that the CRL participants can get to know each other both as individuals and as researchers. These efforts target both individuals and larger groups within the CRL. A GM CRL leader commented, "[Person X] does an excellent job of keeping us informed and involved, and his faculty involved." Another GM CRL leader stated,

> The partnership is going to survive or fail on the personal interactions between these two people (the CRL co-directors). You need a champion at the university to get graduate students and to make important the work being done at the university. At GM, the champion has to link the work on the projects to work at GM on the product.

This leadership role is analogous to a central individual in a kinship system who organizes family reunions and makes sure everyone is talking with, or at least knows what is going on with, everyone else. This individual helps preserve the ideals of the family. He/she also maintains a clear sense of the obligations and a measure of when some generalized reciprocity is needed, where balanced reciprocity requires some form of exchange in a particular direction, and where negative reciprocity might be creeping in and might need to be prevented or mitigated.

The Primary Elements of Reciprocity in Partnerships

We originally looked for a synthesis of reciprocity that fit our needs for understanding dual (market and reciprocity) exchange systems such as collaborative partnerships (cf. Trotter and Briody 2006 for a review of current constructions). We discovered that reciprocity had been elaborated in useful ways, but we did not find a synthesis that explained our data. Subsequently we constructed a partnership-reciprocity model that identified the underlying cultural conditions within reciprocity that have a direct impact on partnership success. We have used this model to provide best-practices guidance to GM.

The primary elements of our reciprocity model include (1) a set of culturally agreed-upon definitions of relationships, (2) rules about social obligations that people use to establish, maintain, and/or eliminate relationships, (3) the values attached to different kinds of relationships, and (4) the cultural meaning of the items exchanged in a reciprocity relationship. We then used that model (Trotter and Briody 2006) to elaborate and inform our relationship-dynamics model. A goal of our analysis was to identify the elements of reciprocity in partnerships that would allow the theory to be applied in partnership cultures for positive, long-term benefit.

Relationship Definitions

Every group has an extensive set of cultural definitions of relationships in that culture. These definitions identify which relationships are appropriate. They provide the information needed to distinguish among the varying obligations attached to relationships. They also establish the cultural value or importance of the relationship. Typically the most important cultural relationships begin with kinship and family relationships. They then expand to relationships that decrease in importance and obligation from close friends, to more distant kinds of acquaintances, and finally to the expectations of strangers.

Cultural variation in relationship definitions can cause ambiguity that needs to be resolved. Problems with relationships occur when two individuals or sides of a partnership either have a different definition for their relationship or value the relationship differently even though they see it as the same kind of relationship. Two individuals may see each other as a friend. If one of the two, however, attaches a different value to the friendship (e.g., seeing the other as a boyfriend), problems can occur because both the expectations and reciprocity obligations are out of balance.

Earlier we cited the difficulties GM participants experienced in allocating sufficient time to the CRL partnerships and their own perceptions of not contributing fully or appropriately. The relationship definition in this case, as evident in the behavior of GM participants, would be incongruent with the behavior of the university CRL participants.

Relationship Rules

Every culturally defined relationship carries a set of obligations with it; those obligations are normally expressed as rules and norms. Those rules can be described in terms of the exchanges that are important for establishing and maintaining or destroying relationships. CRL participants may adhere to or disregard agreed-upon rules as the context of their interactions change. The rules area of reciprocity is the major element that allows CRL participants to adhere to, and manipulate, the cultural conditions of reciprocity. By following the rules, individuals can manage their part of the relationship dynamics. Manipulating the rules allows modification of the relationship. Mutually or unilaterally redefining the relationship changes the dynamics from one set of obligations and rules to another set (e.g., from unknown to known partner, from a trust relationship to a relationship characterized by distrust).

Relationship Valuations

All cultures place values on relationships. Some relationships are considered priceless, while other relationships are considered of little or no cultural value. Thus, relationship valuations range from high to low, from good to bad, or from excellent to terrible, depending on the culturally correct scale used by each participant in the relationship. Relationship value judgments are cultural composites of a number of value dichotomies such as close-distant, intimate-aloof, clear-ambiguous, family-acquaintance, important-unimportant, helpful-harmful, voluntary-required, or consensual-forced.

There may be actual formulas for combining these value dichotomies in some cultures, but for the most part, we learn them from informal rules, and we learn that different combinations of these value judgments attach to different kinds of relationships. Our general cultural model of reciprocity in partnerships indicates that more obligations, higher expectations, greater expected continuity, more rules, and broader cultural requirements are attached to relationships that have the highest number of positive elements and intimacy, while decreasing requirements attach to less positive or intimate relationships.

The Meaning of the Exchange in Reciprocity Relationships

The meaning of the items exchanged is an important part of maintaining an appropriate relationship. It is often more important to convey the correct meaning of the relationship in the exchange than to focus on the market value of the items being exchanged. The cultural meaning assigned to the items exchanged ranges from appropriate to inappropriate or acceptable to unacceptable. The cultural meanings attached to those goods and services are either shaped by, or have an impact on, perceptions of the meaning of the relationship, as well as the meaning of the exchange. Individuals can get into trouble in a relationship or feel that they have not fulfilled their obligation to the relationship by giving the wrong kind of gift. For example, during our site visits to the CRL universities and during joint work reviews at the CRL universities, we noticed how much care was taken that we were well fed. Universities place a high value on reciprocity relative to corporations. Since food is a major component in how reciprocity is expressed, university personnel would consider it inappropriate not to provide appropriately for their guests. This same kind of emphasis on food was not as evident when CRL reviews occurred at GM.

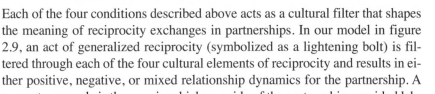

Reciprocity Filtered Through Four Cultural Elements

Each of the four conditions described above acts as a cultural filter that shapes the meaning of reciprocity exchanges in partnerships. In our model in figure 2.9, an act of generalized reciprocity (symbolized as a lightening bolt) is filtered through each of the four cultural elements of reciprocity and results in either positive, negative, or mixed relationship dynamics for the partnership. A concrete example is the case in which one side of the partnership provided laboratory equipment and space for a collaborative research project without expecting a direct return or payment for either the space or equipment.

The result of this type of exchange can be characterized in terms of the degree of congruence or cultural dissonance in how the relationship affects each collaborating partner. If the partners express congruence about their mutual definitions of the relationship, adhere to the relationship rules, value the relationship highly, and engage in exchanges that each side considers appropriate, then the collaborative relationship would be evaluated favorably. We would say that the relationship was in the process of being established, built, or maintained. It would be judged as successful. If the partners' definition of the relationship is more incongruent than congruent, and if the partners tend to disregard rather than adhere to relationship rules, are more likely to assess the relationship poorly, and engage in exchanges considered more inappro-

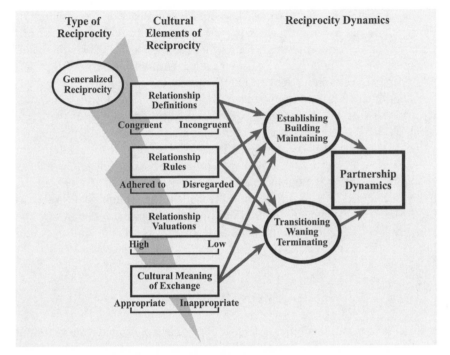

Figure 2.9. A Model of Cultural Interactions and Reciprocity

priate than appropriate, then the partnering relationship would be negative. As such, it would likely be transitioning, waning, or terminating, and its success would be limited.

Linking Reciprocity Models with Relationship Dynamics Models

We see the two cultural models (relationship dynamics and reciprocity) as being intricately linked. Successful partnerships take both into account and can use both separately or in combination to achieve partnership success. Part of our interest in and exploration of the relationship between reciprocity and other relationship dynamics evolved out of a need to understand the underlying rules, roles, values, and meanings that produced the interactive parts of partnerships, as well as from our need to provide culturally appropriate recommendations for making different parts of the relationship-dynamics model work in various types of partnerships. For example, the rule elements of reciprocity are directed at all four components of the relationships-dynamics model, but they appear to impact communication and the quality of interaction segments of the model most heavily.

The roles element in reciprocity has significant impact on the structure of partnerships and in the joint-work portion of the model. Values, and the importance of cultural meanings for both exchange and relationships, are demonstrable and important in all four elements of the model. From an applied perspective, joining the two models allows for specifically targeted actions and interventions. When partners are engaged in any form of reciprocity, they have to know the rules, value, and cultural meanings of the items being exchanged (e.g., expertise, experience, assistance), because the cultural value of these items is constantly defining the meaning of the relationship. They have to demonstrate that they are reinforcing the relationship by the exchange rather than questioning it or destroying it. Misjudgments about the items exchanged (e.g., too little time investment, unwillingness to travel to the partner's site) damage the relationship rather than the reputation of the partnering organization, though continued misjudgments will spill over into the reputational realm as well.

CONCLUSION

We used a four-part theoretical framework to collect data and create a cultural model of collaborative partnerships. The framework, detailed in chapter 1, allows us to explore the evolutionary, structural, symbolic, and cognitive aspects of partnerships both individually and in combination. Our GM-CRL data clearly support an evolutionary or life-cycle model of partnerships. Each life-cycle stage can be linked to definable network structures, roles, activities, issues, and decisions. They can be linked to specific stage-based reciprocity dynamics and can be linked to critical cultural models and meanings that create the relationship dynamics in those partnerships. This framework and the accompanying findings can then be translated into recommendations for successfully initiating, maintaining, and exiting from collaborative partnerships.

At their core, successful CRL collaborations are based on strong partnering relationships. Sharing a common framework—including an agreed-upon definition of the nature of the relationship, rules about partnering behavior, a comparable value attached to the relationship, and a similar meaning for the items exchanged—creates a strong foundation for the relationship. Moreover, managing the types of reciprocity well strengthens partnering ties, which allows for a focus on the collaborative work. The following sections summarize a number of the key findings that can be turned into lessons learned from this exercise.

Each of the CRLs have at least one—and more often two or three—individual called key players, whose primary role is to keep communication lines open, solve problems, and help solidify relationships. These life-cycle processes of CRLs are facilitated by the various roles of individuals in this chapter. They are the glue that holds the collaboration together, in large part because they foster connections between individuals on both sides of the partnership. Without their efforts, CRL work would be much less successful because the coordination of CRL activities, resources, and deliverables, including oversight of the technical work, would be lacking. They also support the formation of relationships between many individuals by creating processes at the outset of the partnership (e.g., site visits, technical discussions, joint presentations) that build and strengthen the collaboration by building on the relationship (i.e., social capital) investment in the CRL. Participants need to be brought together on a regular basis to develop multiple ties within the CRL.

The primary partnering relationships can be described and modeled as a dynamic cultural system that demonstrates the ways in which relationships are influenced and shaped by communication, joint work, quality of interaction, and social structure. Our composite model demonstrates that partnership success is largely dependent upon the development and maintenance of strong, productive relationships between the partners. Without strong relationships, there is neither a commitment to the partner nor the likelihood of achieving partnership goals. Each of the four key components of relationship effectiveness is important to the model, varies over time in predictable ways, and contributes to the success and failure of partnerships. At any particular time, relationship effectiveness is an aggregated outcome of these four key components and subcomponents, their interaction effects, and any change over time, since these partnerships go through stages in predictable ways that can be captured in a dynamic model.

Our findings demonstrate that while partnership outcomes are the goals of the partnership relationships, reciprocity enables the partnership to achieve those outcomes. Collaborative partnerships are mixed-exchange systems with both market exchange and reciprocity active. While market exchange is particularly salient at the start and end of the partnership cycle when negotiations occur, reciprocity emerges as soon as partnering relationships are built, and it continues throughout the cycle. CRL partnerships require a greater emphasis on reciprocity than on market-exchange mechanisms. CRL partnerships, with their broadly defined goals and five-year time frames, cause the relationship aspect of the partnership to take on a much stronger role in the success of the partnership, though the market exchange makes the partnership possible. The longer the partnerships last, the greater the likelihood that relationships are critical. Reciprocity is needed in long-term collaborative arrangements because the market-exchange mechanisms are unable to sustain the relationship indefinitely.

Participants experience all types of reciprocity as their CRL relationships evolve during the partnership cycle. Organizational-culture differences between GM and its university partners appear primarily during courtship stage negotiations and start-up stage discussions. GM participants tend to adhere more to the principles and practices of market exchange, while the university philosophy is oriented largely toward generalized reciprocity. For example, GM is oriented toward protecting and marketing intellectual property, while CRL universities seek to share knowledge with the wider community.

Some reconciliation of these different views reduces the likelihood of negative reciprocity so that the work of the CRL can be advanced. The transition from a market perspective to a reciprocity perspective takes time and effort but typically occurs during the start-up stage. Even if initially unaware of the centrality of relationships to partnership work, all CRL participants come to recognize and appreciate their value. The dynamics holding the partnerships on course (e.g., the development of trust, an increase in the overall quality of relationships) emerge as the key focus.

The concept of balance, as evident in the emphasis on balanced reciprocity, pervades the midterm and mature stages of the CRL partnerships. Participants expect their counterparts to work diligently toward their goals, share ideas, and complete tasks. If these expectations are fulfilled, the relationship and the work flourish. If the relationship lapses or any obligations associated with it lapse, the partnership is at risk. During the transition stage, increasing tension and fear of negative reciprocity arise. University participants experience heightened ambiguity about the future status of their CRL—whether it will be renewed, modified, or terminated. Judgments are underway about the value of the partnership from both a relationship and market perspective. Thus, a relatively high level of distrust often characterizes a CRL university's relationship with GM at transition, even if relationships between individual counterparts remain intact.

Partnership participants offer informally stated rules about how partnerships work best, such as the frequency of interactions, balance between work and relationship activities, and resolution of CRL tensions. Participants also spend significant time developing, maintaining, and/or improving their partnering relationships. Because market-exchange mechanisms can create power differences between the partners, participants must work to keep the partnering relationship in balance. With market resources moving in one direction, there may be a tendency for the GM side to rely solely on the CRL partners to complete the collaborative work. It is only when both partners are involved, however, that the partnering relationship can grow and the joint work advance. In addition, despite a market-power differential, the relationship dimension of the partnership can operate independently of the monetary exchange and still be in balance.

Our integrated model of reciprocity and relationship dynamics illustrates the connections between the types of reciprocity, the cultural processes of reciprocity dynamics, and relationship dynamics. The types of reciprocity exchange filter through the cultural processes of reciprocity dynamics that feed into and have a direct impact on partnerships. Those relationships have both a direct and an indirect (though substantial) impact on the joint-work outcomes for the GM-CRL partnerships—through their direct impact on quality of interaction—and both direct and indirect impact on communication.

THE MODEL AND THE CASES

Models developed in a vacuum are often interesting thought experiments, but they do not match as closely with reality as we would like. While we were developing our culture-theory framing of partnerships and expanding and empirically testing the model in this chapter, we had the opportunity to interact with and learn from other researchers who were pursuing similar goals and processes in the partnership field (cf. AAA, SfAA sessions).[4] One of the results of those interactions is the presentation of the case studies in the next two sections of this book. Each case study expands on the details of the model and offers a number of critical lessons learned about partnerships that are either congruent with, or independent of, the model. We hope these first two chapters are useful in understanding the cases, but we also believe that the ethnographic cases and their associated metaphors are powerful in and of themselves.

NOTES

1. This project would not have been possible without the sponsorship and support of Alan Taub, executive director of GM R&D. We enjoyed the opportunity of working closely with the GM-CRL co-directors, and we were grateful for the warm welcomes we received when we made site visits to the four CRL universities. We appreciated the willingness of so many GM and CRL participants to interview with us, respond to our social-network survey, and provide us with feedback during our validation sessions. Their input was invaluable. Finally we thank the reviewers of earlier papers based on this data set who provided us with many helpful suggestions: Marc Robinson, Dan Reaume, Phil Keenan, Kurt Godden, Linda Catlin, Jan Benson, Debra Elkins, Mike Whinihan, and Bill Jordan.

2. All names of the university partners are pseudonyms.

3. Figures 2.1, 2.2, 2.3, and 2.4 were constructed using NETDRAW, a network visualization program (Borgatti 2002c).

4. We convened or participated in sessions with a partnership theme in 2003 and 2005 at the Society for Applied Anthropology meetings and in 2004 at the American Anthropological Association meetings.

Section 2

DEVELOPING PARTNERING RELATIONSHIPS

3

A "Dreamcatcher" Design for Partnerships

Christina Wasson

THE DREAMCATCHER PARTNERSHIP STRUCTURE

This chapter examines the web of partnerships that surrounds the Department of Anthropology at the University of North Texas (UNT).[1] The structure of this web resembles the dreamcatchers that are found in Native American cultures (see figure 3.1). The Department of Anthropology forms the core of the structure, and myriad partners are linked to this core in a radial web-like pattern. The department itself, however, consists of a circle of faculty members who are not, in fact, connected by a central node. That is, the department has a chair that plays many important administrative functions, but his role in directing faculty members' partnering relationships is minimal. Faculty members develop their partnering relationships through their own initiative and networking activities. As a consequence, the partnership structure described in this chapter has emerged from the entrepreneurial spirit of its members. It resembles a dreamcatcher in that it has a hole in the middle. Dreamcatchers were originally made by members of the Ojibwe tribe to ensure that their babies only had good dreams. "When bad dreams come, they do not know the way through the web and get caught in the webbing, where the first light of day causes them to melt away and perish. The good dreams, knowing the way, go through the center of the web and slide down the feather to the sleeper below" (Shupe 1995).

This partnership structure is notable for its complexity. First, there is not one big partnership but rather an interconnected series of small partnerships, many of which have fairly modest goals. Second, there are many partners, and the partners are highly diverse. Third, the interactions and goals characterizing

Figure 3.1.   Dreamcatcher (Dick 2004)

the partnerships fall into a number of different categories. Finally, the temporal cycles of the partnerships vary markedly.

At the most general level, what the Department of Anthropology regards as the desired outcome of this partnership structure is the accomplishment of core departmental goals in the areas of teaching, research, and service. Key

I webs more complex than A markets?

goals include training master's students in applied anthropology and conducting applied research projects. This overall desired outcome, however, is not dependent on the success of any particular partnership. Rather, it results from the aggregate successes of many small partnerships and the ongoing effort of all faculty members to develop relationships with a variety of community organizations, businesses, and practitioners. The discussion of partnership outcomes in this chapter will therefore be different than what you read in the chapters that examine a single relationship between a small number of partners.

A key finding about this case study is that when profit is not the motivation for developing and maintaining partnerships, the motives become more diverse and the webs become more complex. The marketplace logic that underlies structures such as chains of customer-supplier relationships no longer applies in a direct way. Instead, we find organizations such as public universities and nonprofit organizations developing elaborate webs of relationships—sometimes with multiple interactions between nodes—as an essential set of tools that they draw on to accomplish their missions. Although this tale of the UNT Department of Anthropology is a story in progress, it may nonetheless be useful as an emergent model of how to manage partnership structures with similar structural, temporal, and political complexities.

The most relevant prior research for framing this story is the literature on partnerships in the nonprofit sector. While private universities are generally nonprofit organizations, UNT is a public university and thus technically belongs to the governmental sector. In its cultural logic and practices regarding collaboration, however, UNT, and the Department of Anthropology in particular, most resemble the nonprofit sector.

In the United States, "The nonprofit sector has grown explosively since World War II," and two key factors in this expansion have been (1) the way that nonprofits are able to combine "public service with private initiative," and (2) the advocacy role that they often play (Powell and Clemens 1998, xv). Both of these factors characterize the applied anthropology program at UNT, as well as the College of Public Affairs and Community Service in which it is housed. The partnerships described below illustrate the service and advocacy orientation of the faculty, as well as their entrepreneurial qualities.

The literature on nonprofits highlights the role of resource scarcity as a "strong motivation to enter collaborative ventures" (Murray 1998, 1192; Foster and Meinhard 2002). Like nonprofit organizations, public universities tend to suffer from resource scarcity, especially in these days of state budget crises. The motivations for the partnerships in this case study, however, go much further than that. An applied anthropology program is literally unable to accomplish its core mission without partnerships. Partnerships are essential for giving students practical experience and for providing faculty members with applied research opportunities. Various chapters in this volume show that other nonprofit organizations also find partnerships essential for accomplishing their core mission.

Figure 3.2 provides a social network diagram of the partnerships of UNT's Department of Anthropology. Although the diagram will be described in more detail below, in this section I present some theoretical frameworks for interpreting it. A striking feature is the relative paucity of ties between actors. Recent research in collaboration networks has shown that there is not an ideal design for such networks; in some cases, dense networks may be the most useful for the actors involved (Coleman 1988); in other cases, structural holes may be beneficial to participants (Burt 1992). "The optimal . . . design is contingent on the actions that the structure seeks to facilitate . . . identifying the benefit sought from a social structure is therefore . . . critical in identifying the form of social structure that is most . . . facilitative . . . there is no simple, universal answer" (Ahuja 2000, 452).

The dreamcatcher design is hardly a dense network, but it does not exactly fit Burt's notion of structural holes either (1992). Burt argued that actors (people or organizations) benefit when the other actors with whom they have ties *do not* have ties with each other. According to Burt, such networks benefit ego by providing a broad range of information while allowing ego to control the flow of information between the other actors (1992). This theory, however, does not appear to explain the dreamcatcher design.

First of all, the lack of partnership ties between faculty members does not mean that information does not flow between them. On the contrary, the department is highly collegial. Faculty members have strong cultural and social ties. The lack of partnership ties between them can better be explained by the political economy of the public university, which rewards faculty members for initiating projects that they control individually and which provides disincentives for collaboration. This point is explained in greater detail later.

Second, the paucity of ties between the partners of faculty members indicates the breadth and diversity of faculty members' interests. As a relatively small department, professors cover a wide range of areas in order to accommodate the students' interests. It also highlights the entrepreneurial energy of faculty members in constantly seeking new contacts and expanding their networks. None of the faculty members interviewed, however, mentioned that they preferred partners who lacked ties to their other partners. Indeed it is difficult to imagine what benefit such structural holes might produce. In a number of cases, faculty members were involved in multiparty collaborations in which their partners were linked to each other.

Another partnership model that is superficially similar to the dreamcatcher design is the "spider's web" joint venture, which links "many firms to one

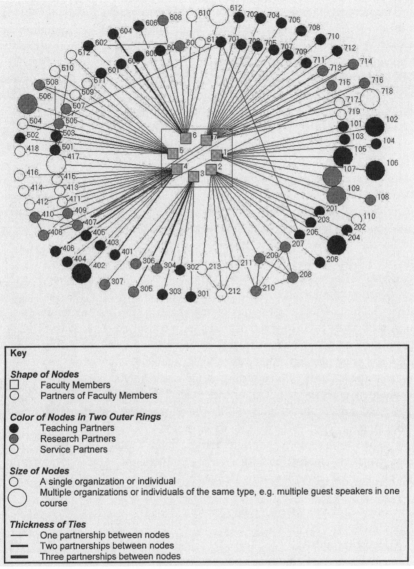

Key

Shape of Nodes
- ☐ Faculty Members
- ○ Partners of Faculty Members

Color of Nodes in Two Outer Rings
- ● Teaching Partners
- ● Research Partners
- ○ Service Partners

Size of Nodes
- ○ A single organization or individual
- ◯ Multiple organizations or individuals of the same type, e.g. multiple guest speakers in one course

Thickness of Ties
- —— One partnership between nodes
- —— Two partnerships between nodes
- ▬▬ Three partnerships between nodes

Figure 3.2. Social Network Diagram of Partnerships of the UNT Department of Anthropology

pivotal partner" (Harrigan and Newman 1990, 419). The goal is to "keep out-siders at bay while [the central firm is] strengthening its own position" (Harrigan and Newman 1990, 419). Although the structural design looks similar, the motivation behind the spider's web is clearly different from what leads to the dreamcatcher design.

The dreamcatcher design is thus a type of partnership structure that has not previously received much attention in the literature on collaboration networks. A contribution of this chapter can be to make readers aware of this structure as a useful option under a set of conditions that resembles those of UNT's Department of Anthropology. For instance, informal communication with faculty members at other universities indicates that it is a common structure for other applied anthropology programs' partnerships.

The concept of the "collaborative entrepreneur," developed by Takahashi and Smutny (2002), helps illuminate the partnering activities of faculty members in the UNT Department of Anthropology. They examined the ways that partnerships emerge in the nonprofit sector. Adding to previous research, they identified two key factors. One was the opening of a "collaborative window," a confluence of problems, potential solutions, organizational conditions, and environmental conditions that together constitute an opportunity for a partnership. The second factor was the presence of a collaborative entrepreneur, someone who recognized the window and had the will and the ability to initiate the partnership. This emphasis on the agency of those who initiate collaborations is appropriate to an examination of the UNT Department of Anthropology, since the dreamcatcher design is largely the result of the entrepreneurial efforts of individual faculty members. They go on to argue that long-term collaborations may be difficult to sustain because the qualities of a good entrepreneur are not necessarily the qualities of a good manager. This part of their argument, however, is less pertinent because the majority of partnerships in this case study are designed to be short in duration, and they do not involve an extensive intertwining of organizations. The dreamcatcher model draws on the strengths of the entrepreneurial mindset while minimizing the effects of its weaknesses.

Applied anthropology programs and the organizations they team with have complementary motivations for creating partnerships. Applied anthropology programs need partners to provide the following:

- Practicum and internship opportunities
- Class projects
- Guest lectures
- Advice on curriculum and course design
- Jobs for graduates
- Applied research projects
- Service opportunities

At the same time, various organizations and applied anthropology practitioners benefit from partnering with an applied anthropology program, because the program can provide the following:

- Interns
- Free research through class projects and practicum
- Employees when students graduate
- A means for practitioners to stay current with research
- A professional community for practitioners

Several different types of organizations and individuals can be useful partners. These include:

- Applied anthropologist practitioners
- Organizations that hire anthropologists (the contacts within the organization may or may not be anthropologists)
- Organizations that offer research opportunities for class projects, practicum, and so on (the contacts within the organization may or may not be anthropologists, but they appreciate what anthropological research can offer)

THE PARTNERSHIPS OF
THE UNT DEPARTMENT OF ANTHROPOLOGY

Data on the Department of Anthropology at the University of North Texas were collected using several methods. First of all, I have been teaching in the department since fall 2001 and thus may be said to engage in a form of participant observation, rather loosely defined, with an emphasis on the participant aspect. Second, I interviewed all relevant faculty members; the conversations were recorded and transcribed by a research assistant. The only faculty members who I did not interview were (1) a professor who is emeritus and therefore no longer actively engaged in partnerships, and (2) another person who was hired only weeks before I collected data and therefore had not yet had time to develop partnerships. In total, I interviewed six faculty members and collected the same kinds of data for myself. I was thus able to analyze partnership information for seven faculty members. The analysis presented here is department-centric. I did not conduct interviews with partnering organizations. This seems like a worthwhile endeavor for a future project; combined with the departmental data, however, it would have produced too much information to present in a single book chapter.

The term "partnership" is not a widely used term in the UNT anthropology department, and in this sense it is an etic concept rather than an emic one. The practice of collaboration, however, is widespread. Based on an examination of our partnerships, and in order to identify a comparable set of data, I have developed this working definition of partnerships in our department:

A collaboration between a faculty member of the UNT Department of Anthropology and one or more other individuals or organizations that furthers the mission of the department.

- The partner must agree to a certain level of personal engagement, at a minimum, an activity such as a guest lecture.
- The collaboration must lead to an activity *with an outcome*; this is what differentiates it from networking.
- Relationships between students and external partners are included only when there is also direct contact between the faculty member and the partner; thus practicum sites count, but class projects initiated and conducted by individual students do not.

Under this definition, I did not include future projects that were under discussion at the time of the interview, grants that had been applied for but not received in the past, or services that the department simply paid for.

Partnership Types

In the interviews, faculty members described a wide variety of partnerships. I grouped these partnerships into twelve categories that faculty members used to describe their activities in their interviews. For clarity of presentation, I further grouped the twelve categories into forms of teaching, research, or service.

A total of ninety-nine partnerships were listed, but the number of partners is actually somewhat greater, because some of the partnerships include multiple individuals. For instance, Tyson Gibbs regularly invites a series of alternative health specialists to his class "Holistic Health and Alternative Healing"; I grouped all these specialists as a single coded entry (102). I used this system of listing multiple partners under one entry whenever there was a group of partners in which they all played equivalent roles, and their total number was large (i.e., coded entries 102, 105, 106, 107, 109, 204, 402, 417, 506, 612, 718). Multiple partners are represented by a larger circle than single partners.

Each of the twelve categories of partnerships is described below. First, its goals/outcomes and temporal structure are described in general terms. Then an example is provided. Finally, the relationships that were developed or maintained are briefly discussed.

Teaching

Guest Lecture: Many faculty members invite guest speakers to talk to their classes. The goal is to illustrate topics that the class is learning about and to provide models for students of successful practitioners in these fields. The duration of this activity is, of course, very short—usually just an hour or so. An example is the prepracticum course, where numerous guest speakers are invited over the course of the semester to help students learn about the varieties of applied/practicing anthropology. The professor who teaches this course has developed connections with practitioners whom she then asks to speak in her class. At the same time, she develops new connections every year. Some participants from previous years may be unable to return—for instance, if they have moved.

Educational Program: Some faculty members have designed special programs to benefit particular groups of students or to focus on a particular topic. In terms of their duration, two are summer programs, while the third is an interdisciplinary minor. For example, one faculty member offers a field school in Mexico that teaches students about ethnographic fieldwork in the context of community development. She draws on her extensive network of contacts in Mexico to organize each field school. She has developed this network over the course of many years, and the field school is just one of many activities that has emerged from it.

Practicum: All students in the applied anthropology master's program must conduct a project for a client. This project is called a "practicum." It is the capstone experience for students, and it allows them to integrate all the knowledge they have gained through course work with managing a client project on their own (although they are supervised by their advisor). It is usually conducted over the course of six months, although the duration can vary, depending on how many hours a week the student works on the project.

An example of a practicum is one student's work with the Denton Housing Authority. She studied the homeless population in Denton and made recommendations to her client about how local social service agencies could better coordinate their efforts to serve this population. Although advisors sometimes draw on their own networks to help students find practicum clients, this student found the client on her own. However, once a practicum is underway, the student, the faculty advisor, and the client form a triangular partnership in which each participant communicates with each other participant. All three members hold a kickoff meeting at the start of the practicum, and the client completes two evaluations of the student that go to the professor.

Class Project: Several courses in the applied anthropology master's program are organized around class projects in which the students solve problems for real clients. These projects give students hands-on experience in how to design research projects, engage in ethnographic research, work as a team, and manage client relationships. They typically last for one semester. For example, the design anthropology class in fall 2004 conducted a project for

Microsoft on how 18–24 year-olds use their mobile devices. Such partnerships may either emerge from a professor's directed search or from their pre-existing networks. In either case they tend to build and strengthen networks.

Applied Anthropologist Visits/Symposia: Occasionally faculty members invite applied anthropologists to visit the department. Such visits benefit students by giving them access to anthropologists who are experts in areas other than those of the students' own faculty members. The visits also help create an intellectual community in the department. A visit or symposium typically lasts one to several days. A creative example of this is a series of videoconferences—a virtual symposium—that a faculty member organized between the UNT anthropology department and colleagues at a university in Mexico. They compared border issues in the areas of community development, public health, and environment. The faculty member drew upon her extensive network of anthropologists in Mexico.

Research

Grant: Many faculty members apply for grant money, which then enables them to conduct research projects. The grant agencies range from the National Science Foundation to small foundations. The duration of a grant varies from about six months to several years. For example, one faculty member obtained a grant from the North Texas Future Fund to develop a list of best practices for the teaching of English-language learners. The funding agency is a consortium of local chambers of commerce. It is common for researchers to work on grant projects collaboratively. In this case, the grant recipient put together a team of eight people to accomplish the tasks in the desired time frame. Most of the team members were in UNT's School of Education. Thus the grant was an opportunity to build relationships across disciplines.

Research-Based Center: Several faculty members have ongoing relationships with multidisciplinary research centers at UNT. They conduct a range of activities through such centers. The duration of the relationship with the center is ongoing; particular activities may last a few months to a few years. As an example, one faculty member is a founding member of the Virtual Collaboration Research Group at UNT's nationally known Center for Collaborative Organizations. This group is developing an edited volume, looking for grant opportunities, and engaging in its own organizational development— for instance, by creating an advisory board of corporate managers. The group provides an opportunity for members of multiple departments at UNT, multiple universities, and the private sector to develop relationships with each other.

Publication: Publishing articles and books is, of course, a central activity of academics. At times, working on a publication can be a collaborative activity. Faculty members may co-author articles or co-edit books. Writing a publication and getting it published typically takes several years. For example, one faculty member co-authored an article with a medical researcher who had hired her to conduct a research project for him on how physician assistant students dealt with the cadavers in their anatomy course. After she completed the project, she and her former supervisor decided to develop a journal article about the results. Thus began an ongoing collaboration that has led to other projects as well.

Other Research Project: Finally, faculty members conduct research projects for which they do not have funding. They engage in such projects because they are interested in the topic and sometimes in order to develop publications. Such projects can last anywhere from a few months to several years. For instance, one faculty member designed an almanac for low-income populations. He identified a need in these communities for a single, easily understandable source of information on topics ranging from health care to bill payment. He worked with local social service agencies to obtain the information that would go into the almanac, to get feedback on the design of the almanac, and to help distribute the almanac. He also obtained funding from the family medicine department at UNT's Health Science Center to produce the almanac.

Service

Service-Based Center or Program: Some faculty members are active in UNT centers that have a service orientation rather than a research orientation—in other words, they provide assistance to local populations. Such partnerships are also ongoing in terms of their time frame. An example is the International Resource Council for New Americans (IRCNA). This center provides legal, medical, and social-service referrals for immigrants and refugees. It was a partnership between the UNT College of Public Affairs and Community Service and DFW International, an organization that promotes and links North Texas ethnic and New American groups. A faculty member in the anthropology department was the director of the IRCNA. This role furthered his relationships with the dean of the College and the head of DFW International. It also helped him connect with a diverse group of individuals and agencies that provide services to immigrants.

Professional Organization: Some departmental faculty members are active in professional associations, and occasionally their activities may be structured as a partnership. The goal of professional associations is generally to promote the discipline they represent. Membership in such an organization is likely to be ongoing, but participation in particular activities may last from a few months to a few years. For example, one faculty member partnered with a group of students to start a Local Practitioner Organization (LPO) in Texas. LPOs are regionally based professional associations for applied/practicing anthropologists. The start-up activities included designing an organizational structure, a mission, and the LPO's first events. This faculty member drew upon her relationships with the students as well as with practitioners to get the LPO going.

UNT Lectures/Symposia: Occasionally faculty members organize university-wide lectures or symposia. These usually last no more than a few days. For example, a professor who had spent time in Saudi Arabia arranged for a group of nine Saudi faculty members to visit UNT from King Saud University. They gave many lectures and class presentations during their three-day visit. The UNT professor was able to organize this event due to the relationships she had developed when she spent a year in Saudi Arabia. This event also helped build relationships between the visitors and UNT.

Faculty Members' Criteria in Selecting Partners

Several of the faculty members I interviewed talked about choosing partners based on the potential for balanced reciprocity in the relationship. For instance, one professor said that she wouldn't feel comfortable creating a partnership in which her primary goal would be just to get something out of it for her or her students. She looks for opportunities where she or her students can reciprocate and provide a service to the partner organization.

The reciprocity needs to go the other way also. A second faculty member said that she looks for someone she can trust; trust is a prime quality for her. If she has a gut reaction that another person is a taker and not a collaborator, someone who might try to run away with the data or the glory, she will not collaborate with them. A third faculty member summarized that he wants both partners to benefit equally. The concern with balanced reciprocity echoes Ring and Van de Ven's argument that "equity, defined as fair dealing" is as important as efficiency in assessing collaborations (1994, 93).

In addition, faculty members mentioned criteria that were specific to the roles for which they were seeking partners. For instance, one person selected speakers for a symposium on affirmative action based on their expertise in the particular issues that she wanted them to address.

How Partnerships Were Initiated

There were two main ways that faculty members found organizations and individuals to partner with. First, partnerships were often an unplanned outcome that emerged as a result of faculty members being active in a particular community. Several mentioned that they found partnerships through "dumb luck" or "serendipity." On closer inspection it usually meant that they had developed networks of relationships in their fields of interest. For instance, one faculty member with interests in Latino issues joined the organizing committee for the Hispanic Friends of UNT Conference. Through this network, she met the head of UNT's Office of Equity and Diversity. She developed a working relationship with him, and through their conversations, they developed an idea for a class project.

At the same time, it was also common for faculty members to search for partners directly. For instance, one faculty member wanted to create a class project on sleeping disorders. He actively searched for someone to collaborate with him. He sent out a prospectus to people in the field; one of the recipients referred him to the medical practice that he ended up working with. As a second example, a faculty member interested in Native American issues sought out local Native American organizations and volunteered to work with them on projects.

Challenges that Occurred in Partnerships

By far the biggest challenge that faculty members encountered in their partnerships was working with partners from other disciplines—in other words, the challenges of multidisciplinary collaboration. Six of the seven faculty members mentioned such challenges. A variety of issues arose. Most common was the challenge of translating an ethnographic research approach into terms that were meaningful to partners in fields such as medicine, business, or quantitative disciplines. In addition, a professor who invited speakers to his holistic and alternative healing class encountered suspicion. Some healers wondered why someone at a university would be interested in their work. They were concerned that they were being set up for a joke or other trap. A third issue was difference in temporal rhythms and timeframes between partners. For instance, one faculty member had to ask for extra time to complete a project when she worked with a consortium of chambers of commerce. The consortium was not familiar with the temporal cycles of university life.

In addition, there were challenges mentioned by fewer faculty members. A challenge that emerged in partnering with people in other departments at

UNT over the subject of grants was the question of how to divide the indirect costs. When grants are run through a university, the university adds on a considerable fee, currently forty-six percent of the requested funds at UNT. This money, called "indirect costs," is distributed to various parts of the university. A certain percentage goes to the department. If grants are co-authored by members of several departments, each department will want to receive the full departmental indirect cost allotment. Splitting it up across departments can require delicate negotiations.

A few faculty members encountered personality issues with a particular partner. In each of these cases, the challenge was magnified by political contexts in which they felt that they had limited power to act as they might wish. None of the challenges described here led participants to abandon a partnership. At worst, they produced experiences that were more difficult and less rewarding for the partners. More often, partners successfully negotiated solutions.

CULTURAL ANALYSIS OF PARTNERSHIPS

A visual representation of the partnership structure in the form of a social-network diagram reveals some interesting patterns (See figure 3.2). All of the partnership connections between faculty members and their partners are included. The faculty[2] members are placed in a ring in the middle of the diagram, since this is a department-centric analysis. Partners form a radial pattern around the faculty.

One obvious feature of this structure is its complexity. There are many partners, and the partners are highly variable in size, economic sector, and so forth. Furthermore, the same partner may be engaged in several partnerships with a single faculty member. Alternatively one partner may have connections to multiple faculty members or to other partners. Finally, although not visible in the diagram, each type of partnership may have a different duration and temporal rhythm.

Figure 3.2 also shows that faculty members are mainly reaching outward in their partnerships. No faculty members are engaged in substantive partnerships with each other. And very few faculty members share a partner. This pattern is different from many business partnership structures. It does not necessarily mean, however, that the department is fragmented or lacks cohesion. On the contrary, members of the UNT anthropology department are a cohesive group. They share strong social and cultural ties. In the diagram, the square around faculty is a visual representation that the department is ideologically unified and that members share a set of values and understandings about their work and their roles. This camaraderie is due in part to members of the department having such strong cultural and social ties that they are able to focus their energies outward.

From the "emic" perspective of UNT anthropology department members, the structure of the department's partnerships partly reflects the growth phase in which the department finds itself. In 2005, when data were collected, five out of the eight faculty members had been in the department less than four years. The master's program in applied anthropology was only a few years old. In the near future, the department was planning to launch an online master's program and eventually a PhD program. As one interviewee pointed out, these developments illustrate the department's energy and its outward movement. "We are all out there" actively developing new relationships, as another put it, highlighting the enterprising behavior of her colleagues. The relative independence that characterizes faculty roles and relationships encourages this entrepreneurial spirit. As another faculty member pointed out, it appears that the department is maximizing the number and diversity of its partnerships.

The lack of partnerships between members of the UNT anthropology department also reflects the cultural logic of academia. Faculty members are rewarded for connecting with external partners; they are not rewarded for collaborations within their department. They gain more symbolic capital from projects they have initiated themselves than from joining another faculty member's projects.

In addition, several interviewees noted that this type of partnership structure is fundamental to the operation of any applied anthropology program. One person argued that the department would not survive without partnerships. Applied anthropology can only be taught by modeling it and by involving students in it through guest lectures, class projects, practicums, other applied-research projects, and service activities.

Furthermore, at UNT the Department of Anthropology is located in the College of Public Affairs and Community Service (PACS), essentially an applied social sciences school (in most universities, the department would be housed in the College of Arts and Sciences). One interviewee noted that PACS values partnerships as a way of linking with the community, and it rewards faculty members for creating partnerships. Indeed, the dean of PACS was himself an applied anthropologist.

CONCLUSION: COMPARING THE DREAMCATCHER DESIGN TO BUSINESS PARTNERSHIPS

The dreamcatcher design, or some variant thereof, is not unique to the UNT Department of Anthropology. On the contrary, it is common for nonprofit

dreamcatcher shape → nonprofit (vs business) partnerships

organizations to engage in multiple collaborations and for these partnerships to be diverse in terms of the types of partners, the temporal rhythms of the relationships, and so forth (Foster and Meinhard 2002; Murray 1998; Takahashi and Smutny 2002). Comparing the dreamcatcher design to business partnerships can therefore lead to insights about differences between for-profit and nonprofit partnerships.

In terms of structure, the dreamcatcher design is characterized by a large number of different partnerships—about a hundred in the case study presented here. As a consequence, no single partnership is essential. Although it is critical for many universities and nonprofit organizations to develop partnerships to accomplish their mission, each particular relationship has a fairly limited purpose, and each can be replaced by another without much trouble. The failure of a single partnership will not bring disaster to the dreamcatcher structure as a whole. Similarly, in the dreamcatcher structure, the partners are never large organizations; they are individuals or small numbers of people. Even if a faculty member engages in a partnership with a corporation, for instance, she is only forming a connection with an individual or a lab or a small unit within the corporation.

By contrast, the archetypical structure of a business partnership is a link between two organizational entities (Glaister and Buckley 1997; Harrigan and Newman 1990). Sometimes this link is formalized as a joint venture, which then constitutes a third entity, the "child" of the parents (Harrigan and Newman 1990). However, the original connection is essentially between two organizational partners. It may thus be visually characterized as a barbell, two organizational entities that are connected to each other. Of course, large numbers of employees may be involved in such organizational partnerships, and mapping their relationships would produce a much more complex network diagram. Furthermore, large organizations are typically involved in a number of partnerships at any time.

The contrast between what I am calling the "barbell" and the "dreamcatcher" structures is that in the former, the two organizational partners are much more invested in one another than faculty and their partners are in the latter. In barbell structures, the failure of the organizational partnership can have serious consequences for many people. It is thus a higher-stakes endeavor. In a barbell relationship, having a successful outcome is much more important, yet also much harder to achieve than in a dreamcatcher structure. Meschi has noted, for instance, that while international joint ventures "receive undivided support from practical and theoretical specialists, in terms of profitability, attractiveness, and performance," they are also "one of the worst performers in the business environment" (1997, 211).

The point of these comparisons is not to argue that one type of partnership structure is better than another. Rather, it is to illuminate the diversity among the partnerships that organizations may develop. Each form of collaboration has a different set of strengths. The barbell structure mobilizes much more significant levels of organizational resources; it enables the accomplishment of substantial projects. The goals of individual dreamcatcher partnerships are more modest but also carry less risk and vulnerability. Their aggregate effect supports the organization at the center of the dreamcatcher in significant ways, but since the partnerships are developed by many independent actors, they do not collectively move that organization in a particular direction.

NOTES

1. I would like to express my appreciation to Megan Ko, an outstanding research assistant, who helped me greatly by transcribing the interviews, completing innumerable edits to the social network diagram, and carrying out other tasks. In addition, I extend thanks to my collegial colleagues for their time and thoughtful responses during the interviews and other discussions about our departmental partnerships.

2. Faculty members include Tyson Gibbs, Doug Henry, Lisa Henry, Mariela Nunez-Janes, Ann Jordan, Alicia Re Cruz, and Christina Wasson.

4

Cultural Training Partnerships

Who Has the Power?

Mary Beauregard

INTRODUCTION

"**G**oing global" has been a strategic focus for many U.S. corporations for many years.[1] Corporate managers discovered that differences in behaviors, attitudes, thought processes, and values of national cultures influenced their efforts at achieving success in the global workplace. Cultural competence has become a new qualification for gaining a competitive edge in the world market.

Cultural training is not a new concept (Landis et al. 2004). Cross-cultural training is a common experiential-learning mechanism used by firms to train members to manage cultural diversities inherent in global strategic alliances (Parkhe 1991). For decades, corporations have prepared top executives and their families to adjust to differences they encounter when assigned to a position in a foreign country. This expatriate preparation addresses everything from etiquette to shopping and transportation in the new culture. More recently, another type of cultural training has been offered to employees. For those who visit the foreign office regularly—or conversely for those who may never step foot in the target country but who work with foreign nationals virtually or in the U.S.—workforce training is a valuable new tool.

MCB Associates International

MCB Associates International[2] offers cultural-training workshops that orient employees to the subtleties that cultural differences present in business interactions. MCB has its roots in Detroit, Michigan, the erstwhile "automobile capital of the world." Automotive manufacturers and their suppliers are demanding customers when it comes to setting the standards for training services. Establishing strong relationships, providing expert consultants, and delivering effective workshops are critical to acquiring and keeping clients. Forming and sustaining partnerships with these firms is one side of our business. The other side is forming and sustaining partnerships with the cultural experts who conduct the training. MCB brings the pieces together, aligning corporate goals with the expertise of the consultants, successfully fusing these entities to produce and deliver our product.

MCB Associates International evolved from an organization that sold language training, translation, and interpretation services, but that recognized that speaking a foreign language was not the only way to connect with the global work force.[3] We organized a cultural-training department. We began selling basic programs to our customers. After the programs began, it became evident that the participants needed more powerful, practical applications of the cultural theories. Clearly, forming partnerships with the trainers would provide an opportunity to hone their skills and would offer programs that were better suited to the challenges of the global client. We began working closely with the trainers to adjust training methods. Our team developed a copyrighted model employing cultural variables in order to form a framework for addressing work issues across cultures. After six years of learning about the needs of the clients and the abilities of the trainers, we decided to concentrate fully on cultural training. We formed MCB Associates International.

Accompanying this shift was our desire to nurture the partnerships that had already been established—without damaging ties with my former employer. Our focus on pragmatic cultural solutions allows MCB to continue developing programs and to sell training for my former employer while cultivating new alliances and designing new workshops.

Defining Partnerships

The term "partnership" can have "multiple, overlapping meanings extending from 'partnership' as a business agreement to 'partnership' as kin relationship" (Goldberg and Comins 2001). Partnerships are relationships between two or more individuals or two or more groups. With our corporate client, a partnership is "a relationship between two or more entities wherein each accepts responsibility to contribute a specified, but not necessarily equal, level of effort to the achievement of a common goal" (University of New Hampshire National Infrastructure Institute, www .ni2ciel.org). MCB provides a customized training service; the corporation provides its dilemmas as program objectives and then reimburses us for our customized service. Initiating and managing this partnership requires many levels of contact and an ability to sell an intangible: soft-skill training. "Partnership arrangements tend largely to focus on meeting the needs of a client. These arrangements are formed to extend the coverage of these needs where an organisation's coverage may not exist or may not be to the standards required" (Callan and Ashworth 2004).

MCB's second partnership is with consultants and trainers: "Partnerships involve collaboration to enable delivery of a service or product, and within the partnership, there is a sharing of resources to add value to the product or service for suppliers and customers" (Batorski 2002). The trainer is an external partner but also an employee who is respected and appropriately managed. We *need* this partner, yet we direct and guide him to our client's goals. Our relationship with our trainers is delicate, critical, and essential to our existence. We work nonstop to maintain connections that might not be active for months. Successful partnering with consultants takes time, personal attention, diplomacy, and energy.

Where Do We Get Our Energy?

MCB's cultural metaphor is an electrical transformer (see figure 4.1). We are a broker of training, a manager of partnerships, a developer of content, and a program facilitator. The high-voltage challenges of our partnerships flow from two directions: toward our clients and our cultural consultants. Like elements of raw electricity, they are not yet harnessed or connected, and they are not consumer friendly. Through MCB, their potential is aligned and transformed to satisfy consumer demand, changing the power to voltage that meets the end users' needs. A successful training program is a win-win-win situation for all three parties.

Figure 4.1. MCB as Transformer

PHASES OF ALLIANCE EVOLUTION AND LEARNING

There is a great variety of partnerships, each evolving over time. In some cases, the evolution follows a predicted process. In others, particular elements exist that affect these stages. Our partnerships are unique. Most of the partnership literature is focused on a two-way, ideal relationship rather than on alternative structures such as our transformer. One such example is Iyer's (2002) evolutionary model. It includes both qualitative and quantitative studies, short-term studies (e.g., Barkema, Bell, and Pennings 1996; Doz 1996), and longitudinal case studies (Iyer 2002).

The four evolutionary phases that partnerships travel through are adapted from the works of Dwyer et al. (1987), Wilson (1995), Doz (1996), and Doz and Hamel (1998).

- Phase I—Awareness and Partner Selection: Recognition by a firm or another as a feasible exchange partner
- Phase II—Exploration: Search-and-trial period in which the purpose of the partnership is established
- Phase III—Expansion: Stage of increased mutual interdependence and growth in benefits accrued to the partners
- Phase IV—Commitment to Relationship: Mutual pledges of continued interdependence and to the maintenance of the relationship

These phases are combined with the following learning dimensions (Doz 1996; Doz and Hamel 1998): environment, skill, goal, task, and process. The resulting framework is used to examine where the activities of MCB and our partners match these phases and dimensions and where they differ.

Phase I—Awareness and Partner Selection: Where Do We Begin?

We begin with a sales call. Because our corporate clients are deeply engaged in the tasks of daily business, they may not recognize that solutions to their cultural dilemmas are available. Soliciting these corporations to offer our service raises their awareness of potential assistance.

The American adages that business is business all over the world, or that what works in the U.S. culture will work in others, are less strongly held beliefs today. When market share is lost, unemployment rises, and budgets are trimmed due to global competition, the environment changes. Even though corporations might believe they need to understand cultural differences, training programs are often eliminated during reduced growth. In this environment, people purchasing training for their corporations are looking for tangible, cost-effective solutions to problems.

Our trainers are affected by this external environment and by various internal environments. The trainer may be a foreign national, an international corporate expatriate, a learned cultural anthropologist, or even all three. We adjust to each of these contexts, creatively tapping the ability of that consultant for the corporate environment.

MCB's skills and abilities must be demonstrated to the client during the first meeting or first phone call. Posing appropriate questions and providing examples of how our programs have improved cultural relations is critical to winning a client's confidence. Differentiating ourselves from the competition is essential in this phase. Corporations are looking to streamline their processes and to use internal talent. "Firms scout for compatible partners to complement their own resources and to contribute to developing new capabilities" (Wilson 1995). Our prospective client is skilled at looking for a solid return on investment (ROI) and purchases of soft-skill training can be risky because they do not always show an immediate ROI.

Selecting our trainer and finding the best match for our client is a time-consuming process. The ideal trainer should have knowledge of cultural theory, work experience in a global setting, and an ability to engage an adult audience or an expatriate child who is curious yet hesitant about a new life in a foreign world. Both adults and children must learn something new and useful.

In this first phase, the partners have related but dissimilar goals. The corporation is interested in selecting the best provider, within budget, and securing a long-term relationship. MCB wants to establish contact and meet with experienced decision makers who recognize the potential of our programs based on our credentials and capacity for future service. As we go about selecting our training partner, we aim to match a trainer's abilities and unique experience with the client's profile and therefore uncover a new partner for future collaborations. The candidate strives to understand our needs and to see what opportunities might exist in the future.

The corporation has very little to do in this dimension; it may request a quotation and proposal. If directed to move forward, MCB has many tasks to complete. We attach a cost for our product, and we offer a measurable value to the corporation. We may provide the client with program evaluations and endorsements from past trainings, illustrating our ability to customize by industry, function, and individual experience. Through the process of submitting quotes and program outlines, we follow-up with the client in the hope of receiving a purchase order and a date for training.

In the meantime, we select trainers. We recruit and interview candidates who furnish credentials and who demonstrate knowledge and training skills.

We need to know the following: Will this trainer be able to facilitate the training and adjust to the needs of the participants? Will he/she assist with meaningful input in developing materials for this program? Ideally a brief mock-training displays the trainer's ability to work within our requirements. Finally we agree upon trainer responsibilities and fees.

In this first phase, we work closely with individuals whose expectations, personalities, cultural conditioning, and values affect partnering. We submit that a sixth learning dimension should be considered to align and connect people as partners through relationships.

Phase II—Explorations: Alignment Through Communication

One of MCB's core competencies is that we know our customers because we inquire and learn. Our responsibility is to uncover and examine challenges of our pragmatic client firm and of that firm's employees. The importance of and focus on the corporate environment grows in this phase. We need to understand the corporate mode of thinking, its strategic direction, and as much of its internal environment as possible (Parkhe 1991). With what kind of industry are we working? Who will we train: engineers, marketing associates, researchers, human resources professionals, financial staff, or all of the above? What facets of business are affected by cultural differences? How do we guide the participants through successful resolution of their challenges? Are there internal staff members who might complement the training and use their native cultural knowledge to make the program more pertinent? At this point, the corporation is exerting the most power in our electrical metaphor, and we must be sure that the power is properly channeled.

The internal environment of the trainers is important to understand here too. We find that we must use the very skills we often recommend to our client when we are working with a culturally diverse set of trainers. "The tricky step for managers is how to dance with dissimilar partners without stepping on any toes" (Kanter 1999). Healthy relationships with client and trainer require good sensitivity.

"This phase of evolution marks the beginning of *interaction* between partners." (Iyer 2002). We demonstrate our commitment by putting our client's goals first; that is, identifying dilemmas and current challenges in order to establish common objectives. Clients expect us to meet their needs but do not always appreciate the importance of their involvement in our enlightenment. We attempt to arrange a meeting with a focus group or obtain written answers to an online questionnaire. We encourage client cooperation. Our customized needs-assessment is central to obtaining a profile of the program participants. Upon completion we begin customization of the program.

The trainer is involved in this labor-intensive process and shares his/her experience organizing data to coincide with our model for training. We foster the trainer's trust and direct the energy, thereby enhancing the trainer's knowledge and ability. There is a great deal of mutual learning, and each partner brings his/her experiences to this development. Diplomacy, tact, and patience are also necessary. "There emerges (towards the end of the phase) a systematic effort by the partners to vicariously learn deeply embedded knowledge such as skills, processes and routines" (Iyer 2002).

We research, edit, and possibly purchase video and "realia" (i.e. everyday objects) for the upcoming program, all of which adds time and cost to development. When all is complete, MCB undertakes the final, physical task of producing resource materials for the training participants. The trainer is ready for the next phase—conducting the program.

Phase III—The Activity: Partnership Execution

We add an activity phase to Iyer's (2002) model. The partners finally come together in a culmination of their efforts on our power grid! We now deliver the transformed energy from its raw state to the consumer, all the while monitoring the transmission lines for any faults.

The trainer's ability to facilitate learning is the most important skill in this phase of alliance evolution, and delivering it in a micro-environment that is conducive to learning is the responsibility of MCB or the corporate partner. The number of participants and type of customization drives this choice. During the activity, MCB's goal and skill as the transformer is functioning, which ensures that the trainer responds to the group's dynamic and that he/she has maximum opportunity to be effective. The trainer or MCB facilitator must encourage active learning and participation where groups work together to solve cultural challenges based on new information revealed during the program. The corporation must actively participate in the process of acquiring new cultural knowledge and skill; there is unilateral as well as mutual learning throughout the workshop.

Phase IV—Expansion: Ongoing Partner Decisions

This evolutionary phase is "characterized by a high interdependence, greater trust, and increased investment for mutual benefit" (Iyer 2002). After the first successful program, the partners move beyond exploring and probing. They see the collaborative efforts as reciprocal learning.

If the client was satisfied with the activity and the program evaluations were positive, there may be an opportunity to expand the partnership by adding new training for other areas of the corporation. While negative reactions usually result in partnership termination, post-training discussions can also be an opportunity to strengthen relationships in either of the partnership realms (i.e., corporate or trainer).

Successful training creates a sense of accomplishment, validation, and relief for the trainer. This baptism by fire demonstrates more than any amount of preparation could exactly what the client needs and wants. On occasions where workshops have received less-than-average evaluations, trainers often see where they missed the mark, and they will adjust methods and material to improve their effectiveness (should another opportunity arise). In the case of failure, it is essential to discuss the reasons behind the failure with the client and to identify what could have been done differently.

The global environment takes center stage after satisfactory training, underscoring the need for cultural competence. Internally, MCB and the trainer can become a part of the corporate context, which once was a private area and they can become a new resource for coaching and consultation. It is here that the trainer begins to trust and appreciate the implicit skills that MCB has as a broker/program designer. These two partners appreciate what has been shared and learned. Trust is established, and mutual goals can be set for the future.

During the expansion phase, the client must assess the value of the program objectively. MCB shares a synopsis of the program evaluations and makes recommendations regarding sequels. If it will help future programs, the client must be willing to transfer some implicit skill knowledge. MCB and the trainer also interpret this assessment, and they extract information, which sets some mutual three-way goals toward further expansion.

Will another workshop take place? The trainer is assigned the task of reviewing and revising, incorporating new information and insight. MCB's role as broker is vital; keeping in contact with the client is imperative. The personal-relationship factor grows, and respect for each partner is emerging, which fosters interdependence and growth. MCB, as the connector, must provide new and innovative suggestions for viewing the cultural obstacles that the client encounters. MCB must continue to match the talents of the trainer with new clients and new opportunities.

Phase V—Commitment to Relationship or Transition? Increase the Power!

This phase is the most advanced state in the alliance relationship (Iyer 2002). It is reached only after a good deal of reward is gained for all three of the partners. Goals are mutually understood and agreed upon. The external and internal environments are monitored and are familiar. The partnerships are still fresh and so we see this as more of a transition phase. The time it takes to establish commitment to the relationship varies between the two sets of partners. For the firm, this commitment is not always made after just one successful workshop, while for the trainer it can be an immediate outcome of that one successful workshop.

The client must continue to "evaluate and revise alliance goals continuously to sustain advantage" (Iver 2002). If MCB has proven its value, the firm will endeavor to maintain this alliance to improve efficiency and effectiveness in the corporation through cultural training. It is important to note that a MCB + Firm partnership can be latent for a period of time without having a negative effect on the relationship. Economic variables and corporate direction can influence when the next training might take place.

The trainer may now realize the importance of a participant-centered workshop versus a lecture-style seminar to foster the training participants' application of new strategies to culturally-based challenges. These skills will benefit all three partners and will be part of the alignment managed by MCB. Perhaps a new alliance goal will include developing a second level of training to sustain advantage in the marketplace. The trainer should be willing to contribute more to this alliance in joint process based on the mutual benefits ahead. The personal collaboration that underlies these processes is instrumental in transitioning to a strong commitment to the relationship.

PARTNERING WITH A MEXICAN PROFESSOR AND A HIGH-PROFILE AUTOMOTIVE CLIENT

The importance of paying attention to each of the phases of partnership evolution, particularly to the expansion phase, is illustrated in a request we received early in our training experience. A prominent automotive manufacturer was increasing exposure with counterparts and customers in Mexico. This manufacturer hoped to ease current tensions between U.S. and Mexican engineers working in Mexico and to formulate guidelines for integrating the different values and work styles into a cooperative collaboration—objectives common to our automotive clients. If this pilot program were successful, we would conduct twelve Mexican cultural workshops in the U.S. and two more in Mexico, which would introduce Mexican employees to U.S. business culture. Our client gave us one skill stipulation: the trainer should be a Mexican national.

We had an excellent U.S.-born trainer who had lived and worked in Mexico. We wished to please the client, however, and not contradict his belief that a Mexican would be a better consultant. We began pursuing local business experts with little success. Next we searched the academic community and met with a professor of management at a state university. He was Mexican born and an advisor to the local government for trade relationships between the U.S. and Mexico. He was an educator who was accustomed to working with groups. He had some experience with the automotive industry and was very knowledgeable about the cultural differences between the U.S. and Mexico. We contracted with Dr. Garcia (a pseudonym) for the project.

I worked on program development with Dr. Garcia, preparing overhead slides and producing a participant-resource booklet with case studies and critical incidents. Our two-week task was to address the needs of the client in a workshop that would incorporate some history, some theory, and some hands-on recommendations and problem solving. I introduced Dr. Garcia to the procedure and explained that even though we were not experts in Mexican culture, our team had other areas of expertise that were critical to the success of the upcoming activity. We understood the firm's needs and expectations, and were sensitive to the adult corporate learner. Our client was looking for practical solutions and new skills for dealing with cultural differences. Dr. Garcia was agreeable, charming, handsome, well spoken, and delightful to work with.

We employed our copyrighted model, and together Dr. Garcia and I reviewed the needs assessments, reviewing the participants' experience and current perceptions of doing business with Mexicans. I often emphasized the main objective of the group: a nuts-and-bolts approach to their current problems.

We planned the agenda and painstakingly reviewed each overhead so that each would correspond with the material that comprised the participant resource manual. We used company-formatted slides and designed each one with the right amount of contrast and bullet points for optimum visibility. We worked on critical incidents and problem-solving activities. Occasionally Dr. Garcia and I disagreed on a minor point of sequence or about material that I felt was too academic or too theoretical for the workshop. We discussed these issues briefly and settled them rather quickly to our mutual satisfaction. When Dr. Garcia reviewed the materials after our progress, he would always compliment me and say that the materials were "fantastic." I grew more confident that we had an excellent trainer and that there was great potential for several programs with this prestigious client on Mexican/U.S. interaction.

On the day of the training (i.e., activity phase), I arrived before Dr. Garcia in order to arrange the room and the ancillary material for the program. I welcomed participants as they entered, setting the tone of the meeting. When Dr. Garcia arrived, I made certain that he had the participant booklet, our final slides, and anything else he needed to begin the program. I planned to stay all day to help facilitate and complete a written evaluation of our new trainer. The clock struck eight o'clock, and I opened the workshop with a brief summary about our company, a review of the plan for the day, and finally, a formal introduction of Dr. Garcia, in which I described his background and experience doing business with the U.S. and Mexico.

As I moved to the back of the room, I watched Dr. Garcia take our well-thought-out slides and move them to a side table. While he was talking to the group, he reached in his briefcase and produced a packet of worn, typewritten slides, with misspelled words and incorrect grammar. He then began a presentation on the sociological and anthropological background of culture. Although his intentions were good, he was rapidly losing twenty-two engineers who were anxious to discuss the nitty gritty of the problems they faced every day. During the morning break, I delicately asked Dr. Garcia what in the world he was doing. His explanation revolved around setting a foundation for the concepts we were going to be covering, which he had previously agreed to present in a much more hands-on manner. My role as the transformer was being short-circuited and there was a real possibility of power failure; the attention and energy of the audience was fading. I politely asked him to discontinue his lecture and to get to our slides and the agreed-upon format. When we reconvened, he went back to his old slides, completed his lecture, and finally got down to business about forty minutes later.

Dr. Garcia had not previously expressed any disagreement or discomfort in conducting the program that we discussed. We followed a protocol for "polite interaction(s) and conflict avoidance" (Wilson 1995, 34). In our exploration phase, our own cultural environments greatly influenced our new relationship. In retrospect, I believe that Dr. Garcia was respectful of my gender, my position as his new contractor, my qualifications as an educator, but not so certain of my cultural acumen and knowledge of what the corporation needed to know about Mexican people. His high-context behavior[4] did not allow him to disagree with me outright. His need to save face and my need to air our differences in the open clashed. The only choice he had was to act on his own in the way he believed was best.

Although his program had a rough start, Dr. Garcia did provide solid explanations and unique responses to the challenges that participants faced. There were negative comments about the opening lecture on the evaluations and some initial disappointment from my corporate contact. I arranged for a three-way debrief outlining how we would approach subsequent trainings. We were awarded more programs and eventually conducted that anticipated work in Mexico. This newly formed partnership with the corporation flourished, extended to other divisions, and lasted for ten years until all outside training was curtailed due to economic conditions. After working together for several months after that first session, and after getting to know and trust each other more, we developed a strong working relationship that spilled over into other areas of collaboration for about six years.

PARTNERING WITH A GERMAN LINE MANAGER AND TWO AUTOMOTIVE SUPPLIERS

Although partnerships might appear to be working, and goals, tasks, and skills seem to be in line, there can still be a disconnect in one learning dimension or another. Ongoing assessment during the expansion and transition phases is important, and the ability to be open to dissolution of a seemingly successful partnership is vital.

We once contracted with a multilingual consultant who had worked in the U.S., Germany, Mexico, Japan, and Brazil. He had held positions in major automotive companies and had acted as an independent consultant to one of the "Big Three" (i.e., General Motors, Ford, and Chrysler). We matched Frank's (a pseudonym) abilities with requests made by two large automotive suppliers for programs on management and communication style across cultures. Working with Frank was simultaneously rewarding and extremely stressful. His business background and global connections impressed us almost as much as they impressed the clients. Our program participants found him helpful and knowledgeable, if cantankerous and a bit overbearing. We made every effort to accommodate his self-described "line worker" style and to reform him through our personal relationship. Yet, in the expansion phase, we found him argumentative and stubborn—even bristling at updating or developing customized material. Often toward the end of a workshop, Frank would insult U.S. business and business people. Yet evaluations were positive, and these clients continued to request programs that Frank could deliver. In the spirit of collaboration, he shared leads with us for translation projects, and our partnership seemed to progress.

Several months after conducting three one-hour minisessions in Spanish for some Mexican nationals, we were informed that Frank had used some off-color humor and had expressed negative opinions about the client's corporate management! We ended our partnership with Frank. No matter what global expertise he offered, we were not willing to ruin our reputation over such behavior.

Fortunately neither of the two corporate connections was lost due to our break with Frank. We were able to replace him and add to the programs we had developed together. Learning to set limits and knowing when to dissolve a partnership were lessons that might have cost us a good and loyal client. Frank was usually able to provide solid advice and insight, but we knew that we had to end our partnership before he offended anyone else.

PARTNERING WITH TWO TRAINERS AND ONE JAPANESE AUTO MANUFACTURER

In 1996, we secured a contract with a Japanese automotive supplier to provide dual-focused, cross-cultural training programs. One program, for the U.S. audience, introduced employees to the differences in Japanese culture and to the realities of working for a Japanese company. The other program, for Japanese nationals, addressed working in the U.S. with U.S. counterparts and management. We presented these programs quarterly. We also received peripheral language-training and translation business from this client.

As time went by, the lead trainer, who was also a consultant on other countries, was unable to stay abreast of the fast-moving changes in Asian business. In spite of very positive program evaluations, we felt that the participants were not receiving current, relevant, and practical information. Approaching the human resource manager, we proposed replacing him. She was hesitant but trusted us to make the decision. This alteration marked a significant step in the commitment to the partnership. We reset and revised our alliance tasks and our partner (i.e., trainer) selection in order to improve efficiency and effectiveness.

We valued our strong relationship with the former trainer and respectfully explained the change to him. We assured him of our confidence in his ability and his continued inclusion on our trainer roster. He was concerned but acknowledged our mutual commitment to providing the best possible product to the client. Our relationship with him is still strong today. The new Japanese/U.S. trainer worked closely with us to develop meaningful critical incidents, learning activities, use of film, and realia. He has conducted these programs with updates for eight years.

Last year, while providing yet another training variation for this client, we noticed new banners in the facility announcing a recently adopted corporate philosophy. The philosophy encouraged ideas our trainers had been teaching for years: an integrative approach to work dilemmas using the best business practices of both cultures. It was an affirmation that we were congruent in this long-term partnership and that we shared goals with this company. Another example of mutual commitment is shown by the current requests from the firm for more than just culture-to-culture training. We have developed and conducted new workshops that incorporate cultural sensitivity in business procedures, such as e-mail etiquette and time and project management. These new opportunities reflect the confidence that our client has in our abilities, as well as our client's commitment to the relationship.

MCB LESSONS LEARNED

The lessons learned through the partnership phases of evolution can be seen in table 4.1. Our partnerships are unique. Our relationships continue even after the training is completed. During these latent periods, MCB is the

Table 4.1.   MCB Lessons Learned

Phase of Evolution	MCB Relationship with Trainer	MCB Relationship with Firm
Awareness and Partner Selection	As employer and mentor, evaluate potential for informative, pragmatic presentation	Illustrate practical return on investment; price program to reflect high customization
Exploration	Establish appropriate working communication style; guide and direct knowledge	Identify problem focus and goals for training; gather needs assessment
Activity	Observe training, facilitating as appropriate; gather additional info about client needs	Suggest alternatives to conventional training; provide action plan module
Expansion	Use training evaluations and MCB training notes; encourage changes in training materials if appropriate	Share training evaluations; discuss firm suggestions improving training; seek new opportunities by providing follow-up and consultation
Transition	Share firm suggestions for improving training; maintain relationships with effective trainers; end ineffective partnerships; network with other trainers	Maintain relationship; update firm on training innovations and access to assorted trainers

connection that remains active—empowering the trainers and nurturing contact with the clients.

NOTES

1. Thank you to clients who have helped us examine our training programs from a "transformer" vantage point during our research, especially Jill Pippin from Nissan R&D. We appreciate Natasha Crundwell, John Gu, Kelly Denawetz, and Mary Alice O'Brien Mecke, who assisted in dissecting things that work from the standpoint of the trainer. Thank you to Dr. David Victor for his cultural expertise and willingness to share his knowledge. Sincere appreciation to Bob and Hortensia Neely, of Global LT, for the diverse experiences and support during all the phases of cultural-training exposure over the past fifteen years.

2. Mary Beauregard has provided MCB Associates services to firms such as GM, Lear, Real Estate One, TI Automotive, Ford, Nissan, Valassis, and Carhartt.

3. "In general, while cross-cultural understanding was frequently viewed as important for doing business in a global economy, foreign-language skills rarely were considered an essential part of this" (Fixman 1990, 25).

4. "People raised in high-context systems expect more from others than do participants in low-context systems. When talking about something that they have on their minds, a high-context individual will expect his interlocutor to know what's bothering him so that he doesn't have to be specific" (Hall 1976, 98).

5

Coordinated Autonomy?

Culture in Emergency Response Partnering

Tara A. Eaton and Dale C. Brandenburg

INTRODUCTION

The status of the front line for emergency and disaster preparedness and response in the United States changed dramatically with the events of September 11, 2001.[1] Since that date, the emergency[2] response community has undergone significant changes. There is a new U.S. government structure with its own cabinet-level secretary; revised structures at the federal, state, regional, and local levels; significant investments in new technology, high-profile research centers, and new initiatives that receive inordinate attention from the press; and heightened awareness of homeland security activities among the general public. A critical problem associated with these changes, however, is that they have not led to transformations between emergency response agencies or their underlying cultural behaviors or strategies.

An effect from the events of September 11, 2001, on the emergency response community has been federal government mandates on agencies that are considered to be core first-responders to disasters and emergencies in large urban metropolitan areas. These agencies typically include police departments, fire departments, emergency medical services, and public health departments. Mandates have required that first-responder agencies work more closely together to prepare and train for any threats to national security or public safety associated with five phases of disasters and emergencies— surveillance, preparedness, response, recovery, and mitigation. At a deeper level, however, these mandates are also asking that first-responder agencies coordinate and build relationships, or partnerships, with each other to achieve this goal. The desired outcome of these activities is the coordination of response efforts, and that is the major focus of this case.

The heightened awareness of the need for closer collaboration among first-responder agencies has forced the issue of coordination to the forefront of partnerships that have heretofore been viewed as implicit. Such partnerships have been encouraged and expanded since the formation of the Department of Homeland Security (DHS) in November of 2002. Thus, to a great extent, many of the partnerships that have existed in name are only now given formal status. In the post-9/11, high-stakes environment, coordinated response to life-threatening events is not something to be taken for granted. This point was again made clear in the response to Hurricane Katrina in August and September of 2005.

Federal mandates from the DHS have forced agencies in the emergency-response community to form new partnerships with the goal of improving interagency communication and coordination. Each agency, however, has its own mission, history, operating procedures, traditions, and culture that we identify as shared and learned beliefs, norms, and symbols of a particular group. Organizational and cultural differences, such as the functional differences between police (law enforcement) and fire (saving lives), are not presently taken into consideration by federal or emergency-planning managers as variables that may affect interagency coordination, despite the fact that emergency-response agencies are cultural entities. Successful partnering could result in greater coordination across response agencies, but a false notion of coordination could lead to increased vulnerability and a greater opportunity for errors.

Since culture appears to play a significant role in first-responder coordination, an anthropological approach is useful in examining the contextual differences that may prevent efficient knowledge sharing and partnering in the professional emergency-response community.

For descriptive purposes, our discussion of the first-responder community of Ridgemont (a fictitious name) is divided into three distinct time periods or phases: Phase 1: pre–September 11, 2001; Phase 2: September 11, 2001 through fall 2003; and Phase 3: fall 2003 to the summer of 2005. Although fieldwork for this case did not begin until the fall of 2002, data was collected that informed all three phases of our discussion. Fieldwork included attending multiple-agency disaster-preparedness exercises, observation and participation in local emergency-management planning committees, education and training-development functions, and disaster-preparedness workshops and conferences. Primary data (interviews and observation) from one nine-month exploratory study with one of Ridgemont's key first-responder agencies is also included.

LITERATURE REVIEW

The partnership we examine is based considerably on events that involve formal and informal relationships among individuals and organizations. This type of partnership follows the concept of "relational exchange," noted by Ring and Van de Ven (1994) as opposed to transactional exchange; that is, organizations cooperate on the basis of inherent know-how (social assets) rather than the development and use of tangible assets associated with transactional exchange. The concept of relational exchange, therefore, is associated with significant social ties as in the social networks that characterize coordination in response to emergencies. The potential absence of social assets, or their limited existence, leads to situations of less-than-optimal coordination.

Since the organizations within our partnership neither share a profit motive nor do they directly share tangible assets, their results are not generally measured in tangible terms. This type of cooperative interorganizational relationship (Ring and Van de Ven 1994) is best studied in a field setting where events that cause organizational interplay can be examined for further analysis. Since the various first-responder organizations have independent operational responsibilities, it is through events such as disaster drills or exercises to prepare for emergencies that interactions and relationships can be observed and documented. These observations relate to an "ongoing dynamic state" (Macneil 1974), where events of the past, present, or future can be logically separated. While formal arrangements between organizations exist through mechanisms called "mutual aid agreements," any event is more likely to be governed by informal relationships because of the dynamism and uncertainty of the emergency/disaster context. The resulting exchanges between organizations are based considerably on trust (Ouchi 1984) as opposed to an established hierarchy that governs interorganizational behavior.

The specific goal of the interorganizational relationships we study is coordination, especially coordination in response to emergencies and disasters. This coordination may be defined as, "the collaborative process through which multiple organizations interact to achieve common objectives" (Drabek and McEntire 2002, 199). In the studies of various disaster-response contexts (Dynes and Tierney 1994; Quarantelli 1996), effective coordination is generally the result of two processes—(1) the formation of social networks and (2) preparation through planning, training, and exercises. Communication and cooperation are viewed as necessary but not as sufficient conditions to achieve coordination (Drabek and McEntire 2002; Auf der Heide 1989). The formation of social networks is also a function of the norms and values of the individual organizations which leads to the development of trust, required in relational exchange. The research literature does not portray a consensus as to what is meant by coordination, its nature, or its degree (Drabek and McEntire 2002). The complexities involved with managing bureaucratic structures, relying on informal processes, using multiple communication methods and technologies, and directing response agencies led one author (Koehler 1996) to suggest that chaos theory may be the most appropriate concept to use for studying this type of organizational partnering. The events and processes we have observed during our investigation offer only a snapshot of the complicated nature of the relationships involved. Additionally these relationships are evolving and dynamic due to changing contextual demands and available resources.

ECOLOGICAL GUILDS AS A METAPHOR FOR FIRST RESPONDERS

The cultural theme we propose in viewing this case is the existence of distinct cultures in forced emergency-response cooperation. We are making the assumption that during the process of forced cooperation, a major contributing variable is culture clash. That is, it is a major inhibitor, not necessarily a facilitator, of organizational cooperation and partnering. The concept of culture clash is not just a social perspective because, as a defined variable, it has been established as a major driver of not only organizational performance and results, but also of individual performance in organizations (Carleton and Lineberry 2004).

Within the context of this collaboration, we have adapted the metaphor of an ecological community, referred to as a "guild" (Simberloff and Dayan 1991), to represent what we call "emergency-response guilds" (see figure 5.1). An ecological guild refers to a collection of functionally similar species coexisting in a particular habitat. For example, different species of birds might maintain a habitat within a single tree. In this example, each species has a role to contribute to the ecological viability of the community within the tree. While there is some overlap in a niche,[3] each species of bird can forage and function within a sustainable ecosystem and without undue competition or compromise to the other members of the community.

Effective collaboration of multiple agencies within a mass emergency/ disaster event can be likened to that which occurs in an ecological guild.[4] In our case study, our target agencies A, B, C, and D could be perceived as constituting an emergency-response guild in that each one has a specific role in the event of a disaster. As these agencies evolve as an emergency-disaster response group (i.e., a guild), they can be considered a "community of practice" (Wenger 1998) of functionally-similar entities. For an emergency-response

Figure 5.1. Disparate First Responder Agencies (Shown as Birds) in the Same Ecological Guild

guild to function effectively, it is important that no specific agency role be redundant and that none conflict with another, so that preexisting cultural distinctions are maintained at the same time as interagency partnering forms. To the extent that individual agencies accept their newly evolving identity as a single interacting group of emergency responders collaborating on a shared mission/objective, effective disaster response could be realized. This would be like four species of birds living cooperatively in a single tree. Thus we posit the emergency-response guild concept as a goal for emergency-response cooperation and partnership, where effective community practice is enhanced by cultural sensitivity across the cooperating agencies.

A CASE OF EMERGENCY-RESPONSE PARTNERSHIPS IN RIDGEMONT

The current goal for larger-scale integration and extension of more formal first-responder partnerships in metropolitan cities, such as Ridgemont, was born out of the attacks on the World Trade Center towers on September 11, 2001 and the formation of DHS soon thereafter. Subsequently DHS distributed mandates to focus on the prevention and handling of terrorist attacks through better coordination between all disaster-response agencies. The philosophy for this partnership has been that conducting disaster-preparedness exercises, such as full-scale drills and table top exercises, will lead to more effective and coordinated responses. A further example is the establishment of regional entities called Regional Medical Biodefense Networks by the Centers for Disease Control in order to coordinate hospital, emergency medical, and statewide public-health communication infrastructures that would respond to major bioterror and related events. It is our position that although the national directive from DHS did succeed in forcing partnerships between metropolitan first-responder agencies by increasing the number of disaster drills and exercises, it has been less successful in encouraging these partnerships to develop greater interagency understanding or collaboration outside the conduct of the preparedness drills.

Much of the information we have collected up to this point suggests that we are observing an evolving organizational and cultural change that does not result in empirically-definitive conclusions regarding the outcomes of the partnership. As such, it is aligned with a diachronic focus. The partnerships are not voluntary but are instead mandated by federal and state guidelines. They are also subject to the whims of government agencies, including federal and state legislatures. Therefore changes in structure and operational requirements will be both constant and expected.

Contextual Aspects

In the years preceding our investigation, emergency response and homeland security had separate functions. Traditionally emergency response was the management of the effects of disasters or crises and dealing with risk and risk avoidance. Crises in this sense meant natural disasters such as earthquakes, floods, and hurricanes. Changes in the Federal Emergency Management Agency (FEMA) during the 1990s resulted in a formal reassignment of the name and function of emergency-management practices to an all-hazards approach that included homeland security following the terrorist incidents. The creation of DHS marked,

> the greatest federal government reorganization since President Harry Truman that is charged with a three-fold mission of protecting the U.S. from further terrorist attacks, reducing the nation's vulnerability to terrorism, and minimizing the damage from potential terrorist attacks and natural disasters (Haddow and Bullock 2003, 213).

What is notable about these changes in emergency management is that little research has focused on how to prepare and structure first-responder responses during terrorist threats (Tierney et al. 2001). This evidence aligns with the lack of coordination we observed between first-responder agencies during phase 2 of our investigation.

Phase 2 of our study in Ridgemont was marked by first-responder agencies trying to address federal mandates without formal implementation guidelines. First-responder agencies struggled to simultaneously develop emergency operations plans (EOPs), run disaster exercises, train employees for disaster response, and obtain protective or needed equipment for disasters (Tierney et al. 2001, 5). Disaster preparedness exercises, "designed to provide the opportunity to test the effectiveness of an EOP and to test the systems, facilities, and personnel involved in implementing the plan," (Haddow and Bullock 2003, 179) were frequently scheduled without complete attendance from all first-responder agencies. These or other private and public agencies that hosted disaster-preparedness exercises did so with varying resources and without using comparable exercise-design standards. Generally exercises during this time were not recorded, nor were they obviously used to inform the design of subsequent exercises. The effect of this cooperative but uncoordinated effort to organize and carry out new federal mandates for emergency response resulted in few true developmental partnerships between agencies.

Phase 3 of our investigation was a time period during which first-responder agencies in Ridgemont had completed one year's worth of homeland security activities. The positive effect of these experiences was fully illustrated during Ridgemont's response to its own local disaster during phase 3, when a power outage resulted in the most coordinated response event in Ridgemont's history since September 11, 2001. First-responder agencies A, B, C, and D, plus other public and private agencies, rallied to keep Ridgemont's citizens safe and at ease during the three-day outage. This event later became a type of cultural legend or a point of reference for first-responder agencies to draw on in subsequent discussions during disaster drills. The response to the outage was considered a success, so much so that the event itself was not characterized as a "disaster" formally, but rather just as the Blackout of 2003. This labeling signified the level of control that Ridgemont first-responder agencies felt they had over the situation during the response. Moreover, the event served as an impetus for first-responder agencies to begin to form more significant partnerships. This shared experiential learning was leveraged to further interagency coordination within the general context of broader public safety issues.

Finally, in many Ridgemont preparedness exercises, consistency of agency participation is varied and is usually dependent on which agency organizes the exercise and on who that agency invites to participate in the exercise. It is not uncommon to attend a disaster drill or tabletop where key agencies are not present or have not been invited, due to some oversight or from just not knowing whom to invite. In addition, emergency-response personnel will regularly float in and out of planned exercises due to real emergencies or duties, thereby interrupting the flow and sustainability of a focused discussion. In one exercise, a two-hour apartment building evacuation drill was cancelled fifteen minutes before its scheduled start time due to an actual fire emergency across town. In summary, emergency-response drills, as they are currently designed and conducted, are neither formalized nor necessarily dependable mediums for emergency-response personnel to fully collaborate or form partnerships in meaningful ways.

Characteristics of Ridgemont First Responders

There are recognized major role players among the Ridgemont's response community represented primarily by four agencies that depict our emergency response guild. Other city agencies are also included in most exercises but are generally not at the planning table. The cultural dynamic among these agencies is seen as a major hurdle to better coordination. For example, agency B and agency D tend to be highly individualistic agencies that work separately from other agencies during emergencies. They have deep and distinct histories that make it difficult for either one to adapt to the other's procedures for communication. Agency A and agency C, in comparison, work together more often than with either of the two other agencies; however, they, too, primarily work individually within their own organizational functions.

A tabletop exercise during phase 3 illustrates this point. During this exercise, agency C was working in partnership with other agency Cs in communities surrounding Ridgemont. Their goals were to talk out a response to a bioterrorist threat and to compare results across agency Cs. We observed that Ridgemont's agency C contacted agencies A, B, and D as one of its last tasks during the exercise. This was especially significant since one of the goals of the exercise was to test for interagency communication and coordination.

Other cultural/functional issues with the Ridgemont first-responder community are that agency A is organized in such a way that it functions through an assortment of public and private suborganizations, which make coordination and communication difficult for the other primary agencies (B, C, and D). Also, in general, there are several different coordinating bodies in Ridgemont that are not working in concert and in some cases overlap. For example, in one large-scale tabletop exercise, agency B did not inform agency C about special arrangements for the transport of victims from the scene of a disaster. Instead agency B called on agency A, who in turn was to notify agency C of the transportation arrangements. Both agency A and agency C have direct relationships with agency B; yet, because agency B is used to dealing primarily with agency A, the communication process proved to be inefficient in the case of a large-scale emergency scenario.

Finally, there is no single line of leadership or designated governing authority that is acknowledged by all of these response agencies and thus is similar to our ecological guild, where no single species dominates the environment. One area organization has the responsibility to assist in the coordination of efforts across the primary agencies, but also to support organizations and private businesses. This is the Local Emergency Planning Committee (LEPC), an entity that exists in most locations throughout the country. The LEPC has only an advisory capacity, however, and agency D, in particular, does not send representatives on a regular basis to the monthly LEPC meetings.

Four observations are relevant to understanding the people elements of the case. First, with regard to organizational characteristics, there appears to be a paramilitary cultural orientation to the work of emergency management, a pattern that is especially prominent in agencies B and D. Second, the primary first-responder agencies tend to associate communication during disasters as a technological issue only, where good communication is using the latest communication devices, like an 800 MHz radio system.

Third, in examining the inter-organizational context, there have been and continue to be organizational turf battles among the public agencies. For example, agency B and agency D have a long history of criticizing each other for being less competent than the other. Within Ridgemont specifically, we observed that agency D during phases 2 and 3 often did not show up for exercises hosted or coordinated by agency B, although the cause could have been related to a shortage of people attending the exercises. Fourth, the events of 9/11 have affected the emergency-response community in that agencies have changed their attitudes and procedures with regard to disaster response and to their role in the war against terrorism. These changes have added considerable stress to this ecological setting and need to be explored and synthesized to guide interagency partnerships.

PARTNERSHIP OUTCOMES

Relationship Outcomes

Relationships have been established in Ridgemont because of forced partnerships; the level of development between any pair of agencies, however, is not consistent. It is difficult to ascertain whether the relationships were successful beyond the boundaries of the partnership; all parties involved in the Blackout of 2003, however, agreed that the response to that event was a success. One outcome was the successful integration of agencies to provide a coordinated response since such integration had only existed as plans prior to the event; subsequently this integration solidified the identification of overlapping agency responsibilities. An inhibitor to building relationships was the highly individualistic nature of particular organizations that have worked successfully on their own for a long time. Thus they are like the species of birds who do not relate their individual roles within the environment of a single tree.

A second observation of Ridgemont's emergency-response community is that none of the emergency-response agencies involved is realistically prepared (due to shortages of resources and capabilities) or is currently achieving the high level of performance necessary to partner and achieve greater coordinated response during disasters. We believe that while strategic alliances among the agencies are demanded, some agencies are neither capable nor motivated, nor do they view such partnerships as mandatory for meeting the evolving new demands of coordination. To refer back to the cultural image of an ecological guild, a core emergency-response agency is like a species of bird that functions independently and whose functioning has worked well for the majority of its history, leaving little motivation to partner with other birds.

Our research has led us to view the relationships of the first-responder community as a product of cultural behaviors and beliefs that may or may not be compatible with current and future demands of these organizations. The introduction of a super-organization represented by DHS requires a reexamination of the cultural and structural underpinnings for what is meant by coordinated response. While its purpose seems to engender systemic action, in practice it leads to questioning traditional authority and lines of communication, which may, in the short term, lead to dysfunctional actions. Thus what we are viewing is a system in the midst of transformation where the outcomes and goals are not fully appreciated or determined.

Our concepts concerning what coordination is and how it is implemented in the first-responder community is linked to the thinking of Auf der Heide and Quarantelli. Auf der Heide (1989: 39) presents this picture of barriers to turning communication into coordination:

- The "Robinson Crusoe syndrome" or "We're the only ones on this island." Organizations are accustomed to operating autonomously and fail to change this approach in disasters where multiple organizations are involved and are dependent on one another.
- Terminology and procedures used to exchange information vary among organizations. There is a hesitancy to depend on other organizations, often due to a lack of trust or familiarity, or due to political, jurisdictional, and personal disputes.
- There is no mutual agreement as to who has the responsibility for the collection and dissemination of various types of information, or to whom it should be distributed.
- Persons possessing information do not realize that another person needs it.
- The information needs of other organizations are not understood.

One may conclude that what is initially seen as communication issues are fundamentally also political and cultural. The politics and culture of highly authoritative organizations, ones that need to build trust in their own organizations, often do so grudgingly with other organizations. The complex nature of multiple-agency coordination and the politics involved is described by Quarantelli (1983, 105):

Cooperation is adversely affected by preexisting personal, political, and jurisdictional disputes . . . Such differences as those between city and county or public and private interests had a pervasive negative influence on cooperation. The consequences of such disputes may range from the exclusion of organizations from planning meetings to charges that an organization is transgressing another's jurisdiction or responsibility. Unfortunately jurisdictional disputes unresolved on an everyday basis, do not tend to get resolved in disasters.

Coordination requires knowledge (Auf der Heide 1989) about other organizations, especially information about job roles and functions, available resources, current needs, terminology, and professional competence. Such elements are viewed as necessary to establish the trust among organizations necessary for achieving a high level of cooperation. The acquisition of knowledge needs to be developed both at the individual and organizational levels to foster cross-agency coordination. In Ridgemont, the acquisition of such knowledge is sponsored by the LEPC, and it is up to individual agencies to take advantage of these opportunities. The improvement in this arena was recognized through subsequent large-scale, multiple-agency exercises.

Partnership Goal Outcomes

It is necessary to understand what *good* emergency preparedness and management look like, and the issue of providing an operational definition of coordination in Ridgemont remains unresolved. The converse, however, seems to be well recognized; that is, when coordination is lacking, the results are obvious, such as the immediate aftermath of Hurricane Katrina. This lack of definition and understanding generates a state of fluidity where statements of specific objectives are often in conflict.

A current assessment is that improved coordination has been achieved, but only in the sense that multiple agencies are regularly participating in preparedness exercises. It is an open question as to whether the agencies are working as an ecological guild to build a community of practice. There are many agencies that point to the Blackout of 2003 as spurring the development not only of dialogue and networking among agencies, but also of greater willingness to recognize the contributions made by other organizations in working cooperatively. In a recent situation, representatives from fifteen area agencies were called to work on a regional response plan. Two of the agencies that had not offered participation in such ventures in the past immediately volunteered for the effort. In terms of sustainability, there is no indication that emergency response partnerships have dissolved or will discontinue.

CULTURAL EVALUATION OF THE PARTNERSHIP

The cultural theme we propose is the existence of disparate cultures in forced emergency-response cooperation. It is our view that cultural disparity prevents openness among response organizations to understand each others' coordination-response strategies. Such strategies, using more fluid command structures, would be built on coordination issues resulting from an effective community of practice. Referring to our ecological guild, Ridgemont's emergency-response agencies, or "species," operate separately from one another and thus prevent true coordination through partnership. Second, because many of these agencies believe that they were forced to coordinate with each other, success is measured by whether agencies participate in designated co-ordination efforts (i.e., exercises) and not by the quality of the exchange during the exercises.

For the most part, successes are not regularly acknowledged or celebrated. More important, it is the failures that attract attention. The consequences of not performing well are often carefully acknowledged, and most often corrective actions result. In some cases, individuals are recognized for their contributions, but seldom is the entire agency or organization recognized. The only observed mention of success took place at the end of preparedness exercises when the sponsoring agency usually thanked the other agencies for participating.

The theme of cultural disparity among emergency-response agencies in a stressful environment hints at a social explanation for the lack of interagency coordination among these agencies. Coordination issues cannot be fixed through the purchase of expensive communication technologies (i.e., 800 MHz radios) or by going through the motions of preparedness exercises. The theme of cultural disparity also suggests ideas for what response agencies must do to be successful in improving coordination despite their individualistic tendencies. One of these ideas could include collectively forming and identifying a new response identity such as the Disaster Response Network of Ridgemont instead of agencies A, B, C and D of Ridgemont.

KEY LESSONS LEARNED FROM THE PARTNERSHIP EXPERIENCE

For Partnership Participants

Based on our observation of the city of Ridgemont, we offer recommendations to improve collaboration and the formation of true partnerships between emergency-response agencies exhibiting cultural differences. First, the preparedness exercises should be structured so that they facilitate true knowledge-sharing and learning between organizations rather than simply serving as opportunities for collective interaction. Stated differently, executing drills does not automatically translate into increased coordination. Second, when preparedness drills are successful at facilitating knowledge sharing, these successes should be publicly recognized and celebrated as positive indicies of experience. Third, standard operating procedures or communication procedures need to be shared among all response agencies. Although we understand that standard operating procedures have been kept secure from outside agencies, we believe that the post-9/11 environment requires more information sharing and interagency understanding for complex all-hazard response environments.

A fourth recommendation relates to interorganizational strategy development. In emergency preparation, there are local needs and external requirements coexisting in constant flux. Regardless of the level, these demands are associated with relationships between individuals and organizations. A consistent statement we heard from many leaders was that effective coordination was the result of individual relationships (not necessarily organizations). This conclusion, also supported by Auf der Heide (1989), states that confidence and trust are built from personal relationships. To achieve coordination, an integrated strategy to support relationship building is required.

Finally a formal process of legitimization is needed for the integration of new organizations within the ecological guild. We noted the increase in the number of agencies and organizations participating in drills and exercises, especially from the medical community and agency C. The issues of integration include not only trust but competence and skills, historically recognized performance, leadership recognition, and the organization's work culture—all of which can either facilitate or inhibit the integration process.

For the Research Community

Current discussion of disaster within academe views disaster as a process or event involving the combination of a destructive natural or technological agent and a technologically- and socially-vulnerable population (Oliver-Smith 1996). This definition of *disaster* suggests that relying heavily on information technology (IT) devices as solutions for improved coordination between agencies may in fact contribute to the vulnerability of a technologically-interdependent population when a disaster occurs (Hart et al. 2001). It also suggests that our observations of organizational differences among emergency-response agencies may contribute to a "socially produced condition of vulnerability" (Hoffman and Oliver-Smith 2002, 4). In this view, vulnerable populations are less prepared to adapt to the changing features of their natural, social, and technologically constructed environment during a disaster. Societies do cope with disasters over time, however, with appropriate environmental, ideological, and cultural adaptations that include innovation and persistence in memory, cultural history, worldview, symbolism, social-structural flexibility, religion, and the cautionary nature of folklore and folk tales (Hoffman and Oliver-Smith 2002). It is our view that Ridgemont and other communities must bring a more comprehensive set of cultural issues to the foreground to form true partnerships and to decrease their vulnerability to disaster.

As the frequency and seriousness of natural and technological disasters increases (Hoffman and Oliver-Smith 2002), a holistic and cultural approach to understanding the sociocultural and organizational factors involved in disaster readiness has a direct role in the protection of homeland security. Since September 11, 2001, the U.S. media has provided Americans with a pervasive obsession over terrorist and disaster awareness, a concern that has affected both public and private organizations across the country. Disaster awareness has generated a strong response from emergency-response communities, where preparedness plans and procedures for disasters are being renegotiated and disaster consciousness is on the rise. In this way, the events of 9/11 have mobilized cultural change within U.S. disaster prevention and management. Moreover, these events have generated values among society that affect the way U.S. citizens behave, as well as how they view themselves, their security, and their future. For example, since the anthrax incidents on the East Coast after 9/11, post offices across the nation have developed new procedures for sorting and handling suspicious mail. As Hoffman and Oliver-Smith put it, "Disaster exposes the way in which people construct or 'frame' their peril, the way they perceive their environments and their subsistence, and the ways they invent explanation, constitute their mortality, and project their continuity and promise into future" (Hoffman and Oliver-Smith 2002, 6). We contend that cultural analysis can provide valuable sociocultural information and perspective on the self-revealing nature of disaster and can suggest ways of improving disaster management.

Finally, the Ridgemont first-responder community is an excellent example of how the concepts of organizational complexity, organizational learning, and organizational culture can shed light on community health and safety issues. It also demonstrates how forced partnerships cannot penetrate to a deeper level without cultural acceptance from all partners. Emergency-response agencies are steeped in cultural traditions such as safety, work, danger, military structure, and a tendency to seek out technological solutions. One could argue that the complexity within and between the organizational cultures of emergency-response agencies provides a salient explanation for the difficulties involved in interagency coordination and communication during disaster and disaster-preparedness exercises. Coordination is thus an evolved state formed through the combination of formal structural mechanisms, such as mandated planning and exercises, with informal relationships that include social networks and shared experience.

Therefore, a holistic and cultural approach can be effective in understanding not only explicit meanings, such as those conveyed in emergency-management procedures, but also implicit meanings, such as those found through interagency interaction, emergency-response agents' interpretations of agency values and characteristics, the formation of an ecological guild, and the organizational culture surrounding emergency-response partnerships.

NOTES

1. We would like to thank our research participants for their time and support during this exploratory observation and study. We would also like to acknowledge, specifically, Dan O'Reilly and Jessica Price for their help in editing the case. A special thanks is also given to Thelma Alcordo and Shane Eaton.

2. There is considerable distinction made between disasters and emergencies in the literature. The players involved, however, remain virtually the same so we adopt the term "emergency" to apply to all such events including disasters, terrorist attacks, and catastrophes.

3. In biology, the term "niche" refers to the specific role a species occupies within an ecological community.

4. We are indebted to our colleague Dan O'Reilly, who suggested the metaphor. Dan is a member of the biology faculty at a local college.

6

Practical Strategies for Partnership

An Inside-Out View

Cristy S. Johnsrud, Linda L. Lampl, and Susan E. Squires

INTRODUCTION

Establishing an independent enterprise presents a significant challenge. In today's environment of downsizing, right-sizing, lean management, mergers and acquisitions, and global competition, both large and small firms turn increasingly to partnering as a means to maintain and expand business opportunities, products, and services. Ten years ago, Randy Myers labeled such arrangements "the modus operandi for the new millennium" in his *CFO* report on Silicon Graphics.

> The fact is, no major company goes it alone these days. Spurred on by the frenetic pace of technology and anxious to pursue new revenue streams and economies of scale in research and development and in manufacturing, innovators like Silicon Graphics are entering into cooperative ventures that just 10 years ago would have been unthinkable in many boardrooms. (1995, 26)

The combinations and permutations of partnering are many. Some involve the formation of a legal entity, others are temporary or informal. Small businesses develop strategic partnerships with large or small organizations to expand knowledge, skills, and abilities and to access new markets without hiring new employees. Large firms partner with one another and/or smaller, more agile companies to capture innovative thinking or technologies, to outsource certain operations, and to meet contracting goals imposed by private and government clients.

This essay describes how three geographically dispersed, women-owned consulting firms formed a strategic partnership c. 2002 to promote their skills in practicing anthropology in new markets.[1] The work presented here

Figure 6.1.   Car Mirror: Reflecting the Path We Took as Partners

is itself a product of individual and collective reflection, constructed by the threesome over a six-month period. The metaphor we use is a car mirror (see figure 6.1). The experience was somewhat like taking a road trip with three drivers, each of whom took the wheel from time to time and relied on back-seat drivers and the mirrors to re-image the path taken.

Unlike traditional research-based reports, the data and analytical comments presented here address the experience and outcomes from the inside out — that is to say, through the lenses of the participants rather than through the filter of the external observer. Consequently the narrators are more participants than observers, with all that such a juxtaposition of roles implies, including the perception of reduced objectivity. The authors created best practices in vivo and extracted lessons learned after performance.

Theoretical Approach

After much discussion, we placed the partnering experience within a number of scholarly traditions and schools of thought in order to correspond to the spectrum of training and know-how available within the group: experiential learning, autoethnography, and collaboration.

Our experience in partnership formation and ongoing activities was influenced by "experiential learning" as envisioned by Kolb[2] (1984) and Schön (1983). It is important to acknowledge that the experiences reported here generated multiple learning opportunities, both individually and collectively, and created a "learning lab" in the tradition of masters from Kurt Lewin (1947) forward; the strategy was to "learn by doing" (Kolb 1984).

The partnership allowed us to test theories—and recommended actions—about collaboration, process, and outcomes; to project ideas about what might happen, what might not, what might go right, and what might go wrong in specific collaborative projects; to carry out project tasks; and to evaluate processes, outcomes, and experiences for higher-order learning. By identifying and understanding particular experiences, we hope to contribute to the theory of partnering, collaboration, and interorganizational linkages as well as to the more practical, hands-on side of doing work through collaborative teams.

We drew from "autoethnography" (Ellis and Bochner 1996; Reed-Danahay 1997) to illustrate the practical aspects and action associated with the formation and operation of a partnership. Autoethnography is an increasingly recognized and useful approach that combines personal narrative with the broader cultural context in which experiences occur. It grew out of attempts to understand the self within a societal context, especially to reveal hidden barriers or issues, otherness vs. mainstream norms. With roots in postmodernism, feminism and post-colonialism, autoethnography seeks to clarify the construction of identities at odds with particular social contexts (Reed-Danahay 1997; McLaurin 2003; Tenni et al. 2001; MacCormack 2001; Ellis and Bochner 1996). The experience portrayed here represents the construction of an egalitarian, democratic, collaborative partnership in the midst of a culture of competition that characterizes business in general. Separately this story calls attention to the fact that small businesses can form and maintain partnering agreements just as well as large organizations.

Both the experiential nature and the self-examination aspects of the perspective we take in this essay equate to looking into the rearview mirror to see where we have been, what the roadway was like, and how it compares with what lies ahead. In the picture, we see the reflection of the road already traveled and a part of the vehicle in which the journey was and is being undertaken. The vehicle symbolizes the partnership structure, and the mirror reflection image can be likened to looking back to see and understand our experience.

The roots of collaboration and its newer manifestation of partnering are grounded in the work of Lewin (1947) and others who in the 1930s and 1940s pioneered the concept of group dynamics (See Burnes 2004; Marrow 1947).

Since that time, the theoretical traditions related to collaborations and partnerships have expanded to include both process and conditional aspects. For example, a number of theorists have focused on process-related aspects of partnership, including Tuckman (1965), who first recognized "stages of group development and maintenance" and later added to that discussion (Tuckman and Jensen 1977). Those explorations were followed by "stages of collaboration" (Hord 1986; Lieberman 1986; Swan and Morgan 1993) and "cornerstone domains for collaborations" (Squires and Uhl 1993). Michael Schrage (1990, 41) defined the process of collaboration succinctly:

> Shared [sic] creation: two or more individuals with complementary skills interacting to create a shared understanding that none had previously possessed or could have come to on their own. Collaboration creates a shared meaning about a process, a product or an event . . . the true medium of collaboration is other people.

Other scholars have examined collaboration as a structure of interorganizational relationships (Blankenship 1977; Priess et al. 1996; Wenger et al. 2002; Johnsrud 2002; Johnsrud 1994). Freeman (1993, 33) elaborates on collaboration:

> The condition that occurs when two or more people or organizations join forces over a long period of time to produce something neither can achieve alone. In the process, each participant contributes something significant and different, derives something of personal and/or organizational benefit, and acknowledges the mutual dependence on the other required to achieve the mutual desired results.

Lessons Learned

The three of us approached the idea of partnering from different perspectives: We held knowledge of different literatures and had separate experiences in the development and teaching of the ins and outs of collaborative relationships and partnering. While knowledge of the literature and teaching are different from practice, each partner brought tales from previous partnerships that did not work. We believed that in this relationship, the partners would walk the talk or practice what we preached. Consequently we attended to process from the beginning.

In retrospect, we created on-the-fly best practices—an outcome that was not surprising given individual foundations in experiential learning. We suggest the habits are transferable and may be used by other businesses—small and large—to negotiate and manage partnerships for positive outcomes in process and the product(s). These practices are

1. Establish a shared vision or culture for the partnership.
2. Provide a basis for dialog, communications, and understanding.
3. Agree upon leadership and management protocols.
4. Balance partnership needs and individual firm responsibilities.
5. Protect each partner's corporate identity and distinctive competencies during and after the collaboration.
6. Build—and work to maintain—mutual trust.

We examine each of these practices later in the chapter within the context of our partnership experience and consider the lessons learned.

HISTORY OF THE PARTNERSHIP EXPERIENCE

Coming Together

Network and activity theory support the importance of professional contacts as a source in the search for a job (Granovetter 1974; Nardi et al. 2000). We suggest that professional networks also contribute to finding partners suitable for temporary or topic-specific projects.

We met in the 1990s as three anthropologists working in leadership positions in a voluntary professional association.[3] While we shared an interest in the promotion of anthropology outside the academy, none of our individual, day-to-day work situations looked alike. For example:

- Cris Johnsrud worked in a university-based center that facilitated technology transfer among government agencies, academic institutions, and business enterprises. She had a background in journalism and teaching and had long worked with engineers and others in the technical workforce. Johnsrud holds a PhD in anthropology.
- Susan Squires worked at the time in a small California-based product-design firm and held previous experience—both internal and external—with Fortune 500 companies. She had a background in teaching, management, and design anthropology and recently co-authored a book about the fall of Arthur Andersen (Squires et al. 2003). Squires holds a PhD in anthropology.
- Linda Lampl cofounded and served as the working president of a small, science-based consulting firm that had provided services to clients in

government, academia, and Fortune 500 companies from 1978 to the present. She has conducted fieldwork in coastal areas of Florida in the oil and gas industry, and in policymaking agencies. She has a background in journalism and environmental issues and holds a PhD in organizational communication.

While we developed a working relationship within the context of the professional association, we did not move to extend that connection until 2001 when Johnsrud floated the idea of combining forces to expand business opportunities. During this period, Johnsrud and Squires left their respective positions to establish separate independent research and consulting enterprises. The first serious discussions began over coffee at the 2001 Annual Meeting of the American Anthropological Association (AAA) in Chicago.

With the spark struck, conversations continued. Telephone conferences—paid for separately—lasted for hours as we discussed the benefits and drawbacks of forming a partnership. Johnsrud and Squires came to the partnership with single-person firms; Lampl brought a five-person organization to the table, which meant that the needs and interests of those "invisible" partners would always be part of the agenda. Lampl was skeptical of the value for her firm's bottom line: exploratory work takes second place to payroll. All of us struggled with the mechanics of such a working relationship:

- What types of opportunities could the collective pursue?
- How would decisions be made?
- How would responsibilities be allocated?
- Who would be in charge? When? For what purpose?
- Who would own the products that might be produced?
- What ideas and time would each organization be willing or able to share?
- How would funds be managed and distributed?

If answered honestly, each question implied a level of trust. Stating these concerns established a working agenda for the group; we revisited these and other questions that emerged time and again as business opportunities developed. We personified Kolb's (1984, 38) experiential-learning model: "Learning is the process whereby knowledge is created through the transformation of experience." We debriefed on a regular basis, discussed our experience, and decided what to do the next time.

As discussions continued and trust grew, each of us began to share more professional and personal data, our distinctive competencies, and, eventually, information about opportunities for a collaborative project. Overlapping expertise areas facilitated communication and nurtured rapport. Shared training in cultural anthropology and its theoretical and value systems was an important unifying and organizing force. We each had experience in ethnographic field work, teaching, and training and in evaluating programs, processes, and projects. We also had a commitment to educate policymakers, managers, service providers, and other client groups about the value of anthropologic perspectives.

Despite the similarities, significant differences and needs remained. Johnsrud and Lampl were based in Florida; Squires was located in California; Johnsrud was a start-up firm; Squires was a young firm with a defined market niche and a well-developed suite of offerings; and Lampl was head of an organization with an established collaborative culture, organizational structure, decision-making process, and client base. Each partner needed to balance the work of the partnership with existing and incoming projects, client obligations, and business development strategies in her own firm. Lampl had the added responsibility of establishing and maintaining a link between the partnership and her own organization so that the home team was in the loop. Lampl wanted to avoid a key problem recognized in small group research: agreements and changes made in and for a temporary, small group may fall by the wayside once the participants return to the influence of permanent groups.

Some Tools Used for Group Development

The early conversations and decision making took place in the virtual environment, mostly by telephone. We also used the telephone for brainstorming and problem solving; this fostered discussions regarding questions and apprehensions. The teleconference provided an arena in which we could reach mutual agreement, if not always a consensus, on a particular strategy, approach, or solution. We supplemented voice communication with e-mail for tasks such as setting meeting times or raising questions. By agreement, we did not use asynchronous communication such as e-mail as a mode for problem solving.

Individually skilled in the mechanics of strategic planning for others, we turned the spotlight on the emerging collaboration and developed what-if scenarios—just as we might have with clients. During this phase, we worked to build a shared vision of a potential partnering arrangement, how it might behave, and how it could adapt to a variety of different clients and services. It soon became apparent, however, that the emerging partnership needed a real project to hold our interest and move the relationship beyond discussion.

THE FIRST PROJECT: RESPONDING TO AN RFP

The first opportunity to negotiate roles and move the learn-by-doing into a project-based experience came in 2002 as a published request for proposal (RFP) from a federal fishery agency. The RFP provided an opportunity to test our mettle at working with one another and to debut the fledgling partnership to a real audience.

The time frame for development and submission of the proposal was short, which meant this project required an intensive, all-out effort. We quickly agreed that Lampl's more-established firm would lead the proposal effort and manage the contract if successful. Johnsrud and Squires provided supporting information and budget requirements; they also participated in the development of the approach to data collection and analysis as set out by the agency issuing the RFP. We did not win the contract. While disappointed, everyone—including the individuals within Lampl's firm who also worked on the proposal—was pleased at the rapidity with which we all were able to produce a competitive proposal, establish a level of comfort and trust sufficient to share financial information, and cooperate on decisions related to research activities and contract management. The proposal process allowed us to work out specific roles and responsibilities and to evaluate performance in a defined or real world context. While a failure in a contractual sense, the partnership matured.

THE SECOND PROJECT: A CRADA WITH THE U.S. NAVY

A second opportunity appeared during a casual conversation at a conference between Johnsrud and a technology-transfer officer from a federal laboratory. This interaction led to discussions about how an anthropological perspective might help the U.S. Navy mitigate the loss of tacit knowledge with the retirement of civilians and uniformed personnel. Could anthropological approaches improve the capture of tacit knowledge for use by Navy instructional designers to create job aids and knowledge banks?

The partners considered the implications for developing products or a program to help the Navy. Since the Navy laboratory was located in Orlando, Florida, Johnsrud and Lampl were delegated to meet with key researchers and managers. Results from the initial meeting were favorable, and all three partners attended subsequent meetings with Navy representatives over a three-day time period. The next step was to develop a formal agreement for the design and implementation of a training workshop on ethnographic methods for use by knowledge-management professionals.

The CRADA with NAVAIR TSD Orlando

The military and its branches speak a language of their own, and the partners became conversant in some of the Navy's vernacular. The Naval Air Systems Command, Training Systems Division (TSD) at Orlando, Florida, is known as NAVAIR TSD Orlando. NAVAIR and other research and development laboratories under the Department of Defense have the authority to enter into agreements with individuals and organizations in order to develop services or products that might benefit soldiers—the military's ultimate customer—via better training and enhanced safety. The Cooperative Research and Development Agreement, or CRADA, is one such vehicle or type of contract.

We worked out the details of the CRADA and its attendant Statement of Work between ourselves and then between the partnership and the Navy. The CRADA was officially signed by the commanding officer for NAVAIR TSD Orlando and by Lampl as the partnership's designated prime contractor for this agreement.[4] Under the official agreement, Lampl's organization and its subcontractors were responsible for a workshop to teach ethnographic methods to NAVAIR TSD. We would develop and deliver all materials and the workshop. We then would make changes based on Navy representatives' suggestions. The U.S. Navy agreed to copy our materials, provide other supplies as needed, enroll personnel for the workshop, and designate space and support for the workshop. In the end, both the Navy and Lampl's firm (and its subcontractors) held claim to the training content of the workshop, and therefore both could offer the workshop for sale after making revisions.

The workshop was held in March 2004. Workshop evaluations were collected on paper and online (Lampl et al. 2004). While we did not script each module, we used PowerPoint as a guideline and were comfortable with each other after the months of development. There were few surprises. During the workshop, we made some changes based on observations within our group, while others were made at the suggestion of the participants.

We conducted the official debrief in May 2004, with Squires attending via teleconference and Johnsrud and Lampl attending in person. Revisions were submitted in September 2004. The CRADA was officially completed in November 2004. The Navy and members of the partnership were satisfied with the results. We continue to pursue additional markets for the revised workshop within other parts of the Navy and other federal agencies.

Debrief From the Navy Experience

The work with the Navy provided opportunities for us to grow and mature. For example, the California-based Squires could not always join the Florida-based Johnsrud and Lampl in data collection activities or in observing Navy activities related to the workshop. While the situation could have led to distrust or uncertainties, it did not. Attending to one another's needs averted such problems. Johnsrud and Lampl included Squires in meetings with clients or prospective clients via speaker telephone or, when impossible to mesh schedules across time zones, explicitly designated an empty chair as Squires in absentia. Johnsrud and Lampl made sure that Squires received detailed briefings of all events. The partners planned upcoming meetings and agreed to responsibilities before such meetings in Orlando occurred.

The development of the workshop and subsequent marketing materials provided multiple opportunities to compare individual perspectives and styles with regard to ethnography, training techniques, and approaches to preparation of workbooks, brochures, and elevator slides.[5] We jointly designed a PowerPoint template specific to this workshop and divided training topics according to each partner's distinctive competencies, experiences, and interests. We also reached a consensus regarding fundamental teaching and learning objectives for the workshop, ownership and use rights for the materials produced, and basic ideas as to how to handle opportunities for subsequent work.

ANALYZING THE PARTNERSHIP EXPERIENCE FROM THE INSIDE OUT

At the beginning of this chapter, we introduced six best practices critical to a successful partnership. The practices are discussed within the context of the shared experience and scholarly approaches to the study of collaborations and partnerships.

Best Practice No. 1. Establish a shared vision or culture for the partnership.

A shared vision continues to emerge for the partnership as each of us looks for new opportunities to learn by doing together. This vision stresses the relationship between the individuals based on a strong ethic of participatory democracy where each is an equal partner in the endeavors by and for the AnthroAllies. Specific areas of responsibility will be determined according to the strengths, interests, and availability of each partner, and we expect these *loose*

to change over time as opportunities appear. We return to these topics at the beginning of each new project. We address problems or questions early and often, and we make frequent evaluations to ensure continued progress. We recognize that we have created a subculture with shared understandings that emerged comparatively quickly as a result of approaching the partnership from the perspectives of cultural anthropologists.

Best Practice No. 2. Provide a basis for dialog communications, and understanding.

Establishing a basis for communication is the most critical operation of the partnership experience. We used every means of communication available to us, including extended telephone conference calls, electronic communication, face-to-face meetings, and combinations of telephone conferences and face-to-face meetings. It is important to triangulate among all of the partners to ensure that each person shared the same understanding of activities, events, and dialog. A fundamental element early in the partnership development stage was to avoid mismanaging our agreements. We set an expectation to articulate assumptions, question goals, and conscientiously seek consensus. Each of us relied on the others to speak up and to state explicit preferences for or against particular approaches, responsibilities, tasks, and outcomes.

This approach to communication, with its emphasis on mutual understanding, helped us establish trust with one another and with the partnership as a whole. Early on we established an expectation to communicate clearly, courteously, and respectfully with one another. Collective vision became a beacon that enabled the partnership to chart a course that maximized benefits to each as part of the whole. This inside-out experience of stressing communication and understanding reflects research findings by those who study partnership arrangements from the outside looking in, including Tuckman (1965), Tuckman and Jensen (1977), Hord (1986), Lieberman (1986), Swan and Morgan (1993), Squires and Uhl (1993), and Johnsrud (2002 1994).

For example, Squires and Uhl (1993) identified four "cornerstone" domains for a successful collaboration: engagement, negotiation, performance, and assessment/evaluation. Engagement is a phase in which the group or just a few individuals develop an understanding of the collaboration. In the beginning, people have different ideas about what the collaboration is and about how it should proceed. Without opportunities to clarify ideas and intentions, individuals may feel an escalating loss of purpose and control over their efforts. Negotiation occurs as collaborators develop an action plan in which objectives are made clear and the meaning of success is defined. This phase involves (1) taking into account the resources, needs, and constraints of each member, (2) exploring conceptual and practical similarities and differences of each member, and (3) clarifying accountability for performance assessment and evaluation of the action plan and collaborative process.

Similarly the works of Tuckman (1965) and Tuckman and Jensen (1977) illustrate the importance of communication in the "development sequence in small groups." Tuckman originally identified four phases in partnership development: forming, storming, norming and performing. Tuckman's later work with Jensen added an adjourning phase. The first three stages focus on the processes for establishing a shared vision through communication and understanding, a vision that supports an underlying emergent-partnership value system (or culture). Performing focuses on group performance with the client and the group process. Adjourning acknowledges the need of each group, team, or partnership to attend to the tasks of the aftermath (e.g., debriefing, gaining closure).

Best Practice No. 3. Agree upon leadership and management protocols.

While we found it fair to operate the partnership as an internally-egalitarian democracy, potential and existing clients and purchasers of the partnership's services may not be comfortable with such arrangements. Clients often require a single point of contact, evidence that someone is in charge. Both the Navy and the federal agency insisted that a single firm serve as prime contractor, with the remaining two partners linked to the prime as subcontractors.

Each partner had experience in contract-consulting arrangements, and each understood the need to differentiate private, internal operations from the public partnership face. It was imperative for us to agree on which one of us would serve in a leadership capacity, under what circumstances, and to what extent. In some situations, the client group determines who will assume the role of project manager or director. For example, the Navy preferred using the Lampl's larger, more established firm as the lead organization. In other cases, we anticipate that one of the other partners could step into the director's role, depending on the market niche. The group's agreement, however, is that leadership and management responsibilities are customer or client driven, not partnership driven. We expect this formula to preserve a mutual sense of equality within the partnership, maximize the collective effectiveness, and discourage the internal competition so prevalent in business. We intend to maintain a work-with instead of a work-for relationship among the partners, regardless of which organization serves as the official lead. To date, we have not encountered situations where a partner felt strongly about serving as project manager or director. Instead, decisions about who should lead will be guided by the needs of the client, the distinctive competencies of the partners for the project, and the time or level of effort available for project work.

While this arrangement seems somewhat second nature to us now, we recognize that leadership and management issues often doom promising collaborations (Priess et al. 1996). In fact collaborative partnerships are exceedingly difficult to establish when the partners have been enculturated to expect competition, both in the business world and in academic environments. Competition is codified in the culture of business in such well-known phrases as "stealing customers away from the competition," "queen bees versus worker bees," "climbing the corporate ladder," and "disruptive marketing." The culture of academic competition is often codified by phrases such as, "publish or perish," "sole authorship," and "peer-reviewed journal." These and similar expressions reflect the underlying values of distrust, individual competition, and Foster's (1965) image of "limited good" where "more for you means less for me," ideas that reinforce the culture of competition.

Consequently the development of a viable collaborative partnership based on decision making by egalitarian, democratic processes represents something of a departure from business in the culture of competition. This issue was the focus of much discussion in the formative phases of the partnership.

Best Practice No. 4. Balance partnership needs with individual firm responsibilities.

Another issue we identified was the balance between the needs and demands of the partnership projects and the needs and demands of each individual's business enterprise. Partnership activities at times must take second place to the urgent demands and opportunities within an individual's own business. We experienced occasional difficulties in scheduling telephone conferences or in developing materials related to a partnership project because of the needs of individual organizations. We developed informal routines, however, for times when one partner experienced a conflict in demands; generally the other two groups were able to develop alternative ways to complete tasks. In the worst case, this issue can lead to serious problems if one or more partners become "out of phase" with partnership activities (Squires and Uhl 1993). We were fortunate in that we were able to adjust and modify activities to accommodate the occasional absence of a partner. We recognized that such adaptation signifies a strong level of comfort among the partners to accommodate the needs of a particular individual.

We also learned that to accomplish project goals, the partnership had to be a high priority for each of the other organizations, where activities ofthe individual firms were adjusted to accommodate the needs of the collaborative. This commitment was illustrated in the Navy project. Every aspect of the training project, including construction of the seminar goals and preliminary survey research, the individual topic presentations, the in-class ethnographic projects, and the form and content of audio-visual materials, was developed in full collaboration.

Best Practice No. 5. Protect each partner's corporate identity and distinctive competencies during and after the collaboration.

Maintaining separate corporate identities while engaged in collaborative activities was critical to this partnership. We each entered the partnership in order to maximize individual business activity, increase marketability, and increase revenues, not to create a new, permanent organization. Sublimation of individual business identities to the partnership was unacceptable from the outset; maintenance of the individual corporate identities was critical. Since each of us brought distinctive and overlapping competencies as well as unique perspectives to the collaboration, we believed that it was important to receive recognition for individual roles and performance. For this reason, we did not brand the partnership with a publicized name. Nor did we develop a website devoted to the partnership as a marketing tool. While we used the term "AnthroAllies" as an internal reference to the partnership, we maintained individual corporate identities in the marketplace.

To ensure that individual brands were maintained in the collaboration with the Navy, we included the logo and individual contact information for each partner on all course materials as well as on all official correspondence. In this way, each of us had proof of involvement in the project. We also had the ability to use portions of the materials for individual business-marketing activities. This agreement also provides the customer with alternative points of entry into the collaboration. For example, if a seminar participant was interacting with one particular partner, the participant might be more likely to use that person as a point of contact for future projects. Personal preferences matter.

Best Practice No. 6. Build—and work to maintain—mutual trust.

Perhaps the most important ingredient in collaborative partnering is a high level of trust among the partners. This element is crucial when one partner is under contract for a collaborative project, as was the case in the Navy training project. As related, the partners selected Lampl's larger firm to act as the lead, which required not only the concurrence of the other two partners but also the agreement of Lampl to carry the responsibility. The other two participants, while named and acknowledged in the document as participants, did not have signature authority or responsibility on anything related to the CRADA as a legal document.

The CRADA codified legal constraints, performance expectations, and accountability between NAVAIR TSD Orlando and Lampl's firm exclusively. If the collaborative relationship among the partners had been dissolved at any point during the life of the CRADA, Lampl's firm would have been responsible for executing the terms of the agreement. Consequently the risk to the lead partner was significant; Lampl assumed a great deal of trust in the willingness, motives, and capability of the other collaborators to produce the desired results. Likewise the other partners had to trust that the lead partner would honor the egalitarian, democratic norms of participation established in discussion and would allow for equal visibility and stage time in the execution of the training seminar.

We view the development of such a high level of trust as a point of pride. We are aware that, while trust may be the most important element of successful collaborations, trust relationships are difficult to achieve and maintain given the distinctly different operating styles and corporate goals of the three independent consultants as discussed in this chapter.

SUMMARY: LESSONS LEARNED

This essay focused on a partnering arrangement between three women-owned firms. We examined key issues and the approaches this partnership devised to meet the challenges. In the multiple debriefings and as reflected in the mirror of our individual and collective experience, we recognized five key lessons learned:

1. Communication should take place early and often. We established multiple lines of communication as soon as we each committed to work out a partnership; we kept the lines open with frequent telephone calls and e-mails. Partnering relationships are fragile, particularly in highly competitive cultures. We found that a constant awareness of the other partners was essential.
2. Establish the nature of the partnership with the client early. Clients find the partnership, or team, concept confusing, despite the fact that strongly hierarchical systems like the Navy or other corporate or government organizations regularly work in teams and allow for teaming agreements. We made known the essential nature of this partnership to the client prior to any formal agreements.
3. Apply the rule of "early and often" to communication with the client as well as communication within the group. Establish points of contact

and a defined image to the client and stakeholders. Even though the partnership itself has more than one face, we select one person to serve as the primary contact point for a given client. This strategy benefits the client by providing a sense of stability and responsibility in the relationship. It also simplifies communication, and avoids confusion.

4. Avoid competition within the partnership. Potential partners may find it difficult to participate in teams, since many people in the U.S. particularly have had little opportunity until recently to acquire the skills needed in teams and partnerships. We established mechanisms and project-specific products to promote equality and democracy within the partnership in order to overcome the potential for competitive tendencies.

5. Maintain openness to the approaches used by your partners. We treated each partner as a source of new knowledge and inspiration and worked to learn from each other rather than compete. We maximized the benefits for each individual by combining—not annihilating—the differences in expertise, unique talents, and distinctive competencies.

We offer these best practices and lessons learned as a starting point for others who want to explore a partnering arrangement between businesses. Just as journeys differ depending on the destination, the road traveled, the traveling companions, and the vehicles utilized, we recognize that the partnership experience will differ for others depending on the nature of the project. Guidelines are just that: guidelines; experience is the proof.

NOTES

1. We use individual names and sometimes speak of ourselves in the third person or use personal pronouns to reflect the personal nature of the experience.

2. Kolb's work in learning theory and development of the experiential learning cycle emerged in the 1970s. We refer specifically here to Kolb's later work *Experiential Learning: Experience as the Source of Learning and Development* (1984).

3. National Association for the Practice of Anthropology (NAPA).

4. While Lampl's corporate entity signed as the official prime contractor, the other partner companies also participated in the CRADA signing ceremony and were acknowledged in all other materials related to the CRADA. Continuing in this egalitarian mode, the names of the three individuals and their consulting firms appear on all materials developed and delivered for the training workshop.

5. The term "elevator slide" refers to a one-page handout popularized in the cultures of venture capital and federal technology funding. The effective elevator slide contains compelling information about everything that is to be pitched to a potential funder who is so busy that his/her attention span is limited to the duration of an elevator ride.

Section 3

SUSTAINING PARTNERING RELATIONSHIPS

7

An Educational Partnership for Immediate Effect

Julia C. Gluesing, Kenneth R. Riopelle, Kenneth R. Chelst,
Alan R. Woodliff, and Linda M. Miller

INTRODUCTION

The purpose of this case study is to provide a concrete, longitudinal perspective on a university-industry partnership that spans fourteen years and that illustrates key principles of partnership formation and continuation.[1] The case frames the partnership as a negotiated working culture (Brannen 1998; Gluesing 1998) and stresses the importance of cross-cultural adaptability skills (Gudykunst 1994; Kelley and Meyers 1994) in sustaining the partnership over the long term within a context of changing conditions (Gluesing et al. 2003). Negotiating a working culture means that partnership participants engage in actions and interactions that help them come to terms with their differences and thereby reach mutual agreement in order to achieve a common objective or goal. The negotiated working culture emerges when the partners have moved beyond their diverse values and ways of working in order to create a new way of working that is more than just a mix of their separate identities. Negotiating a working culture requires that participants be cross-culturally adaptable in their interactions with one another.

The four major dimensions of cross-cultural adaptability are (1) emotional resilience, or the ability to bounce back from difficulties and maintain a positive attitude; (2) perceptual acuity, or the ability to notice and correctly interpret diverse cues that are present in interactions; (3) personal autonomy, or being true to one's own values while adjusting to new ones; and (4) flexibility and openness, or keeping an open mind about seeing events in new ways or trying new ways of doing things.

This case study is based on an ethnohistorical methodology (Baba 1988) that is useful for positioning events on a time line and for assessing their effect on partnership interactions. In this case, there are three phases that characterize the partnership events. The case also is written from the personal experiences of the authors as participants in the partnership throughout the life of the partnership. It also incorporates findings from data gathered through interviews and through focus groups conducted with students, faculty members, and corporate executives involved in the educational program.

This chapter begins with an overview of the partnership structure and the values held by each partner. This overview is followed by a description of the evolving conditions that have influenced the partnership in each of the three phases that characterize its development from 1990 to the present. The chapter continues with an evaluation of the success of the educational partnership from three perspectives: (1) the key drivers of the partnership, (2) the partnership outcomes, and (3) the negotiated working culture. The chapter concludes with a list of lessons learned that are relevant considerations for the development of long-term partnerships among diverse participants.

To illustrate the negotiations and the developmental process of the educational partnership, we use the metaphor of a high-performance automotive race track throughout the chapter. The metaphor is particularly applicable and revealing in the discussion of this partnership since the partners are located in the heart of the U.S. automotive industry.

PARTNERSHIP STRUCTURE AND VALUES

A partnership involves two or more parties working together to achieve common interests and goals. Wayne State University, Ford Motor Company, and Visteon Corporation have developed a win-win educational partnership by providing an engineering-management master's degree program for working engineers in Southeast Michigan that delivers immediate performance impact to both academic and business partners. The impetus in 1990 for creating the partnership was the belief among Ford senior managers that neither the traditional MBA nor the existing advanced-engineering master's degree alone adequately prepared the future technical leaders for the challenges of the global marketplace. A new approach was needed to cross the disciplinary boundaries between business and engineering. Consequently Ford Motor Company entered into dialogue with Wayne State University, which resulted in the creation of the Engineering Management Masters Program (EMMP)[2] to meet the educational needs of Ford's technical managers. EMMP was extended to Visteon Corporation when it was spun off from Ford as a separate company in June of 2000.

In EMMP, high-potential engineers are selected by management to participate in a three-year, two-evenings-a-week curriculum of forty-five credit hours, which results in a Masters of Science degree in Engineering Management. The degree is a hybrid of business and engineering courses as well as content from anthropology to address national and corporate cultures and culture change. The curriculum is team based and includes two years of class studies and team projects in areas such as global technical-leadership, quality management, global marketing, robust design, information systems, and the management of technology change. The third year of the program involves a team leadership project in which participants apply the knowledge gained to a current strategy or opportunity in the company. The program requires commitment by management to sponsor candidates and to support them during the program. It also requires that the faculty members teach on the corporate campuses and not at the university.

The partners have been collaborating to engineer and fine tune an educational experience that serves as a testing ground for the development of high-performance leaders and teams. The partners are continually striving to improve the teams' managerial and technical skills, as well as abilities that will enable the teams to successfully navigate the mountains, valleys, and curves along the track in uncertain and changing business conditions.

The overall goal of the partnership is to produce winning results for the company and university partners who sponsor and work with the teams on the test track and for the team members themselves. The test track represents the intersection of the two value systems—academic and business—that had to be negotiated in order to arrive at a working culture of collaboration that enabled the partners to drive around obstacles and avoid pitfalls and to achieve winning outcomes. The partners were able to negotiate a new working culture while staying true to their own core values because the construction of their test track was driven by a shared value for quality education. The winning outcomes for industry partners are a strong return on investment, (in the millions of dollars), and the development of future leaders who are tested over a three-year period. The university wins with tuition revenue and with the opportunity for faculty members and graduate research assistants to conduct cutting-edge research in a global laboratory that produces conference presentations, journal publications, and PhD dissertations and that attracts external funding.

Table 7.1 lists the core cultural values, in the authors' assessment, that were important to each partner in the negotiation of the goals and in the structure of the EMMP program. This depiction of the partners' values is derived from the authors' long-term association with the EMMP program and its participants

Table 7.1.   Partnership Values

Ford Motor Company	Wayne State University
Shared Value for Quality Education	
Corporate Profit, Customer Satisfaction, and Shareholder Value	Scientific Discovery, Education, Community Service and Economic Sustainability
Competitive Advantage	Academic Prestige
Short-Term but Lasting Results	Long-Term Continuous Learning
Working Solutions to Problems	Research and Experimentation
Practical Tools and Techniques	Theoretical Concepts
Knowledge Application	Knowledge Generation
Team Expertise	Individual Expertise

and also from a review of program documents and transcripts from interviews and focus groups.

As an automotive corporation with publicly traded stock, the Ford Motor Company has a history of operating more than one hundred years in a very competitive market. The highly competitive global-market conditions mean that Ford has had to place greater emphasis on short-term generation of profits, while at the same time accelerating the delivery of high-quality exciting products to ensure the future. Because of the complexity of the automotive industry and the products they produce, success requires teamwork and expertise of multiple perspectives and skill sets that can apply knowledge and use tools and techniques to provide practical solutions in a cost-effective manner.

Wayne State University is also an organization with 100+ years of history. On the other hand, it is a public, nonprofit, Tier One research institution that values scientific discovery, education, and community service and that is also concerned with sustaining economic viability rather than profit margins. The university values academic prestige, long-term and continuous learning, the development of new knowledge, the testing of theory through experimentation and ongoing research, and the expertise and reputation of individual faculty members in specialized fields.

The EMMP story is about how leaders of both organizations, based on a shared core value for quality education, were able to open themselves up to new educational practices and to be flexible and resilient enough to design a unique degree program that has been able to withstand multiple hazards on the educational test track. Figure 1 illustrates the metaphorical EMMP test track that was built at the intersection of two different value systems.

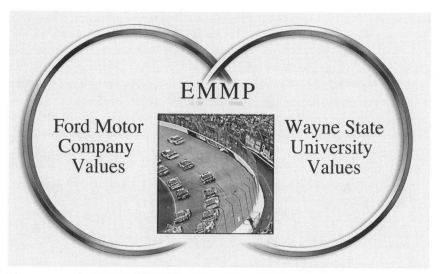

Figure 7.1. The EMMP High-Performance Educational Test Track

THE EVOLVING CONDITIONAL CONTEXT
OF THE EMMP PARTNERSHIP

Changing external and internal conditions have had both positive and negative influences on the development of the partnership and its outcomes over the years. These conditions have occurred on both sides of the partnership and have required openness and flexibility on the part of the companies and the university to sustain the partnership. The partners have had to recognize opportunities and then take advantage of these opportunities before they slipped away, and they have had to adjust rules, reallocate resources, change personnel, and develop new regulations to cope with changing situations.

In its fourteen-year history, the EMMP partnership has undergone three phases of evolution that correspond to changing internal and external conditions: (1) an initial start-up phase during which the program was developed, (2) the maintenance phase characterized by program refinement, and (3) revision and growth, the program's current phase, in which Visteon Corporation was added as a partner and in which the Industrial and Manufacturing Engineering (IME) department is expanding the partnership to the supplier community and to the global market. The partnership has been dynamic and evolving from its inception. There are three phases that have defined that evolution and represent the major turning points in the partnership's development: phase I (1990–1996), the start-up phase, involved WSU and Ford; phase II (1997–1999), the maintenance phase, also involved WSU and Ford;

and phase III (2000–present), a revision and growth phase that involved multiple pairings, including Ford-WSU, Visteon-WSU, auto suppliers-WSU, and other universities-WSU. These three phases represent major turning points in the partnership's development.

There were important external and internal conditions that affected the EMMP partnership throughout the three phases of its development. The external conditions are the primary opportunities and constraints that have fostered the direction of the partnership over time. Additionally the three-phase development of the partnership reflects the changing internal conditions at the executive, classroom, and administrative levels that have shaped the day-to-day challenges to the partnership and its evolving structure and relationships.

Phase I: Start-Up, 1990–1996

During phase I of the partnership, that is, the start-up, from 1990 to 1996, the external impetus for the partnership came from new pressures in the automotive industry. Ford Motor Company began to see that staying competitive in a globalizing industry would mean that the company could no longer be satisfied with managers who were only technically competent. They began to take a long view of trends in the industry and their human-resource-development needs in order to prepare managers for the future. Business-management skills were identified as a top requirement for Ford to succeed against tough domestic and foreign competitors. At the beginning of the 1990s, Ford Motor Company was also at the start of a period of financial growth and had resources to expand its educational investment.

At the same time that the Ford executives decided to approach Wayne State University as an educational partner, the university leaders were engaged in outreach to industry and the community, which pushed the delivery of the university's educational programs to sites off the main campus. Following challenging negotiations that were meant to overcome hurdles in cumbersome business processes on both the university side and Ford side of the partnership, as well as the allocation of responsibilities and revenues to the business and engineering schools at WSU, the WSU board of governors approved the EMMP degree, and the partnership began work in the fall of 1992.

After the formal EMMP degree was conceived, designed, and approved, and after the specifications for the "high-performance educational test track" were developed, the next task was to recruit the students and faculty members who would build the track and make it operational. The intent was to a recruit a class that could be diverse functionally (e.g., product development, manufacturing, powertrain, marketing, information technology) and also work at a managerial

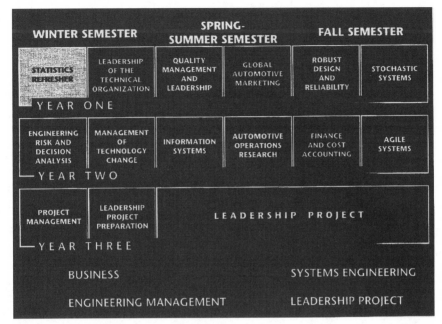

WINTER SEMESTER		SPRING-SUMMER SEMESTER		FALL SEMESTER	
STATISTICS REFRESHER	LEADERSHIP OF THE TECHNICAL ORGANIZATION	QUALITY MANAGEMENT AND LEADERSHIP	GLOBAL AUTOMOTIVE MARKETING	ROBUST DESIGN AND RELIABILITY	STOCHASTIC SYSTEMS

YEAR ONE

ENGINEERING RISK AND DECISION ANALYSIS	MANAGEMENT OF TECHNOLOGY CHANGE	INFORMATION SYSTEMS	AUTOMOTIVE OPERATIONS RESEARCH	FINANCE AND COST ACCOUNTING	AGILE SYSTEMS

YEAR TWO

PROJECT MANAGEMENT	LEADERSHIP PROJECT PREPARATION	LEADERSHIP PROJECT

YEAR THREE

BUSINESS　　　　　　　　SYSTEMS ENGINEERING

ENGINEERING MANAGEMENT　　　　LEADERSHIP PROJECT

Figure 7.2. EMMP Curriculum Overview

level to promote greater cross-fertilization of ideas and learning in a spirit of experimentation. The students would be the high-performance racing teams that would push the limits on the EMMP test track.

The classroom content also was structured around teamwork. In all thirteen classes, students were assigned to teams of three to five members and were expected to work on class projects. Each class was essentially a hot lap around the EMMP test track to prepare the students for the final endurance race, their leadership projects.

Faculty members were initially recruited from the ranks of the Industrial and Manufacturing Engineering department and from the School of Business Administration, according to their areas of research specialization and match with the courses in the EMMP curriculum. Faculty members had to give up their old cultural habits of one-way knowledge transfer through lecturing and instead become open to a new teaching paradigm in which the faculty members learned as much from the students as students learned from them. Each faculty member had to become part of the team, working with the students to excel on the test track.

Another important development in the first phase of the partnership was the creation of an oversight committee for the leadership projects. The oversight committee helped students think about upcoming projects so that the projects would be manageable and would have the greatest likelihood of being completed in the final endurance race, given the members on the team and company sponsorship and directives.

After the first two years of operation, both the Wayne State faculty members and the Ford partners held a shared value beyond quality education, the value of working on real-world problems, because the leadership projects produced excellent results beyond anyone's expectations. Ford executives realized that a team of talented employees could serve as internal consultants to the company, producing results equal to or greater than the highly paid consultants that the company was bringing in from the outside. Executives understood that they could leverage the internal knowledge, creativity, and commitment of their own engineers to solve the really tough problems and implement solutions. The leadership project teams performed well on the tough terrain of real-world operations.

The first phase of the EMMP partnership also required an administrative infrastructure to support the operation of the partnership. Each partner was willing to create work-arounds to negotiate the right administrative structure for the degree program. The negotiations worked because Ford and the university could see the potential for win-win outcomes and because they very much wanted to make the partnership a reality.

Phase II: Maintenance, 1997–1999

From a cultural perspective, the partnership can be characterized as maintenance during the second phase from 1997 to 1999. The steep learning curve had been climbed, and the test track was being adjusted for peak performance. The external conditions for Ford Motor Company remained bright. The company continued along the path of strong economic growth and was making forays into e-business in the dot-com era. The company also was experimenting with businesses, ancillary-to-core automotive design, engineering, and manufacturing by purchasing a quick-lube business in Europe and junkyards to advance recycling efforts, looking at the business from cradle to grave. Wayne State University also was experiencing a period of growth. The health of the Michigan economy stabilized the base of funding for higher education. Under the direction of a new president in September 1997, Wayne State began a vision of expanding the university's research programs and developing global education as a priority.

In the classroom, relevant real-world value remained a shared top priority at both Ford and at Wayne State as the university reaped the benefits of this approach to teaching. Both partners decided the time had come to conduct a formal quantitative and qualitative evaluation of the program's process and outcomes. Some courses and instructors were clearly producing winning results on the test track, while others were lagging behind. Wayne State also saw the need for program evaluation. Faculty member performance was an issue in some cases, and there was continuing pressure to recruit faculty members with real-world experience who could relate to the students' work environments.

Several outcomes of this formal evaluation process are worth noting. First, people became aware of the lasting effect of the leadership projects one and two years after their completion. For example, a leadership-project team member carried on the work of his team and a previous class team of implementing a prototype[3]-optimization model into Ford Motor Company's cycle plan, or portfolio of products to be released each year. The model was put into use on the European Transit vehicle, and it reduced costs by an estimated $12 million. The model also dramatically shortened the planning process, established global procedures, and created a common structure for dialogue between financial controls and engineering.[4] It is estimated that the prototype optimization model now saves Ford Motor Company $250 million annually.

Second, the winning results also were being shared by WSU. In collaboration with Ford Motor Company executives, the results of the prototype optimization leadership projects were submitted to INFORMS, an academic association devoted to operations research, where the project became one of the top three finalists for the prestigious Edelman prize. The preparation for this submission strengthened the relationship between Ford and WSU because it required a high degree of collaboration to put the submission package together.

Third, the evaluations provided detailed information about what had to be done to improve the program. Not all was working in top order. Plans were made for revision and for new faculty member recruitment. The evaluation results also pointed out the need for a leadership-project handbook that would guide students, faculty members, and corporate sponsors through the project process.

The phase II partnership transitioned to phase III with sustained commitment between both partners to continue their relationship, to reinforce the winning elements they had put into place on the educational test track, and to improve the parts that were not working as well as possible. Despite the bumps and breakdowns along the way, high-performance racing teams were being produced, and both partners were seeing winning results.

Phase III: Revision and Growth, 2000–Present

In phase III of the EMMP partnership, external events were to alter conditions for the partnership. The economic recession, the increased competitive pressures

in the automotive industry, and accelerating globalization, combined with the catastrophe of 9/11, created a downward spiral for Ford Motor Company and for
Wayne State University alike. Both organizations quickly entered a period of re-
trenchment that spurred reorganization, and both have emerged in a growth
mode. Ford initiated a back-to-basics strategy that rid the company of anything
that wasn't a part on a car. The cutbacks did not spare education and training;
The EMMP program, however, survived because WSU EMMP graduates had a
high retention rate, with ninety percent continuing their employment at Ford—
and because the leadership project returns to the company were clear. Geographic proximity helped in this case too, since the costs for education delivered
locally were minimal in comparison to the costs of the educational partnerships
with more distant universities.

In its financial housecleaning, Ford also decided to spin-off its internal
component divisions to create Visteon Corporation, which would soon become an independent global supplier to the automotive industry, with engineering centers located around the world. In 2001, Visteon leaders decided to
establish an EMMP separate from the one it shared with Ford during the transition to independence. Visteon's human-resources and engineering executives defined Wayne State as a strategic university partner and created a board
of directors to provide program oversight. The company executives saw
EMMP as a vehicle for culture change within the company. The leadership
projects have been the start of longer-term changes in the very way business
is conducted.

For Wayne State, many changes ensued as well. Following 9/11, there
were new visa restrictions that reduced engineering enrollment, and there
were budget cutbacks to the university from the state of Michigan. During
this period, there was increasing pressure on the university to improve its
ranking as a research institution in the hopes of attracting more external
funding.

To increase the IME department's standing in the university and nationally, as well as to highlight the successful educational partnership with
Ford and Visteon, a new emphasis was placed on participating in professional conferences, making presentations, writing and submitting journal
publications, obtaining National Science Foundation grants, and enhancing
the skills of the PhD-level graduate assistants working on EMMP. Through
a series of meetings, a negotiated review process has been established at
both Ford and Visteon to promote co-authorship of papers and presentations and publication of leadership project research and results. These
agreements represent a level of trust that also has paved the way for PhD
students to conduct their dissertation work at Visteon apart from the
EMMP leadership projects.

At the classroom level, the EMMP class structure and curriculum has undergone revision and subsequent growth in phase III. The relevant, real-world value of the subject matter taught in the EMMP classes received additional emphasis and was adjusted at Ford to accommodate the expansion of Ford's internal technical-education programs. Visteon leadership assigned internal subject-matter experts at the managerial level to align the classes in the curriculum in order to ensure that the class projects would help move the company forward in its strategic objectives.

For both Ford and Visteon, the EMMP program has been adjusted to begin not on the university calendar with a start in September, but rather on the corporate-business calendar, which begins a new planning year in January. This alignment with the corporate calendar has been initiated to allow the leadership projects a chance to work on new business initiatives for a full year, which corresponds to the business cycle and expectations for results.

Phase III was a turbulent time for the EMMP partnership. External conditions prompted many changes in the high-performance educational test-track that threatened the program's viability and very existence. Nevertheless the test track weathered these conditions well and is producing more well-honed racing teams than ever before. The partnership was expanded, and a new Visteon test track was created. The WSU IME department also is looking to meet new competitive demands in the global marketplace and is making plans for additional tracks with suppliers and in partnership with other universities in a global program. Reduced revenue in the domestic automotive industry, globalized product development, and the moving of engineering and manufacturing offshore are putting pressure on companies to move to a consortium model of education, especially among the automotive suppliers. Wayne State University is establishing partnerships with universities in other countries to deliver EMMP on a consortium model.

THE SUCCESS OF THE EMMP PARTNERSHIP

The EMMP partnership has been successful for three reasons. First, key drivers have been present throughout the life of the partnership. Second, the partnership has produced win-win outcomes for both the companies and the university. Third, the partnership has been based on a negotiated working culture of collaboration that is oriented around the superordinate goal of winning and has been built upon the cross-cultural adaptability of the participants.

The Key Drivers

There are five key drivers that together helped initiate and sustain the partnership over the long haul:

1. Shared Geographic Context
   The close proximity of the companies to the university provided easy access to frequent face-to-face communication in the initial negotiation of the program elements, as well as the delivery of courses on the corporate campuses. Shared context facilitated knowledge-sharing and accelerated understanding among the partnership participants, because they experienced the same taken-for-granted industry and regional conditions.
2. Partners' Motivation to Make the Partnership Work
   Each partner was strongly motivated for different reasons to make the partnership work. Competition put pressure on Ford to develop leadership skills in its technical workforce, and the university was motivated by a continuous source of graduate student enrollment and research opportunities.
3. Shared Priority for Real-World Education
   Both partners believed in education that produced immediate results and that was grounded in solving real-world problems.
4. Flexibility and Willingness to Create Work-Arounds
   The partners did not allow obstacles on the test track to keep them from achieving a win on the test track.
5. Ability to Commit Resources to the Program
   The companies had the financial and human resources to initiate and maintain the program. The university was also willing to support faculty members and administrative personnel to deliver the program content.

If any one of these drivers had not been present, the partnership may not have been quite so successful. It even may have failed.

Win-Win Outcomes

Over the years of the EMMP partnership, the participants have been able to negotiate win-win outcomes for each partner, despite the diversity of what matters most at each institution, because they share a value for quality education that produces real-world results. Of course the partnership test track has had its share of bumps, detours, breakdowns, wrong turns, accidents, and construction delays. External events and changing internal conditions have conspired to alternately constrain and expand the partnership relationships and to emphasize some values over others. The partners have adapted well, however, to generate wins for everyone. Wayne State University wins in the partnership because faculty members and PhD-level graduate research-assistants gain access to a global enterprise that serves as a living laboratory and that leads to seven positive academic-partnership outcomes: (1) first and foremost, the university receives tuition and fees that amount to an annual budget for EMMP of $2 million, with $1.5 million allocated to research and $500,000 in tuition. Also the university does not have to concern itself with job placement at graduation, since students are already employed full time in an engineering position; (2) EMMP provides funding for faculty members and fourteen doctoral students to conduct applied research and thereby gain practical experience working with technical managers on important and complex engineering problems. These class projects and final leadership projects now produce an annual stream of conference presentations and publications based on the team-based research conducted at the companies; (3) PhD students, who serve as graduate research-assistants to the teams of company master's students, have the opportunity to further their own studies and research interests working on real-world problems; (4) the EMMP program is also a recruitment tool for qualified PhD students. In many instances, the company master's students' success on the test track is motivation for them to continue their studies and to seek a PhD degree at Wayne State; (5) the university's faculty members have the opportunity to conduct research on topics of interest and to partner with the companies in larger-scale projects, such as those funded by the National Science Foundation; (6) the EMMP program is an attractor of new faculty members who want to come to Wayne State University because of the program opportunities, and; (7) the faculty members sometimes have the opportunity to provide consulting services to the company partners.

Ford Motor Company and the Visteon Corporation, the industry partners, also win in significant ways that contribute to their desired business outcomes: (1) the year-long leadership projects often have had an impact in the millions of dollars either in cost savings or revenue generation; (2) each semester, every class project contributes to advancing the companies' strategic initiatives. Because the students are experienced working engineers, the team-based class projects have had a major effect beyond their coursework; (3) both companies are beginning to leverage the public-relations value of the EMMP leadership projects by presenting results and talking about the program in professional meetings and conferences; (4) each graduating class produces a company-knowledge network of trusted cohorts. This network serves the company by equipping future leaders with a common set of concepts and tools. It also serves the students by helping them build a valuable social network of alumni contacts that reaches across the enterprise and that they can draw upon to help them in their daily work; (5) students have the exceptional opportunity throughout the program to gain experience working with top-level managers in their companies outside their functional areas and thereby increase their visibility among these senior executives; (6) senior executives recognize the value of having an EMMP leadership project team with whom they can work to accelerate strategic company objectives; and (7) the companies' students receive an advanced-engineering management degree, paid for by the companies, that positions them for salary raises and promotion opportunities.

The Negotiated Culture of Collaboration and Win-Win

The EMMP partnership is a negotiated working culture (Gluesing 1998) that follows a process of collaboration directed at winning by focusing on the superordinate shared value for quality education in the real world. The process includes four stages that help balance power and build connections among the partners. The first stage of the process involved a period of learning about one another's values, priorities, similarities, and differences. The partners learned that they had different values for the most part but that they shared both a desire to win and an appreciation for quality education that produce immediate impact. During stage two of the process, the partners negotiated how they would work together. The EMMP partnership developed the administrative infrastructure, customized courses, the delivery model, the oversight committee, and the problem-based real-world emphasis in the classroom. The third stage of the process was about adjusting and strengthening the partnership. The EMMP partners conducted curriculum reviews and focus groups with participants, and they made adjustments to the program start, to faculty member and student recruitment, and to the changing competitive and financial conditions that strengthen the educational test track. Finally, in the fourth stage of the process, the partners focused even more on the real-world aspect of the educational process, with an increasing emphasis on implementation of the leadership projects. The working real-world, win-win culture had been negotiated and renegotiated and was fully shared by the partnership participants.

The EMMP partnership is a business and educational partnership in which winning results are paramount. Understanding this focus is critical to understanding the culture of the partnership. The meaning of a win is different for all the partners. It is evident in the the successful outcomes for the university and industry partners and it is tied to their diverse values.

Winning, however, is the final goal for all the partners and is powered by their common value for quality education. Without the continued win-win for all partners, the relationships and the partnership itself would have ceased to exist long ago. The partnership relationships are important as enablers of the teamwork and of the negotiated collaboration that keep the mechanics of the partnership working in changing and often challenging track conditions. The relational trust in the partnership, however, is based upon the continued ability of the partners to create winning racing teams that contribute to the tangible outcomes valued by each of the partners for different reasons.

As a metaphor, the image of the high-performance test track that produces winning racing teams fits the partnership well and is useful because it focuses attention on teamwork, on learning the specific skills, and on blending the diverse talents that are necessary to drive well under difficult conditions while keeping the car on the road, overcoming unexpected obstacles, recovering from mistakes, continuing to push to the finish with inoperable or damaged parts, and winning. These elements are indeed the fundamentals that have made the partnership successful on the test track.

Many relationships at multiple levels within and across organizational and disciplinary boundaries went into developing the partnership at start-up and have been necessary to maintaining it and to growing the partnership over time. The difficult and ongoing work of developing and sustaining the partnership, however, happens at the college and departmental level for the university partners and at the managerial and administrative levels for the industry partners. This is where the rubber meets the road, to carry on the metaphor. The problems, the tensions, the negotiations, and the solutions take place here in the pit. People on all sides of the partnership create the work around and adjust to new conditions in order to get the students around the track and to the finish line, and to cheer the students on to win. Otherwise, they are often removed from their partnership roles and replaced with new team members who can perform under the conditions of the partnership. Performance is the key.

The greatest tension in the partnership is one that centers on the different values held by the industry and university partners. It is a tension between the theoretical, academic, practical, and real-world values that are important in the two contexts. Essentially the tension has been resolved because the IME department has been able to understand and adjust to the industry demands. In fact the department's image of itself is of an applied educational program that produces real-world results. This image has consistently been the vision in the department's degree programs on campus, so the adjustment to an industry-based degree was not as difficult as it might have been in a more theoretically oriented department.

LESSONS LEARNED FROM THE EMMP PARTNERSHIP

This case description of a university-industry partnership offers six lessons about what makes partnerships successful:

1. Cross-cultural adaptability is necessary.

     While individual contributions to the EMMP partnership have been made at many levels, the strength of the partnership comes from the interactions of people who have collectively exhibited two cross-culture-adaptability skills (Kelley and Meyers 1995): (1) emotional resilience, and (2) flexibility and openness. In constantly changing conditions, it has been the ability of the partnership participants to bounce back and overcome obstacles, to maintain focus on the shared value for quality education, and to remain flexible and open, thereby negotiating new ways of doing things, that enable the partnership to continue and to grow. The cross-cultural adaptability of partnership participants has accommodated continuous renegotiation of program priorities and structure, administrative processes and collaboration practices to maintain alignment, and trust as both university and business conditions change. The test track was repaired and then reconstructed and widened to include more participants from Visteon. The partnership has evolved and has trained new players from the executive, administrative, and classroom levels to work together in the pit.

2. A good vision fosters strategic alignment.

     The EMMP partnership was built upon a vision of quality education that would deliver immediate impact with real-world results. The vision for the EMMP test track provided clear direction for the partnership no matter what obstacles the changes in the external and internal conditions created for the drivers on the track.

3. Champions at the top are necessary for starting the partnership.

     Top executives at the companies and leaders at the university believed in and were committed to the EMMP program. From the start, these champions articulated the vision and released resources to build the track.

4. Commitment at the lower levels is essential.

     While vision is necessary, it is not sufficient to keep the partnership going. Success is in the details, in the working relationships, and in the reciprocal negotiations of the many people involved at multiple levels of the partnership. The working relationships in the pit have to be explicitly negotiated and renegotiated to keep the cars running smoothly and to keep the drivers on the road.

5. Positive results are necessary for continuing the partnership.

     The win-win outcomes for the industry and university partners involved in the EMMP are the reason for being in the partnership. Without successful delivery of a quality education as defined and negotiated in both business and academic terms, the partnership would weaken and eventually dissolve. Winning means the test track is a good one and is worth maintaining.

6. Success breeds success.

As the partners see the immediate effects of their investment and their efforts on all sides of the partnership, they are encouraged to continue working together in spite of differences, changing conditions, and obstacles. Buzz about the success of the partnership spreads and attracts new students, faculty members, and executive sponsors, as well as external funding. There is now an increasing number of industry sponsors for EMMP projects, and there is a critical mass of alumni who provide visibility, support, encouragement, and career advancement through networking for students in the program. The partnership continues, and ties strengthen by word of mouth because of success. The test track is strengthened to simulate the new road conditions created by intensified competition and globalization.

In conclusion, the lessons learned from this case study of the EMMP educational partnership can provide a template for the development of long-term partnerships among diverse participants, partnerships that are likely to face difficult and changing conditions that challenge the viability of the partnership. The four stages involved in negotiating a working culture illustrate the strategies and cross-culture adaptability skills that partnership participants should use. Looking at partnerships as intergroup and interpersonal collaborative efforts that involve well-honed negotiation skills is particularly important in today's globalized business world as well as in intraorganizational and community-based collaborations.

NOTES

1. The authors gratefully acknowledge the leaders, managers, and working engineers at Ford Motor Company and at the Visteon Corporation, as well as the professors, graduate students, and staff at Wayne State University. They have contributed to the continued success of the EMMP partnership with their time, resources, knowledge, eagerness to learn, and collaborative spirit.

2. See the Website at http://ime.wayne.edu//emmp/index.php.

3. A prototype is a preproduction, custom-built vehicle used in testing.

4. See Chelst et al. (2001).

8

Effectiveness through Partnerships

Navigating the Shifting Landscape of Partnerships to Influence Product Development

Tracey Lovejoy and Nelle Steele

PARTNERSHIPS WITHIN OUR MICROSOFT FAMILY

Our work as ethnographers at Microsoft entails building and maintaining relationships with many employees to fulfill our job responsibilities.[1] We work for the Windows Client product-development team, and we sit within a larger user-research group within the team. Our primary goal is to affect product development. The way we achieve this is through partnering with others to design and execute ethnographic research and then drive recommendations based on this data into the product. To this end, we develop partnerships with colleagues on our product team, as well as with colleagues outside our product team, in order to help shape both Windows Client and other products at Microsoft.

Webs of Partnering Relationships—Theoretical Orientations

Our partnering relationships can be described with two theoretical orientations: one is through family-and-kinship literature, which is abundant in anthropology; the other is through organizational literature that focuses on bridging holes within social structures and on the strength of ties between individuals within organizations. From the anthropological perspective, we closely identify with new models of kinship that have emerged in the postmodern era, in which researchers have recognized that kinship is not just based on consanguine relationships. Instead kinship can be better understood as actively putting a flexible social structure in place that ensures a dense web of support for family members, no matter what the actual blood relationships between individuals are. This dense web is built on a series of acts—not on blood—that support us in good times and bad (Weismantel 1995). From the organizational perspective, we see ourselves as actors embedded within a structure that both constrains and enables us to act in ways that can be advantageous to ourselves and, at times, the institution (Baba 1999). Through our partnering efforts, we can act as bridges across organizational holes to share innovation; we can also leverage distant or weak partnerships with others to push and pull information into or out of our efforts to develop products (Burt 2002; Granovetter 1983).

"Partnership" is not a term that is part of Microsoft's language and culture. Our partnerships with colleagues are different from relationships because they contain both personal and professional elements; we not only build a relationship with someone, gaining a stronger sense of rapport over time, but we share a specific professional goal with them that is related to affecting product direction. If we were just introduced to someone, we would not consider that a partnership. An initial meeting turns into a partnership when there is mutual recognition that we can provide value to one another. When we build rapport over time and experience success together, then that partnership can strengthen and grow.

Ethnographer Role

We are both full-time ethnographers. Our role entails multiple responsibilities:

- studying groups of people to understand what they think and do;
- understanding where, how, and why their daily lives intersect (or do not intersect) with technology;
- making recommendations as to how we should improve current products or should develop new products that will meet the needs of those we study;
- identifying the people within the company who have the power to make the changes we think should be made;
- educating those we identify about our data and about how they can build more suitable products for our end users; and
- tracking how our data actually affects our products.

Doing good research is only the first part of our job. In addition, we are rewarded for the changes we are able to make based on our research. We rarely have an effect by simply handing our finished report to a partner. In identifying power brokers who can make change in products, sharing our data with them, and then tracking outcomes, partnerships become essential. Therefore, if we cannot partner effectively, then we are not able to change products with our data. And if we are not able to change products with our data, then we are not doing our jobs. The two main partnership models we work through are partnerships on our direct research team, which we refer to as "immediate family," and partnerships with people who have roles outside of research, which we refer to as "extended family." Developing a dense web of relationships, and creating both immediate and extended family, help us achieve our product-impact goals.

Our Challenges

We face many hurdles in using our partnerships to affect product development. These hurdles include connecting, influencing, and maintaining relevance. For example, connecting and influencing is not as simple as making a telephone call or going to a meeting. We are responsible for identifying the people within the company who have the power to make the changes we think should be made; in a company of 65,000, this can be very challenging.

Ronald Burt's structural-holes theory describes our work practices well. He summarizes his key concept from an earlier article (Burt 1992) by stating that "holes in social structure—or more simply, structural holes—create competitive advantage for an individual whose network spans the holes" (Burt 2002, 155). In such a tremendously large and complex organization, there are divisions and product teams that know little about what the other does. Because our ethnographic work looks at how people live their lives holistically, the results of our work often span organizational divisions, allowing us a unique view on internal company-communication flows, dynamics, and ideas that those attached to a particular feature area or product do not have the luxury of examining and analyzing. Our unique point of view allows us to bridge structural holes and to act as what Burt calls "brokers," engaging in and controlling the flow of information between people, as well as controlling projects that bring people together on opposite sides of the hole.

Once the correct person has been identified, we need to make a connection so that a partnership may be made. We need to understand how this person perceives ethnographic research and then tailor our approach accordingly so that he/she recognizes the value in our work. Some are open to ethnographic work; others are initially resistant to ethnographic findings. They may have a quantitative bias or might not understand what ethnography can bring to product development. Once we have educated them on the value of ethnography, we need to find out how to collaborate with them. Our ethnographic data can be used in a variety of ways, so we work with them to determine which way would be best for their product or feature at whatever point they are at in the product cycle. Whether it is for initial strategy-planning or for creating specific scenarios from which to design, we have to work together to create a partnership that works bèst not only for all individuals involved, but also for the company.

Once we have established our partnerships, the most difficult problem we face is maintaining relevance, or having our data stay at the forefront of the minds of those we want to influence. There are a variety of factors that contribute to this problem: We work on a one-to-many ratio, which means that we each have many individuals and teams we want to influence. It is often difficult to make this scale appropriately within a finite work week. Additionally our target partners are equally busy, and although they may have the best intentions to use our data, without our physical presence serving as a reminder, our data has a tendency to be pushed aside in favor of other people's demands or the most recent stream of data they have received.

Despite all these hurdles, we do affect products through our partnerships at Microsoft. For example, in the partnership case study discussed below, our data has affected strategic product direction as well as feature-level design.

Partnership Metaphor: It's a Family Affair

In an attempt to maintain relevance, we have devised strategies to be effective. First, by building a partnership with a variety of teams across the company, based on reputation (which encompasses the ideas of repetition, credibility, education on the ethnographic process, and results), we have made ourselves part of the consciousness of Microsoft-wide product-development teams. Second, through building local, targeted relationships with other researchers and team members, we gain enthusiastic advocates, allowing our results to scale far beyond the one-to-many ratio we currently face.

What we have recognized in creating and sustaining our partnerships is that it's a family affair. The way we form and sustain partnerships can be illustrated metaphorically with kinship models. In the early kinship models, family relationships were typically defined as those that were based on blood relations—people descended from the same ancestors (Levi-Strauss 1971; Malinowski 1988; Radcliffe-Brown 1940). To get around what they considered "non-standard" examples of family relationships, such as adoption or non-blood relationships, they either ignored what they considered outlier cases or created terms to describe people who did not fit their mental models.

We identify with new models of kinship that have emerged in the postmodern era, through feminist and symbolic critique, in which researchers have recognized that kinship is not just based on consanguine relationships. Instead, kinship can be understood as actively putting a flexible social structure in place to ensure a dense web of support for family members, no matter what the actual blood relationships between individuals are. In addition to this dense web of support, there are certain expectations that come with varying social distances between partners and information exchange that the kinship metaphor helps to clarify in our partnerships.

Weismantel (1995, 689), in her work among the Zumbagua, states, "In a society where 'orphan' is synonymous with 'poor,' a defining characteristic of wealth and success is the ability to fill the house with children. Families like the Izas are big families, strategically assembled from a widespread web of close and distant kin through a variety of economic and social tactics." She goes on to cite an example of how a young boy who is not related by blood becomes a member of a family. He is fed by his new father figure many times, over a long term, and then he becomes a part of this new father figure's family.

We construct our family with our Microsoft colleagues in a similar way. We form rapport through both personal and professional acts so that we can work together effectively to affect product and to raise customer awareness and empathy. The personal and professional acts we engage in with colleagues help build rapport. We analyze data together in order to come to design recommendations (as opposed to analyzing and creating recommendations alone), celebrate life stages together, and socialize. We also make frequent contact via e-mail, schedule meetings where we brainstorm and debate, share meals together, and make other plans outside of work, all of which ultimately cement that family relationship and partnership between us.

The structure of our partnerships is like the structure of a family. We ethnographers are at the center, forming our "nuclear family," where together we develop, field and analyze our research, then decide how to target the results. Partnerships with researchers on our team are like "immediate family." We interact almost daily with our immediate family. We share a common goal: putting customer needs at the center of product development.

Our partnerships with non-researchers are like our extended family. As we create new partnerships with people around the company, we add new members to our extended family. While an imperfect representation, a web gives a sense of how our relationships scale along the family metaphor, how all the relationships are somehow interconnected, and how we often meet new partners through an existing partnership.

To build successful partnerships within the context of our workplace, it is essential that we approach people in a professional, courteous, and respectful manner, no matter the situation. This approach is certainly not a novel tactic; in fact we find that for most people, it is the norm. We have been involved in difficult interactions, however. For example, as mentioned above, those we interact with for the first time may have no knowledge of, or even hold a

loose

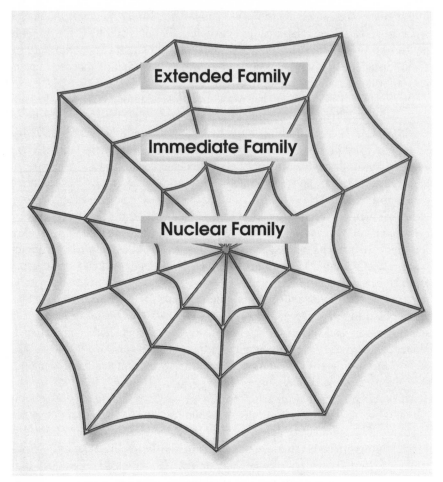

Figure 8.1.   Spiderweb of Relationships in the Microsoft "Family"

negative impression of, ethnography. No matter how we and our work are received, we choose to take the attitude that this person is a family member,
rather than an adversary or critic, and respond accordingly. In the long run,
we find this attitude pays off because it helps establish our reputations as approachable and nice to work with.

CONTEXT OF OUR PARTNERSHIPS

In all of our partnerships, we have a goal: to influence the development of the
products Microsoft builds so that they meet the needs of our customers. The

way we meet this goal is affected by general software-development cycles and by whether the people we want to affect are on our research team (within our immediate family) or on other teams (part of our extended family).

Software-Development Cycle

Microsoft has a software-development cycle. This cycle guides us as to when we should engage with our immediate family partners and when we should engage with our extended family partners. The development cycle has four distinct phases: phase I: planning the product; phase II: designing and building the product; phase III: testing the product; and phase IV: releasing the product.

Planning focuses on initial research that guides the process of deciding what the main goals of the product will be. During the designing and building phase, responsibility for particular product components is assigned to program managers who oversee the development of that area. During the testing phase, the product is used by many people who try to fix as many problems as possible before the product is released. Finally, once the product seems stable and has met the original goals, the marketing campaign begins and the product is released to the public for purchase.

Ethnographer Engagement During Software Development

Within the four phases of the development cycle, some points are more natural for ethnographic engagement than others. Ethnography has the potential to have an effect during phase I when the initial strategy and planning is executed. We conduct longitudinal ethnographies with target audiences during this phase. During the early part of phase II, which is when the product is created, team members are struggling to define their individual feature-area and to understand how it may affect target customers. During this time, we educate our team members about our customers' needs and behaviors, thereby guiding the development process.

As phase II continues and product direction becomes clearer, our engagement declines as the team focuses on completing features rather than taking in new ideas. Once the product reaches a point of relative stability during phase III, the testing phase, ethnography once again plays an important role; we observe how the product performs in real-world environments. During phase IV, the release phase, ethnography's role lessens then grows as planning begins for the next release. During the times when we are not engaged in the current development cycle, we move into exploratory ethnographic research that will feed into future products.

FAMILY DYNAMICS

Setting the Scene: Partnerships with Immediate Family (Researchers on Our Team) and Extended Family (Non-Researchers on Our Team and Other Teams)

Nelle arrives at the 10:00 a.m. product specification, or spec review. Seated to her right is a usability researcher on her team who focuses in this area and who attends every review on this topic. Nelle asks her how the 9:00 a.m. review went. On Nelle's left is one of her favorite program managers, with whom she briefly catches up by asking how his birthday was, then asking when his product review will take place and if he has had a chance to review the feedback she sent via e-mail. Several people are reading the spec for this particular feature area, copies of which are sitting in the middle of the table, while others have their laptops open, either reading the same document online or catching up on e-mail. Nelle briefly skims the document to see what questions she has.

When attendees have finished reading the spec, people begin to pick the document apart, asking questions and making suggestions. The program manager running this review tries to consider all the feedback, while moving the meeting along. As the meeting progresses, Nelle points out several places where small-business-owners' needs could be better met. The hour passes quickly. Recognizing that the program manager had a tremendous amount of information to absorb during the meeting, Nelle heads back to her computer where she formalizes her feedback in e-mail. She cuts out sections of the original spec and rewrites them to reflect small-business-owners' behaviors and needs, knowing that the program manager will probably copy and paste her feedback directly into the original document.

Key Partners in This Scenario

Researchers

Our closest family is our direct team of fellow researchers; we work with eighteen usability researchers to try to affect product development. In our family metaphor, usability researchers are members of our immediate family with whom we are very close; we spend a lot of time together and share a lot of information. Because our ethnographic data has implications for many areas across Windows, it is impossible for us to attend all the meetings to disseminate all the data. The feature-dedicated researchers have the closest partnerships with team members because they engage with them on a daily basis. Therefore, when we have information for a particular feature area, we are able to give that information to the particular researchers and be confident that they can represent the data for us to the people we need to educate. In return, these researchers share information with us on when and how our data can be used to influence product development. Through this reciprocal exchange of information, our work is able to reach many more people than it would otherwise. We therefore view these partnerships as crucial to our success.

Expectations of reciprocity in organizational structures can mirror those of kinship structures (Baba 1999). Balanced reciprocity demands the greatest requirement for trust outside the family structure. In balanced reciprocity, each party gives something of value to the other without the requirement for (a) immediate payback or (b) payback of exactly equal value. The exchange of value is both asynchronous and asymmetrical (e.g., "If you give me something now, I'll give you something different later" [Baba 1999, 335]. In the long term, social distance is reduced between partners in a balanced reciprocal relationship, allowing for high quality and quantity of information flow, which minimizes the risk of the partnership participants.

In other words, we are taken in confidence because of trust we share with our research colleagues. They know that our data is reliable and that it can help them present a more well-rounded picture of our customers. We know that they are more closely aligned with the product-development team and that they can get our data to the right people at the right time and thereby help us influence products. Our partnership has minimal risk because we know what to expect from one another; we develop trust that they will do what they say they will do, and vice versa, through repeated interactions.

Program Managers

These individuals are ultimately responsible for a particular feature area. When we want to influence a particular area, going to the program manager can be the most useful. While fellow researchers help keep our reach broad, partnerships with program managers are often targeted and specific. For example, because communication features is one area on which we focus, we try to develop partnerships with the program managers who work in that area.

In our family model, we consider program managers to be part of our extended family. At times, contact with certain program managers is regular but then wanes during certain phases of the development process. During phases I and II, we have regular contact with the program managers we want to influence. We attend weekly meetings, send regular e-mail messages, and make strategic visits to their offices to discuss certain data. Later, in phase II and into phase III, we are less likely to attend weekly meetings or to stay in day-to-day touch with decisions, but our relationships with research colleagues ensure that our data lives on in these phases.

PARTNERSHIP OUTCOMES

Across our partnerships, our success is varied and still unfolding. Within our immediate family, the partnerships we have created with usability researchers have been successful. In this case, our measures of success include the following:

- a core set of colleagues who understand, value, utilize, and advocate ethnographic research;
- close, lasting, and mutually beneficial partnerships, even where early uncertainty existed;
- a positive tone to our collaboration (and the lack of competition or distrust, which makes all our work better);
- a willingness and eagerness among the usability researchers to create and execute research jointly;
- the ability to extend ethnography's sphere of influence, which helps us overcome the one-to-many ratio; and
- sufficiently strong relationships with researchers, which allow us to disengage from our direct team but still be pulled in when necessary.

In partnerships with our extended family, we are successful, but perhaps not to the same extent as with our research colleagues. We have developed close and lasting partnerships with non-researchers, such as program managers. Our interaction with program managers, however, often dwindles when we disengage from the team during the middle phases of product development. There are times when a program manager will come to us directly for data while we are not engaged, but this is more often done through the usability researcher with whom they work closely. The exceptions are those with whom we have deeper personal relationships. Often, during periods of disengagement, our interactions tend to be more about our personal lives than our work. In the long run, these partnerships are fruitful because there will be a time when we will provide data again and the relationship and credibility are already in place.

Our biggest challenge to success is turnover within a given team. Program managers frequently change teams within Microsoft. In addition, new people (either new to the team or new to Microsoft) join the team. When these changes occur, it can be frustrating because a nurtured partnership disappears and we have to start anew. When we are not in a phase where we are engaged, we fall out of touch with the organizational changes and may not attempt to create new partnerships. When this happens, our impact may be diminished. To some extent, however, we can mitigate this situation through our continual relationships with the usability researchers who have internalized our data and can recall it when necessary.

In terms of evaluating if we have met our stated goal of product impact, the answer is yes, to some extent.[2] Overall, our product recommendations based on field work create a backbone for the planned features in the areas we target; this could not happen without the relationships we have developed. There is difficulty, however, in evaluating our long-term impact. First, in the course of the development cycle, many product plans created in phase I get cut during phases II and III. Thus, although our recommendations directly inform certain areas, those areas are subject to being cut. Ultimately, if the feature area we influenced does not make it into the final shipping product, our effect is reduced. Additionally, by the time the major product cuts happen (latter part of phase II), we have disengaged from the team, meaning that we are no longer there to advocate for the features we believe are the most important to the customer. Our hope is that the usability researchers and others with whom we have partnered will know our data so well by that time that we do not need to be there. Second, because we disengage, we do not follow how and why decisions are made. Therefore, while it may appear that certain product features matched our original recommendations, it is not clear whether our research actually led to the final outcome or whether some other factors were involved.

When trying to measure effect with extended family, one of the key measures we use is whether we are asked to consult and provide feedback throughout the development process. If we are called in, it is clear our work is being valued. If not, we must ask ourselves a series of questions: Is this person too busy to reach out? Are there biases against ethnography or against us as individuals or our work? How important is it for us to continue to try to engage? What is the cost versus potential gain? The truth is, in most partnerships, we are somewhere in between. We are called in for some things, but not others where we think we should have been. In most cases, we have found that the exclusion was not personal, but more a function of not considering us a resource.

Interestingly there is value both in developing close partnerships and in having partnerships in which the connections are more intermittent. This insight may seem counterintuitive, because it is not necessarily in line with our reward structure at Microsoft where we have to develop close relationships to affect product development. There are advantages, however, to having both close, deep partnerships and more distant weak ones. The quality and quantity of information that flows between us and our immediate family is high. While it is less with our extended family, it can be extremely advantageous because we can get fresh perspectives on our team and others within Microsoft.

An unexpected success with our extended family partnerships has been our unique ability to connect people across teams when a project requires it. Because a good portion of our job entails building relationships with people and teams where we think our data should drive product development, we seek out the appropriate people and often become more aware of everyone operating in a given space—for example, small business—than people in other disciplines might be. This success is unexpected, because when we began to connect people together who were working on similar issues, we did not know our organization would value it. As our extended partnerships evolve, we continue to look for innovative ways to partner effectively.

CULTURAL EVALUATION OF THE PARTNERSHIP

Both Burt (2002) and Granovetter (1983) have theorized on the ways partnerships play out between individuals within institutions, exploring the systemic view of actors within a structure that both constrains and enables them to act in ways that can be advantageous to themselves and, at times, the institution. Burt's structural-holes theory shows how an individual agency can act within and against the institution, providing individuals with the opportunity to create advantages for themselves. Granovetter sees the institution as a benevolent non-actor that serves as a petri dish in which connections occur between individuals.

To some extent, these examples describe how we attempt to enact our partnerships at Microsoft. In a large and organizationally complex company, some product teams know little about what other product teams do. Because our work looks at how people live their lives holistically, the results of our work often span organizational divisions, leading us to build partnerships with individuals on many different teams (extended family). These partnerships allow us a unique view on internal company-communication flows, dynamics, and ideas that employees attached to a particular feature-area or product do not necessarily have. Our unique point of view allows us to bridge structural holes and act as what Burt calls "brokers," engaging in and controlling the flow of information between people, and controlling projects that bring people together on opposite sides of the hole.

Granovetter's strength-of-weak-ties theory focuses on the argument that "our acquaintances (weak ties) are less likely to be socially involved with one another than are our close friends (strong ties)" (Granovetter 1983, 201). He sees this as a strength; often in social networks within institutions or organizations, those weak ties can actually be powerful in terms of acting as bridges to give people access to information or resources others know little about.

Granovetter reviewed a number of studies that attempted to explore his concepts, including one by Weinmann (1980). Granovetter found that weak ties provided the bridges over which innovations could cross, but that strong ties are much more likely to allow information to flow faster, are more credible, and are more influential in decision making. The strong ties described above in our immediate-family partnerships fall in line with Weinmann and Granovetter's assessments. Because we have strong, long-term relationships in place with usability researchers, information flows quickly and freely between us. We are able to influence their decision making in feature work effectively. In terms of our weak ties, extended family becomes receptive to our themes after we discuss them. Even though we do not always work together closely, these themes are often a fresh, new way for the useability researchers to look at their existing products. Therefore, they are engaged and receptive.

What these structural theories do not account for is change over time. We do not view partnerships as simply strong or weak in a binary fashion; instead, we foster oscillating partnership strengths based on our needs, our partners' needs, and what we are trying to affect. When we have strong ties with our immediate family members, we have weaker ties with our extended-family members, and vice versa. We are able to optimize our effect across the organization precisely because our strength of ties to others changes over time.

LESSONS LEARNED FROM THE PARTNERSHIP EXPERIENCE

Although our immediate-family and extended-family partnerships vary in their scope, commitment levels, and end results, there are common lessons we can take away from both.

Partnerships are Essential for Success

In the power dynamic of Microsoft, having partnerships is essential for being successful in affecting products. Because we are not actually writing the software code to build the products ourselves, we must partner with those who do, or with those who have the relationships with those who do, in order to ensure that we affect the final product.

Build Credibility

It's not enough to have personal or kin relationships. We build credibility by proving that our work is good and that we are able to translate the data we have into clear design recommendations that make sense to each discipline.

Once our partners recognize that our practices are rigorous, creative, and useful, our credibility is assured.

Mixing the Personal and Professional Helps

Combining the personal and professional can create strong relationships. People remember us when we take the time to get to know them. Having this personal relationship in place makes people feel connected to us again after time apart. Remembering partners' names and knowing something about their personal lives, then folding that knowledge into present interactions, is essential to forming and maintaining partnerships.

Be Kind

We must treat all potential and current partners just as we would treat members of our immediate or extended families, with trust and respect. Engaging with partners in a professional, courteous manner is essential to our potential future success in working with that person.

Face-to-Face Interactions Matter

In the age of digital communication, face-to-face interactions are still important at Microsoft if you intend to shape a product. There is a correlation between long-term product change and physical proximity to our partners. The more time our partners spend around us, seeing us, conversing with us in the hallways or in meetings, the more likely they are to keep our data at the top of their minds and to ask us for data.

Data Lives in and Leaves with Our Partners

By transferring our knowledge to our partners, our expertise lives, in part, in each of them. This key element allows us to overcome the issue of scale. It can also be frustrating, however, when people leave a particular role. Our strategy is time intensive and emotionally intensive. Experiences we have shared with a partner who leaves a role are nearly impossible to transfer to a person who comes in to fill that role. Therefore, we lose exponentially more than the partnership when an individual leaves a particular role or the company; we lose human capital in the form of expertise and support from that person.

Change Can Be Difficult to See

While our ultimate goal is to affect products, it can often be difficult to know with certainty that our data was the driver in any single product decision. It also can be difficult to delineate the level of effect within our extended family. We have informal measurement strategies in place to learn whether our work has affected a product, but they are primarily subjective measurements, not rigorous, qualitative or quantitative ones.

Stay in Touch

The care and feeding of partnerships are crucial in influencing products at Microsoft. We cannot ignore partnerships once they are established. Depending on where we are in the development cycle, each of our partnerships will be more or less active. It is important for us to stay in touch to see how our partners are doing, and to strive to partner together in ways that will produce great products for Microsoft customers. Face-to-face meetings are often the most powerful means of cementing the partnership, but we use electronic means of contact as well. A key lesson from our partnership work at Microsoft is that we know change will happen and our relationship strengths will oscillate over time in relation to the product cycle. This oscillation is part of Microsoft's culture and should be embraced.

NOTES

1. Thank you, Gayna Williams, for supporting our work. Without you, this chapter would not have been possible. Thanks also go to all our collaborators, colleagues, and friends at Microsoft who have worked with us in the past. We appreciate the time and effort you have given to us and our crazy ideas. You are the ones who make working at Microsoft worthwhile!

2. Due to confidentiality, we are not able to discuss the direct feature areas on which our data has had an impact.

9

The Challenge of Partnerships in Complex Cultural Environments

Christine Z. Miller, Jörg Siebert, Julia C. Gluesing, and Amy Goldmacher

INTRODUCTION

The forces of globalization and rapidly advancing technology are primary drivers of the accelerating pace of change in today's business environment.[1] To face the challenges of managing organizations in the evolving global marketplace, students must have opportunities to expand beyond a traditional understanding of the theories and practices of international business. They must also develop the competence to work with new technologies that are linking firms and markets worldwide. Competence includes not only familiarity with the technical tools, but also an understanding of the specialized social and cultural skills required to function effectively in increasingly networked organizations and global virtual environments.

The scope of international business has expanded to include much more than it did even a decade ago when importing, exporting, and offshore manufacturing dominated international business education. New applications of technology have brought major changes in corporate structures and work practices to such an extent that in many firms it is likely that organizational members will work with colleagues, suppliers, customers, or alliance partners in multiple locations around the world. Growing awareness of the changing context of international business was the inspiration and motivation behind the partnership between junior faculty members at Wayne State University and the Institute for Information, Organisation and Management, TUM Business School, Technische Universität München.

Uranium-236 serves as a metaphor to represent this partnership (see figure 9.1). Uranium-236 is an atom formed when Uranium-235, the fuel typically used in nuclear fission reactors, acquires an extra neutron. Uranium-236 is highly unstable: Within a fraction of a second from the time it is formed, it splits into two smaller atoms.[2] In the process, energy is released. Uranium-236

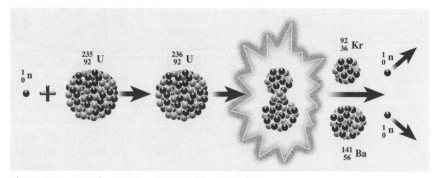

Figure 9.1.   Uranium-236 as Partnership Metaphor

was chosen as a metaphor because both the partnership and the element share the characteristics of fragility and instability, which in the WSU-TUM partnership manifest as disjointedness on multiple levels.

This chapter describes a partnership based on a collaborative virtual-teaming project between junior faculty members at two universities, one located in Southeast Michigan and the other in Munich, Germany. The partnership and collaboration were developed and have been sustained for five years primarily through technology-mediated means of communication, including phone calls and Web-based communication such as chat and instant messaging, e-mail, and video conferences. While there have been several face-to-face encounters over its lifetime, the partnership has, for the most part, lived in the virtual environment. Many factors can affect a partnership's viability. Disjointedness and the resulting byproducts of instability and fragility are the critical factors that inhibit the potential of this partnership in its current configuration.

The genesis and a general description of the partnership are covered in the first section of the chapter. A review of the literature helps to position the partnership in relation to previous research. An analysis of issues that have emerged over time brings to light the challenge of disjointedness that partnerships in complex cultural environments must overcome to survive. This section is followed by commentary from a graduate student in anthropology who participated in an ethnographic study of the virtual-teaming simulation in 2004. The chapter concludes by bringing the partnership into the present and looking ahead to possible directions in which it might evolve.

THE VIRTUAL TEAMING COLLABORATIVE PARTNERSHIP

The WSU-TUM partnership was designed to provide students with an opportunity to explore a range of telecommunication and Web-based technologies while engaging in a technology-mediated cross-border simulation. Based on situations that would likely be encountered in a cross-border business environment (e.g., a merger or acquisition, post-merger integration, managing a multicultural team, development of global strategy), the goal of the simulation was to create a practice field in which students could learn by doing without the risk of real-world losses or costs.

Genesis of the Partnership

The contact that led to the partnership between Wayne State University (WSU) and the Technical University of Munich (TUM)[3] occurred serendipitously through a request in mid-1999 to host a group of German graduate students from TUM and the University of Munich. The group of visiting German students and their advisor were taken on a campus tour, which included an interactive distance-learning (IDL) classroom. During a demonstration of the IDL technology, one of the TUM students commented on how the technology could be used in cross-border international business education. Grasping the idea of utilizing IDL technology to create an experiential learning opportunity for American and German students, a discussion ensued, and the partnership between WSU and TUM was launched.

Following that brief discussion, an agreement was struck to cooperate on developing a simulation for TUM and WSU master's-level students. The course logistics would be handled independently by each university, thereby avoiding the formal requirements for recognition of credits.

The first TUM-WSU collaborative simulation was conducted during the winter-2000 term, with six students participating from each university. The simulation was concluded within approximately eight weeks and, despite challenges of coordination and of learning to work with the technology, the exercise was deemed a success by both the students and the faculty coaches. In March 2000, the six TUM students traveled from Munich to Detroit to participate with the six WSU MBAs in a joint debriefing of the results of the simulation. The WSU faculty members sponsor followed up with a visit and presentation in Munich to TUM faculty members and students in May of 2000.

The first WSU-TUM cross-border technology-mediated business simulation generated excitement and interest within both universities. Based on the success of the first simulation, leaders of the WSU Business School approved a plan to offer an elective course in the MBA program in the winter term of 2001. In addition, a ten-day study tour, one of the first ventures of this kind to be sponsored by the School of Business Administration, would be incorporated as a component of the course. The course attracted approximately forty WSU MBA students, twenty of whom participated in the first study tour. Funding support was provided by the Study Abroad Office, by the management department at WSU, and by students' employers. Subsequent German study tours with groups of between fifteen and twenty WSU students were taken in 2002 and 2004. Each tour included four days in Munich, during which WSU and TUM teams met formally and informally.

Between mid-1999 and the spring of 2001, both universities provided support and resources to the partnership. The initial conditions in which the partnership was established were favorable. Nonetheless, problems that would later challenge the development of the partnership were already beginning to surface. Understanding how these issues emerged over time requires a description of the collaboration and profiles of the students from both partner institutions to provide the context in which the partnership developed.

Defining Partnership

From its inception, the key characteristics of the WSU-TUM partnership have been flexibility, informality, and virtuality. These same characteristics are reflected in the gradual shift of the structure of business partnerships from equity-based joint ventures to less formal collaborative partnership or strategic alliances. It is widely accepted that the change in the nature of business partnerships is being driven by the need to collaborate across organizational, industry, and national boundaries.

The initial decision to establish an informal working arrangement based on the model of a strategic alliance was critical in allowing the partnership to become operational so quickly. Over time, however, the cumulative effects of disjointedness have come to present a serious challenge that the partnership, because of its informal nature and shallow roots, has been ill-equipped to overcome.

PROFILE OF THE PARTNERS

The WSU MBA Profile

WSU is a Carnegie Foundation Research I institute of higher research and learning with an eclectic and diverse student body of over 33,000 and distinguished alumni. WSU's main campus is located in Detroit, Michigan, an area with a long history in the automotive industry. Until recently, most students have lived off campus. New construction of several large dormitories, however, has boosted the number of residential undergraduate students, which is changing the student profile and the character of campus life.

Most of the approximately 2,000 MBA students in the School of Business Administration are older than traditional college students. They typically are returning to school after a hiatus or a change in career path. The majority of these students are employed full time; consequently their course work is completed during evening or weekend classes. In addition, many students are married, some with families, which makes it nearly impossible for part-time MBAs to participate in traditional university study-abroad programs. Consequently special opportunities needed to be created for these students to experience the international environment beyond the traditional classroom setting.

In their jobs, many of the WSU MBAs interact with counterparts from other parts of world, either directly in their current location, or remotely through e-mail, phone, Web-based collaboration tools, and video conferencing. Although the industry is global, many of the people employed in the automotive industry in the Southeast Michigan area are not accustomed to interacting with individuals from outside their immediate cultural environment, despite the ethnic and social diversity of the region in general. Moreover, there is relatively little or no formal training in how to function effectively in either face-to-face or virtual (e.g., technology-mediated) cross-cultural and multi-cultural business environments.

Most students come to the WSU MBA program with undergraduate degrees in disciplines other than business—for example, in engineering or education. Their business knowledge comes from job-related activities that give them a depth of experience with conditions in the work environment. This pattern tends to be particularly evident in the automotive industry, which primarily employs engineers.

The TUM Profile

In comparison, the Technische Universität München (TUM) offers a full-time graduate business program, which awards a diploma in business and engineering or in science. On average, students have work experience of almost three years, although this is not a mandatory requirement for acceptance. Only students who are graduates of the engineering or science programs, however, can participate in the TUM program. Essentially the TUM program is equivalent to what is known in the U.S. as an engineering-management master's program. As of 2005 TUM also offered an MBA degree. TUM accepts students with a specific academic profile that emphasizes technology, business, and European issues, which is quite rare for a public university in Germany. As in other public universities in Germany, students do not pay tuition. Finally, many of the students enrolled at TUM are from other parts of Europe, or from Africa or Asia, which gives the program a strong intercultural composition.

In terms of access to technology, most TUM students do not have Internet access at home, which is generally true throughout Germany, where this service is costly. The use of technology (e.g., online, IDL courses and Web-based course-management platforms) in TUM courses is relatively less than that of WSU courses.

The characteristics described above highlight the major differences between the students from WSU and the students from TUM. MBA students at WSU are typically several years older and typically have work-related experience in an international context but little formal training. TUM MBAs are more attuned to an intercultural environment due the international makeup of TUM's program and because, living in Germany, they experience the influence of the European Union and the direct effects of European integration.

PARTNERSHIP WORK

Beginning of the Simulation

The following section describes the typical sequence of events in the planning and running of the virtual-teaming simulation. The simulation officially begins the first night of class in the winter semester at WSU and the first meeting of TUM classes after their holiday break. The intensity is far greater for the WSU students given that they are presented with the teaming exercise and scenarios. They usually don't know other students in the class and have not seen the simulation before, so they must quickly organize themselves to address the first task. In comparison, TUM students, whose semester started in October, have had several months to become acquainted and to learn about cross-cultural negotiation and other themes that they are likely to encounter in the simulation.

For the next six to eight weeks, WSU and TUM MBAs are engaged as teams in one of two scenarios. Using Web-based collaborative software, e-mail, video conferencing, and other technology-based communication tools, the students interact with their counterparts to conduct due diligence on a potential acquisition target, to negotiate mergers and strategic alliances, and to carry out the activities of a postmerger integration team.

The final task of the simulation requires that student teams prepare a press conference to announce the results and to explain the rationale of their scenario outcomes. In three out of five years, students were able to present the press conference face-to-face with their counterparts when WSU MBAs participated in the German study tour that included four days in Munich. When the study tour did not occur, the final press conference was held virtually as a video conference.

Face-to-Face Interaction: The Study Tour

The best opportunities to strengthen the partnership occur in those years when travel between Germany and the U.S. takes place, and when WSU and TUM faculty members and students participate in several informal and formal activities, including the press conference. Face-to-face interaction provides opportunities for faculty members to discuss the partnership in social settings. While the discussion may focus on the performance of the student teams and outcomes of the simulation that has just been completed, these are occasions when the partnership itself receives the most concentrated and focused attention. It is on these occasions, which typically occur in Munich as part of the WSU study tour, that future direction for the partnership is discussed at any length. These opportunities, however, are limited. Mismatched semester schedules work against interaction between WSU faculty sponsors, TUM senior faculty members, and the chair, who are often away from campus during the semester break.

Problem Focus and Related Research

Data gathered over the course of the partnership through numerous student interviews, surveys, review of documents, and hours of classroom observation provide rich source material for evaluating the perspectives of various stakeholders and the complex cultural environment in which the partnership exits. While prospects for the WSU-TUM partnership appeared promising in the first two years, many issues emerged that revealed the complexities and disjointedness of the partnership.

Many of the issues were interrelated. For example, economic factors in the U.S., and particularly in Michigan, began to affect both university budgets and the ability of individual students to afford the study tour. As Michigan's economy continued to falter, enrollment in the School of Business began to decline, a trend that was exacerbated by corporate cutbacks on reimbursement to employees for MBA coursework. Falling MBA enrollment and the declining value of the dollar relative to the euro put the cost of the study tour out of reach for most students. These and other factors caused support for the course and the partnership to diminish. Consequently five years after its inception, the future of the partnership remained uncertain. The issues that emerged shared a common characteristic: In various ways, they all highlighted the disjointed nature of the partnership. Although many of the issues were dealt with successfully, the cumulative effects of disjointedness ultimately took a toll on the development of the partnership and affected its robustness.

The following section provides a detailed examination of the factors that put the future of the WSU-TUM relationship in question. While each issue does not by itself create an insurmountable problem, together they present a considerable challenge.

DISJOINTED ENVIRONMENTAL ASPECTS CONTRIBUTING TO FRAGILITY AND INSTABILITY

Academic Cycles

Planning is complicated by the fact that semesters at German and U.S. universities run on different calendars. The six-week simulation is scheduled annually during a window when both universities are in session. For WSU MBAs, the simulation begins during the first week of the winter term, whereas for TUM MBAs, the simulation begins at the end of their fall term, immediately before their finals. As the student teams at WSU are finally organized and focused, the students at TUM are turning their attention to studying for final exams. Consequently the attention of the TUM students begins to taper off, while the WSU students are intensifying their efforts to reach an agreement with their TUM counterparts. Everything is, of course, challenged by the fact that students are communicating virtually. Even when using an array of communication media and collaborative tools—e-mail and instant messaging were the most commonly used—the particular contexts affecting the teams were not made explicit by student team members. This was true even when WSU and TUM faculty members explicitly informed their respective student teams about their counterparts' circumstances.

As noted, the partnership had been characterized by annual cycles that commence with each new academic year; Differences in academic calendars complicate interaction. Planning between faculty members begins in late summer with a discussion of how scenarios can be improved, from minor adjustments such as adding additional financial data to scrapping a scenario completely and writing an entirely new case. Again, planning and coordination are done primarily through e-mail. On three occasions, a new TUM faculty member was introduced as the instructor of the class and point of contact for coordinating the scenario. This occurs as TUM junior faculty members, all of whom are completing doctoral programs, shift their attention to completing their dissertations. On the WSU side of the partnership, other faculty members have been involved over the course of the partnership, but the primary contact has remained constant.

Communication between faculty partners peaks during the month leading up to the launch of the new joint simulation. Once the simulation is launched, the role of faculty members shifts from instructor to coach of their respective student teams. At this point, interaction between WSU and TUM faculty coordinators/coaches settles into a weekly pattern, while communication between student teams begins and intensifies.

The topical focus and structure of each of the courses is decided by instructors at each university, and the content and topical focus of the simulation scenarios is a product of faculty partner collaboration. During the first six weeks of the TUM course, students analyze and summarize papers covering negotiation strategies, cultural differences, mergers and acquisitions, teamwork and leadership. TUM students participate in seminars on these topics, which are taught by Accenture staff in the Munich offices. Attending these seminars, in some ways, compensates for having typically less business experience than their WSU counterparts.

The Challenge of Virtuality

From its inception, the WSU-TUM partnership has relied almost exclusively on technology-mediated communications—video conferencing, e-mail, phone, and recently, instant messaging. Because of the different ways in which stakeholders in both locations approached and accessed the technology, both the faculty members who planned and coordinated the simulation, as well as to the students who engaged with their counterparts in the exercise, faced a major challenge. The partnership was based on a collaborative project designed to create an experiential-learning opportunity that exposed students to the challenges of global virtual-teaming. Although all of the students were familiar with the technical aspects of virtuality, they had never systematically explored the social and cultural dimensions of the virtual work environment.

The initial challenge of managing the partnership virtually has been an ongoing challenge in sustaining the partnership. The partnership reached a point at which, in order to grow, it required a greater level of support and commitment from either or both of the sponsoring entities—beyond the informal collaboration between junior-level faculty members. It required additional support, a problem that was exacerbated by the fact that coordination and communication were conducted in a virtual environment rather than in a physical one. The project has remained largely invisible to the faculty members and administrative staffs of both institutions.

Recognizing the invisible nature of virtual work, graduate-level business-anthropology students and faculty members were invited to participate in the collaboration. It was hoped that through their observations, the less-visible aspects of the global virtual-simulation could be brought to light, specifically the negotiation of cultural differences that are known to be particularly problematic in global partnerships.

Role of Business Anthropology Students

In the fifth year of the partnership, a major component to the course was added in the form of participation by graduate-level business-anthropology students. Because of their training in observation and analysis, anthropologists are in a unique position to help navigate the negotiation of global business between members' differing cultural orientations regarding work. The purpose of bringing anthropologists into the partnership was threefold: (1) to provide a fieldwork opportunity for the anthropology students by assigning them to observe the WSU and TUM MBA teams as they worked through the scenarios in global virtual-teams; (2) to expose students from the business and anthropology disciplines to each other in a situation that is likely to occur in a real-world business environment; and (3) to expose the invisible aspects of cross-cultural global partnerships through employing ethnographic techniques.

One of the challenges in today's business environment is to increase collaboration, which requires respect and understanding of the unique skills, perspectives, and practices that different functional and cultural groups can contribute. In an increasingly competitive global-business environment, organizations that are able to master these skills are those that are likely to create innovations that differentiate them from their competitors.

Over the course of the semester, the anthropology students collected data from a variety of sources. First, serving as participant observers and coaches, they observed the WSU MBA students during classes, during virtual interactions online including e-mail, and during two scheduled videoconferences with TUM students. In an online survey and in focus groups, the anthropologists asked all students to compare cultural differences in how they viewed the simulation. The anthropology students presented reports of their observations and survey results, which assisted WSU students in facilitating their simulation interaction. Final results of the ethnographic study of the simulation were presented in Germany.

RELATED LITERATURE AND PRIOR RESEARCH

Cognitive Apprenticeship

John Seeley Brown, Allan Collins, and Paul Duguid's theory of cognitive apprenticeship argues that "activity and situations are integral to cognition and learning" (1989, 32). Using the metaphor of apprenticeship, Brown, Collins, and Duguid challenge the standard separation of "what is learned from how it is learned and used" because "the activity in which knowledge is developed and deployed . . . is not separable from or ancillary to learning" (1989, 32). The authors compare knowledge to a set of tools, because tools "can only be fully understood through use" (Brown, Collins, and Duguid 1989, 33). For example, one cannot learn a language by simply reading a dictionary; one has to use language in context to fully understand what words mean (ibid.). Concepts cannot be taught without also teaching how to use the concepts. Using the apprenticeship metaphor to demonstrate how knowledge needs to be put into use, the authors write the following:

> To learn to use tools as practitioners use them, a student, like an apprentice, must enter that community and its culture. Thus, in a significant way, learning is, we believe, a process of enculturation . . . Cognitive apprenticeship methods try to enculturate students into authentic practices through activity and social interaction in a way similar to that evident—and evidently successful—in craft apprenticeship (1989, 33–37).

Being able to participate in a global business exercise is crucial for students; the apprenticeship approach allows students to practice on a low-risk practice field and helps them to develop the necessary skills for working in today's global-business environment.

Complex Cultural Environments

It is important to emphasize that multiple layers of culture were active at all levels of this partnership, layers that include elements of national, ethnic, institutional, departmental, and professional cultures. Given the complexity of the cultural environment, the only hope for the partnership's sustainability was to continue to build upon the shared perception that sparked its existence: its potential to serve as a vehicle to deliver high-impact experiential learning in a global virtual context.

Although not attractive, characterization of the global virtual-business-environment as a mine field is not inappropriate. As anyone who has worked in the international arena knows, hidden meaning, misinterpretation, and misunderstanding await every step. Only by continually building cross-cultural competency can one hope to avoid making the mistakes upon which many a deal has met an untimely end. These skills cannot be learned by reading a book or by sitting through lectures, although these forms of knowledge transmission can be instructive. The skills that an effective international manager possesses are built from both good and bad experiences and from successes and failures. This learning process takes years. The recognition of this fact, and the possibility for creating a space where individuals could learn through experiences without risking the loss of either a major business deal or millions of dollars or euros, formed the impetus for the partnership. The partnership itself has become a means of building cross-cultural awareness and competence in complex environments.

Cultural Evaluation

The conditional context of the partnership between WSU and TUM is a multilayered cultural context that is illustrated in figure 9.2. Strauss and Corbin (1990, 160–161), in their conceptualization of grounded theory, created an analysis approach that emphasized the conditional context of actions and interactions. Earlier conceptualization of the idea of multilevel cultural context was developed by Steward (1972, 46–47). Cultural influence on classroom activities, and on the partnership overall, occurs at all of these levels and manifests itself in the interactions of the students and instructors in the class itself as they collaborate on the simulation and on negotiating their relationships with one another.

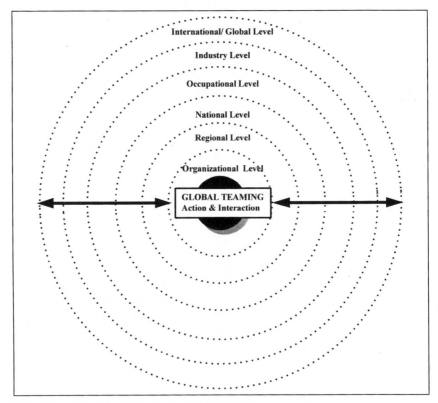

Figure 9.2.   The Cultural Context of the WSU-TUM Partnership

The International/Global Level

This level reflects not just the cross-national nature of the WSU-TUM relationship but also the international makeup of the students who participate in the classes themselves. Education is global in the sense that it involves students who come to each university from different countries and national cultures. While the universities are based in the U.S. and in Germany, the students do not come from those countries alone. The globalization of education has become more of an imperative for preparing students as functioning adults in a global economy. This imperative has led to a more international student body. In turn, the global nature of the student body creates confusion in classroom interactions as students struggle to interpret the meaning of words and behaviors.

The Industry Level

This level refers to the university culture and to the culture of education in general. It is at this level that the partnership finds most of the common ground that holds the partnership together. Both WSU and TUM are engaged in the business of higher education, and this business provides rules about resources, instructor-student roles, and responsibilities and rewards. This shared understanding about higher education provided the fundamental purpose for engaging in the partnership at all. That is not to say that the difference in educational models between the U.S. and Germany was not important. The important point to keep in mind is that all participants in the partnership are interested in creating positive educational experiences and that they share assumptions about what that means at a general level for practice in the classroom.

The Occupational Level

This level highlights the importance of the specific professional or disciplinary cultures that are conditions for interaction in the classroom, including cultural beliefs, value systems, and normative behavior that might be associated with a particular occupation. In the case of the latest collaboration between WSU and TUM, in which anthropologists were introduced to virtual simulation and classroom activities, the MBA students had to learn something about anthropologists and their way of working. Some business students were uncomfortable or even threatened by the anthropologists who were watching them and taking notes about their activities. Others did not understand the value of including anthropologists. The anthropology students, especially those who had not worked in a business setting, struggled with understanding the behaviors of the business students and with explaining their roles and their methods to the business students.

For the MBA students in both Germany and the U.S., and for the anthropology students in the U.S., the relationship was being negotiated throughout the duration of the simulation and the class itself. At the conclusion of the class, however, all of the students had a greater understanding of each other's disciplinary perspectives and ways of working. It is also true that crossing the disciplinary boundaries was often more difficult for the students than crossing the national-cultural boundaries; crossing disciplinary boundaries more subtly affected the interactions because the differences were not as obvious.

The National Level

This level specifically emphasizes the German national culture and the U.S. national culture that affect the interactions in the classroom. Even though the students represent multiple cultures, their educational experiences are taking place in the two countries where the universities are located. The cultural assumptions of the host nations influence the interactions in the classroom in subtle and not-so-subtle ways. Students refer to each other as "the Germans" or "the Americans," and decision-making styles in the simulation tend to reflect the norms in the national culture.

The Regional Level

This level captures the partnership conditions related to the different regional subcultures in the two university locations. While this layer has the least amount of influence on the interactions in the WSU-TUM partnership, it is still worth considering. WSU is an urban commuter university located in Detroit, the students are diverse in age and background, and many students work full time. In contrast, TUM, although urban, has a more traditional student body with full-time students who are younger. These differences create some obstacles for the simulation exercise because not all students in the U.S. can participate during working hours. The diversity also creates additional barriers to shared understanding, particularly related to roles and responsibilities and to expectations for participation.

The Organizational/Sub-organizational Level

This level includes both cultural and structural issues and conditions related to the university and business school primarily. In the WSU-TUM partnership, junior faculty members are generally assigned to teach the class. They are dependent upon the university infrastructure and the buy-in of their own colleges and departments for support and access to resources. There is a gap in how the senior and junior faculty members understand the importance of the course and their commitment to it, as well as in their familiarity with the instructional process and the virtual technologies. The junior faculty members tend to be more comfortable with technology-mediated collaboration tools and with making decisions using these tools.

These methods, however, are not conducive to including decision makers at the level of department chairs or deans. Consequently the level of awareness of the partnership is minimal at the chair and dean level, reducing its level of visibility on the WSU side. In addition, the partnership is not enhanced by perceptions of the associate dean at WSU who believes senior faculty members would not be interested in conducting joint research with TUM faculty members. Unless the gap can be closed, there will remain a cultural divide between junior and senior faculty members and the university administrators about the relevance of the WSU-TUM partnership, and that divide will be sustained if the junior faculty members decide to discontinue the collaborative teaching arrangement.

The Individual/Team Level

This level is the primary cultural context for the actions and interactions of concern to the WSU-TUM partnership. The students and instructors who participate in the simulation exercise, and who interact almost on a daily basis while the simulation is being run, are immersed in a complex cultural context. The nature of the partnership can be understood only by reflecting upon the multiple cultural layers that influence the interactions of the students and instructors that form the basis for the partnership.

The cultural layers are separated by dotted lines in order to convey the interrelationship between and among the layers and the openness of their boundaries. The boundaries between the layers are indistinct and can blend together. Within the layers, there is variation, and students are influenced at the action/interaction level to differing degrees by one or more of the cultural layers within a specific situation. The layers are also in continual flux and become more or less important to interaction under different conditions. For example, a change in instructors at the organizational level on the TUM side of the partnership means that the WSU and TUM instructors must spend time becoming acquainted with one another, as well as negotiate their working relationship, every time the class is taught. If this negotiation is not successful, during the first few days following the start of in-class collaboration, students' interactions with each other will be affected by incomplete negotiations at the organizational level. The decisions at the organizational level among instructors become the most relevant and important conditions for initial interaction at the start of classroom activity. What happens at the organizational level could be more of a conditional influence on initial interactions among the students than national or occupational differences. While such differences might also be influential, they will not be as salient as the organizational influences. The salience of cultural layers is continually in flux and must be constantly negotiated in the WSU-TUM partnership. This realization of cultural complexity and the learning that accompanies it make the partnership important to the participants.

DISCUSSION AND CONCLUSIONS

Returning to the Metaphor: Uranium-236

Insight can be gained by comparing key characteristics of the WSU-TUM partnership to the element Uranium-236, a highly unstable anthropogenic uranium isotope created by a collision between Uranium-235 and a single neutron. The rapid-fire sequence of multiple reactions in the formation of Uranium-236 and the resulting burst of energy when a fragile, unstable atom breaks apart are referred to as a chain reaction. As long as uranium remains, the chain reaction will continue to produce energy. If less than one neutron is available to cause a reaction, the entire sequence eventually will shut down.

In terms of the metaphor, the WSU-TUM partnership has existed in a critical state, generating enough energy from one year to the next to sustain itself. It remains unstable, however, for several reasons. Cultural factors continue to create disjointedness in the partnership.

Partnership Outcomes/Current Status

The partnership between junior WSU and TUM faculty members has affected the education of several hundred students over the course of its existence. Students from both WSU and TUM have consistently given high ratings to their experiences in the collaboration, frequently stating that the collaboration has been a high point of their university course work. For example, when asked to comment on the benefit to students, one TUM student responded, "In my opinion this was one of the courses that provided the most benefit . . . because of the high practical value. I would recommend this course to everybody. Perhaps it should also be offered as a management method [course]." Another TUM student echoed this sentiment stating that "The course was an excellent experience and I recommend it for all students studying *Dienstleistungs* (service) management."

WSU students expressed similar feedback regarding their experiences in the simulation and collaboration. One commented that the opportunity to participate in the simulation, followed by the after-action review (AAR), provided interesting, practical, and valuable learning that they had not found in other courses. Some appreciated the opportunity to work on their interpersonal skills. One student commented, "I looked forward to attending class because it was not a 'standard' lecture where we took notes and regurgitated information; we really interpreted and applied what we learned. I liked that!"

Despite the positive feedback from students, sustaining and expanding the partnership remains a challenge for reasons that have been previously noted. Consequently the roots of the partnership have remained shallow. Finally, if the key members of the partnership leave, the partnership will end.

Lessons Learned: In the End, It's All About the People

Certainly one of the key lessons of this partnership is the enduring power of a good idea (see also Collins and Porras 1997). Considering that the collaboration grew out of the serendipitous visit of a German-student group to the WSU, it is striking that the partnership has lasted as long as it has. The overwhelmingly positive feedback from students who participate in the simulation provides the impetus for offering it again the following year. This is not to say that the learning is painless; in fact, it can be quite challenging for the students to accept the feedback from teammates on their performance. The simulation also requires more commitment and effort from both WSU and TUM students than would normally be required. Despite this fact, and perhaps because of it, the simulation and experience of working on cross-functional global teams continue to draw students to the class.

A second key lesson is that the power of high-impact experiential learning keeps the partnership going. Many students who end up taking the course on both sides do so based upon the recommendation of other students. In addition, the faculty facilitators observe firsthand the benefits to students. This observation reaffirms their commitment to the additional work required for coordinating opportunities for other students to have the same experience. The enthusiasm of students who have completed the course, and their word-of-mouth marketing, results in full classes every time the course is offered.

Key lesson number three is that the importance of the "champions" and "patrons" from both institutions cannot be overemphasized in explaining how the partnership has survived the challenges it has faced in the five years since its inception. Without their ongoing support, the partnership would cease to exist. In the end, it's all about the people.

Further Development of the Partnership

The future may take the form of one or more options that either individually or in combination would effectively increase the level of commitment from the parent institutions. The partnership might also be reconstituted at another college or university.

In closing, Uranium-236 may reveal yet another aspect of the WSU-TUM partnership: Despite its fragility and instability, the partnership, like the chemical element, has continued to generate a great deal of energy by providing meaning, inspiration, and opportunity for the many lives it has touched.

NOTES

1. The WSU-TUM partnership would not have been possible without the commitment and dedication of many individuals in both the U.S. and in Germany. In particular, we thank Dr. Ralf Reichwald, Dean Harvey Kahalas, and Associate Dean Barbara Price, whose support provided the institutional foundations for the partnership. To Dr. Jörg Siebert, Dr. Christian Schaller, Dr. Tobias Fredberg, Dr. Prof Dominik Walcher, and Dr. Jörgen Samsioe, our faculty counterparts at TUM, it has truly been a pleasure to work with each of you. The TUM and WSU student participants deserve special acknowledgment. Their curiosity, hard work, and commitment to developing personal cultural competency continue to carry the core values of the partnership forward. They are the "chain reaction."

2. In the fission process, the atoms formed when Uranium-236 splits can be Barium-141, Krypton-92, Xenon-140, or Strontium-94. Dr. David Z. Robinson enabled us to understand and portray the fission process of Uranium-236 so that we could compare it with partnership functioning.

3. The School of Business Administration at Wayne State University, Detroit, Michigan, and the Institute for Information, Organisation and Management, TUM Business School, Technische Universität München, Munich, Germany.

10

The Making of a Modern Kingdom

Transnational Partnerships in Saudi Arabia

Ann T. Jordan

INTRODUCTION

A significant subset of today's business partnerships is transnational[1] Such partnerships involve a special set of issues as they engage diverse government structures, complex multinational corporations, and multiple cultural systems. As essential as these partnerships have become, they can sometimes seem more trouble than they are worth, given the difficulties of navigating the turbulent waters of cross-cultural negotiation. This chapter describes transnational partnerships for knowledge and technology transfer, and it explains why transnational partnerships are an essential tool in today's global business, even when those partnerships are riddled with difficulties.

This chapter focuses on cultural issues, and partnerships are likened to a three-dimensional puzzle (see figure 10.1). Pieces of multiple cultures must fit together in a layered and complex, but interconnected, manner that most resembles the assembling of pieces in a three-dimensional puzzle. The puzzle becomes a hybrid culture formed from the pieces of diverse cultures. When looking at a three-dimensional puzzle, one only sees the puzzle pieces on the exposed surface. Other pieces are hidden from view below the surface. This is the way in the hybrid culture. The culture one sees is but the surface of an elaborate weave of cultural detail from multiple sources.

This chapter also testifies to the importance of transnational partnerships and to the possibility of their success under even the most difficult of cultural situations. The specific examples used here are from the Kingdom of Saudi Arabia (KSA). The chapter describes transnational partnerships for knowledge and technology transfer that were essential in the modernization of KSA, suggesting that transnational partnerships are an essential component of the political economy of today's world. Then details of one set of transnational partnerships,

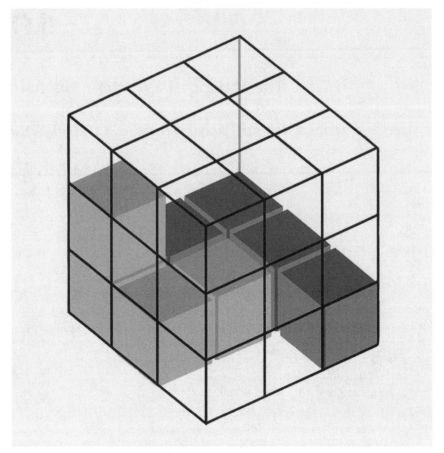

Figure 10.1.   A Three-Dimensional Puzzle as the Partnership's Metaphor

those at King Faisal Specialist Hospital and Research Centre (KFSHRC), in Riyadh, are described in order to illustrate the cultural issues of such partnerships. In conclusion, the chapter includes lessons learned from the study of KSA transnational partnerships. The data for this chapter was gathered during the author's eleven months of research in KSA from 2002 to 2003, including two months of observation and interviews in the KFSHRC.

Definitions of "partnership" abound. The one used here is taken from Dowling et al. (2004) who define partnership in the simplest of terms as a "joint working arrangement where partners are otherwise independent bodies cooperating to achieve a common goal" (2004, 310). Transnational partnerships discussed in the literature are most frequently international equity joint ventures (IJVs), defined as a venture in which two independent organizations partner to create a third (child) organization. The KFSHRC partnerships featured in this chapter are "nonequity joint ventures," because they are alliances where the relationship is established through formal contracts (Glaister and Buckely 1997). To use IJV to refer to the relationships discussed here is misleading since most of the literature considers IJVs to be partnerships that produce a metaphorical child. A more accurate description of KFSHRC and other cutting edge, modern biomedicine organizations around the world is Bartlett and Goshal's (1989) definition of transnational businesses. These authors define them as businesses linking and leveraging knowledge and technological innovation across multiple international partners, while articulating between the local and global simultaneously in any single venture. Any world-class, modern medical establishment must be engaged in transnational strategies like these in order to remain cutting edge.

As mentioned, most transnational-partnership literature focuses on IJVs. In addition, there is a substantial body of literature that suggests that IJVs typically fail and that cultural issues are the reasons for the failures (Meschi 1997; Brannen and Salk 2000; Schuler 2001; Iles and Yolles 2002). This chapter contributes to the literature in that it discusses transnational partnerships that succeed despite vast cultural differences between the partners. The chapter discusses reasons for these successes. Furthermore, literature on partnership success describes success in two ways: process and outcome. Success in the partnership process involves members who learn to work together and thereby achieve mutual understandings. Success in partnership outcomes refers to the partnership reaching the goals it was put in place to achieve. Much of the partnership literature focuses on partnership process (Brannen and Salk 2000; Dowling et al. 2004; Meschi 1997; Doz 1996). Partnership success, as defined by outcome, is less well researched, but general agreement seems to be that it must be measured over a long time period (Schuler 2001; Meschi 1997).

This chapter enriches understanding of both process success and outcome success in transnational partnerships, and it underscores the importance of measuring outcome success over the long haul. In addition, it contributes to an understanding of the relationship between process and outcome success. KFSHRC is an organization in which one could argue that, due to cultural issues, the partnership process was never a success. In fact the partnership environment at KFSHRC could be likened to a pot about to boil over at almost every moment along the way. Outcome, however, was a success. The fact that these Saudi transnational partnerships have succeeded despite such extreme cultural differences is due to the great importance Saudi Arabia places on modernization. This supports Harrigan and Newman's (1990, 425) finding that "propensity" is important in an organization's decision to undertake a

cooperative venture. In this case, there are no other alternatives to modernizing quickly. In his review of the literature on reasons for forming IJVs,
Schuler (2001, 4) lists several reasons that are relevant to the KSA case: to
gain knowledge and technology and to become globally competitive. The
Saudis had and still have a focused need to cooperate with transnational organizations in order to continue to modernize the Kingdom and thereby as-
sure its place at the table of world players.

The literature makes a plea for additional richly detailed studies of the dynamic, interactive process that is partnership survival day to day. There is special interest in this in a transcultural context where culture is caught in the act
of evolving moment to moment through small interactions and negotiations
across multiple layers of meaning (Van Maanen and Barley 1984; Adler and
Bartholomew 1992; Ring and Van de Ven 1994; Brannen and Salk 2000).
This chapter describes such a richly-textured environment and thereby contributes to our understanding of its nuances. In addition, it foregrounds the external environment in which these transnational partnerships were created and
subsequently operated. Much of the literature describes partnerships as if they
existed in a vacuum and does not place them in their larger context. That
larger context is essential to understanding not only the success of the partnership but the ways in which day-to-day processes worked. Thus this chapter contributes to the literature by emphasizing the importance of context.

THE SIGNIFICANCE OF TRANSNATIONAL PARTNERSHIPS: THE MAKING OF A MODERN KINGDOM

To understand this remarkable use of transnational partnerships, it is important
to understand the history and the culture of the Kingdom. Situated in the Arabian Peninsula between the Red Sea and the Arabian Gulf, and between the
great continents of Africa and Asia, crossed by ancient spice-trade routes, the
home of the Muslim holy cities of Mekkah and Madinah, in close proximity to
the Suez Canal, and the location of some twenty-five percent of the world's oil
reserves, the lands of Saudi Arabia have always been strategically important to
the world. The KSA comprises four-fifths of the Arabian Peninsula, an area approximately one-third the size of the continental United States. It is an area the
size of Great Britain, France, and Italy combined, but with ten percent of the
population. In 2000, the population of Saudi citizens was 16.2 million with
thirty-eight percent under the age of eleven (Rugh 2002, 53).

Saudi Arabia is a relatively young state. At the beginning of the twentieth
century, there was no Kingdom and no state system in the Arabian Peninsula.
The peninsula has historically been the home of tribal peoples—bedu camel

there's a better metaphor here (absorption depth)

pastoralists transversing the deserts and horticulturalists growing dates and wheat and settled in the oasis. Politically it was composed of many independent entities that sometimes fought each other for control of land, water, and material wealth. In 1902, Abdulaziz al Saud began three decades of military, diplomatic, and religious conquests that resulted in his uniting the lands of the current Kingdom. By 1932, he had become the first king of the Kingdom of Saudi Arabia, a modern state system. In the 1930s, however, KSA was a poor country with few resources other than camels and dates and a master diplomat as a king. It was a traditional Arab country. Education centered on learning the Koran. Transportation was by camel. The rapid rate of change that the Kingdom has undergone in the last seventy years, even the last thirty years, is difficult to appreciate. Today KSA is a modern country of shopping malls, traffic jams, marble and steel buildings, Starbucks, and Saks 5th Avenue.

The Steps of a Change Process

How has KSA managed this rapid transformation to a gleaming, modern kingdom? How has a country with no modern education system and no modern technology or infrastructure been able to develop all of these and to become a world player in economics in just a few decades? Of course the answer lies in the oil resources used to fund such a transition, but money alone cannot bring about this transformation. It is herein suggested that the mechanism for change has been the use of transnational partnerships to conduct knowledge and technology transfer, and that the kingdom has repeatedly used the same process to effect change. The suggested steps of this change process are as follows:

1. Enter into a foreign partnership that can bring needed expertise into the Kingdom; this might include foreign management of the necessary companies.
2. Set up foreign-led training programs in-country for Saudis, and send Saudi students abroad for further education.
3. Train Saudis in all areas of expertise needed to execute the desired business.
4. Saudi-ization: Slowly replace foreign experts with Saudi experts until all the enterprise has been Saudi-ized.
5. Dissolve foreign partnership.

The Saudi government has not stated this process as a formal government policy. Rather it has simply occurred over time in various industries. Some of the steps of the process have been formal policy. For instance, the government has had a formal policy of sending students abroad for study when no equivalent program was available in the Kingdom. Also, the policy of Saudi-ization is an explicitly stated goal and one that has been codified in law for some occupations. The reason for the importance of Saudi-ization is the country's large number of unemployed youth and the prospect that this number will only grow.

As stated earlier, thirty-eight percent of Saudis are under the age of eleven (Rugh 2002, 53). Faced with the prospect of so many youth with no employment prospects, the government is Saudi-izing occupations as fast as practically possible in order to provide jobs for its youth. Saudi-ization refers to that process of replacing all foreigners in an occupation with Saudis. Inkpen and Currall (1998) and Schuler (2001) describe how increased learning increases the bargaining power of the learner in a partnership by reducing the learner's dependence on the teacher partner. This is exactly what the Saudis have intended in many of their transnational partnerships. This is not done surreptitiously. As previously explained, sometimes Saudi-ization is stated as a goal, and sometimes it is formalized into a law.

Partnerships have been formed as the need arises and then are dissolved when the need is gone. Partnerships can change, morph into different forms, dissolve, reconstitute; it all depends on the perceived needs in the Kingdom. Given the global nature of today's business world, it is unlikely that the Kingdom will ever be without some number of transnational partnerships. While it will eventually acquire the levels of expert knowledge and technology use it desires, no modern state can be without transnational partnerships, and KSA will not be an exception. Saudi-ization is not a drive to remove all foreigners from the country, because any country with state-of-the-art technology, cutting-edge knowledge workers, and multinational business interests must have an expatriate population. Such a population is necessary for maintaining multinational business ties and a global edge. Instead, the five step process, including the step of Saudi-ization, is intended to position KSA as a modern global leader in control of its destiny and as a vibrant economy capable of providing jobs for all its citizens.

Explanation for Change Process Success

KSA has been blessed with two characteristics that are a large part of the reason for the success of this five-step process. It is suggested here that this five-step process would not have been possible without two important factors that were not present for most developing countries during the twentieth century. Those factors are:

1. The Kingdom of Saudi Arabia was never colonized. There were no western laws or ways of proceeding that had to be dismantled. Abdulaziz, the first King of modern KSA, began from an Arab and Muslim cultural and religious base and built an Arab and Muslim modern state.
2. Natural resources provided ample capital to spend in this modernization task. While oil was discovered in the 1930s, the resultant abundant financial resources did not appear until the 1970s. It was in the 1970s and under the rule of one of Abdulaziz' son, King Faisal, that the Kingdom began applying the above formula to areas of modernization other than the oil industry.

Many developing nations are using transnational partnerships to accelerate their modernization process. Few, however, enter these partnerships from as strong a position as KSA. Consequently these partnerships are typically not as successful for the developing country (see Andreosso-O'Callaghan and Qian [1999]; Machado [1989–1990]; Dent [2003] for examples of transnational partnerships in other developing countries). To illustrate the use of the five-step process and the importance of these two factors, examples from the field of medicine follow.

KING FAISAL SPECIALIST HOSPITAL: TRANSNATIONAL PARTNERSHIP AS A THREE-DIMENSIONAL PUZZLE

Like other areas of development, in 1970, KSA had relatively few modern health facilities. There were only 74 hospitals, 591 health centers, and 1,172 physicians. As part of its first five-year development plan, the government set out to improve this situation. It contracted with medical establishments in the west to help build a medical system.

The Creation of a Modern Medical System

In 1970, King Faisal laid the foundation stone for the new King Faisal Specialist Hospital and Research Centre (KFSHRC), which was to be a modern tertiary (i.e., specialist) care facility. The government had contracted with a British firm to build the facilities. On the edge of the dessert, on the outskirts of Riyadh, a modern hospital was built—along with a housing compound that provided living quarters for the foreign physicians and other specialists. In 1975, KFSH opened with 120 beds. To manage the hospital, the government partnered with a U.S. firm, Hospital Corporation of America (HCA). So, while the British created the buildings, the U.S. actually created the working hospital. HCA created all the procedures, hired the staff, and managed the development of a modern tertiary-care facility. Doctors and nurses were hired primarily from Europe and North America. Employees remember, "[There was a] bias from the beginning to hire Americans," and,

> Almost 100% of the staff was American at that time . . . The Americans were here and they put in an American system, turnkey . . . There was an infrastructure in place at one time. I tell them, the hospital has really good bones. It was constructed well originally. The policies and procedures were fabulous. The human resource policies really good, financial, everything.

Meanwhile, the Kingdom sent its most promising students to Europe and to the U.S. in order to attend college and medical school. The students' tuitions and living expenses were paid by the government with the understanding that the students would return to practice medicine in the Kingdom.

By the late 1970s, nine to ten percent of HCA's revenue was from its partnership with KFSHRC. Other western medical organizations also partnered with KFSHRC. For example, in 1978, the hospital partnered with Baylor College of Medicine, in Houston, Texas, to begin performing cardiac surgery. The partnership with Baylor would continue until 1985 when KFSHRC cardiology services began to be offered entirely by in-house medical staff. The management of HCA ended in 1981, and Saudis took the lead in hospital administration. By 2002, KFSHRC in Riyadh was a 650-bed tertiary-care hospital that admitted 212,000 patients a year, supported 592,000 outpatient visits, and performed 1,400 open-heart surgeries, 130 bone marrow transplants, and 60 kidney transplants. The hospital had 720 physicians and 1,940 nurses, with a total staff of 7,150 that was composed of 63 different nationalities (KFSHRC Healthcare System 2003: Facts and Stats). In 2003, the last non-Saudi administrator, a U.S. citizen, left the hospital.

Today over fifty percent of the physicians are Saudi. The Kingdom also has its own medical schools. The teaching physicians in those schools were mostly trained in the west; the students, however, will be a new generation of Saudi doctors whose education was acquired entirely within the Kingdom. Thirty years after its opening, KFHSRC is a world-class tertiary-care hospital and a leader in health care in the Middle East. The process of development through transnational partnerships that was outlined earlier is the reason for its rapid success.

Ongoing Transnational Partnerships: A Necessity in Modern Healthcare

Not only were transnational partnerships essential in developing a modern medical system in KSA, they continue to be essential in operating a modern medical system anywhere in the world. World-class biomedicine is a global business. KFSHRC has collaborated with numerous institutions, including Massachusetts General, the Mayo Clinic, Johns Hopkins, Sloan Kettering, and UCLA. For example, KFSHRC has partnered with World Care, a company that contracts with numerous hospitals to provide second opinions and consultations. When the physicians at KFSHRC need a second opinion on a case, they ask World Care to make the connection for them with specific medical institutions. KFSHRC is developing electronic diagnostic systems with hospitals in the United States. In these systems, all the information that pertains to the patient can be sent electronically. A physician located anywhere in the world can actually help diagnose the disease without seeing the patient lying in a hospital bed in Saudi Arabia. KFSHRC is, in turn, a leader in the region and provides expertise within KSA's borders and in the larger Gulf area as well.

Not only were transnational partnerships essential for developing and maintaining Saudi expertise and its leadership position in the region, they remain essential for conducting business efficiently. Outsourcing has become a way of life in Saudi just as it has in the U.S. For example, KFSHRC contracts with CBAY, a U.S. company, for medical transcription. The Kingdom has few trained medical transcriptionists and has tried in the past to entice foreign transcriptionists to move to the Kingdom to work. They tried to recruit from the U.S., South Africa, and the Far East, but they had little luck in recent years. Faced with a backlog of transcription needs, KFSHRC contracted with CBAY to handle medical transcription. Each day, they transmit their medical records electronically to CBAY in the U.S., where records are in turn transmitted to India, where transcriptionists actually transcribe them. Then the records are transmitted back to the U.S., checked for errors and sent on to Saudi Arabia to the KFSHRC. The entire process takes less than twenty-four hours to complete.

Thus the example of KFSHRC sheds light on another aspect of the five-step process. While transnational partnerships were essential for the modernization of the Kingdom, Saudis assume that they will continue to be essential for the running of a modern Kingdom. The Saudi experts at KFSHRC, like their counterparts all over the world, will go wherever it is necessary to go to establish partnerships that allow them to maintain their leading edge in tertiary care.

Hybrid Culture: The Three-Dimensional Puzzle at KFSHRC

The transnational partnerships that brought the miracle of modern medicine to the Kingdom have been fraught with problems. An important set of these problems are cultural issues. KFSHRC is staffed by 7,488 employees of sixty-three nationalities. The differences in culture, of course, cause tension.

But many see this cultural mix as a good environment. One physician describes her department in this way:

> We have one American, one Canadian, three Danish, and one South African. That is for the physician staff. And the rest [of the physicians] are Saudis actually, 6 or 7 . . . Our nursing staff we have a whole mix of everywhere . . . And we have 50 [to] 55 nurses. They come from all over—South Africa, a lot of Canadians, a lot from the Philippines, a lot from other Arab countries as well . . . The support staff . . . I have one from South Africa and one is Philippino, and one is Arab (she is from Palestine). Case managers and coordinators, most of those are Saudis because they have to interact a lot with patients. They have to be native speakers. [Our staff is] a mixture from all over. If we all know the mission, if you know what you are doing, it doesn't matter what the nationality or background of the staff members are.

Others describe the kinds of cultural clashes this involves. For example, the following perceptions are culled from interviews with nurses. (1) British doctors clash with American nurses because the U.K. has a more rigid system than the U.S. British doctors do not expect nurses to question them. (2) English nurses are not taught to do a physical assessment (listen to breathing and heart, check pulse, and so on) when a patient first arrives at the hospital, while U.S. nurses are. (3) Indian nurses do not have the clinical experience or nursing education for this kind of high-tech hospital. (4) Philippinos are excellent at cardiac and pediatric specialties.

Part of the unique nature of the culture at KFSHRC is this multicultural mix that creates the hybrid culture that is herein likened to a three-dimensional puzzle. Although the staff includes workers holding some sixty-three different national passports, a few nationalities make up large percents of the total staff population. Saudi Arabia makes up the largest percentage of the workforce at 38 percent, followed by the Philippines (17 percent), the Sudan (8 percent), Canada (6 percent), India (4 percent), the United States and South Africa (3 percent each). While all these cultural groupings affect the dynamic of culture at KFSHRC, two have extraordinary influence on hospital culture: Saudi Arabia and the United States. Since the hospital was originally created by an American corporation, (HCA), staffed with Americans, and used an American hospital structure, policies, and procedures, it had a strong American hospital culture initially. This is voiced by long-time American employees who are still at the hospital: "There were very few concessions to the Islamic way. We were an island and it was very American." As the hospital has increasingly been Saudi-ized, that culture has been altered in Saudi ways so that by the time of this study, there was a true hybrid culture of which Saudi and U.S. elements were the most prominent.

So the puzzle pieces are predominantly Saudi and U.S., but they are mixed together in surprising ways.

The issue of dress, discussed in multiple interviews with hospital staff, illustrates the transition from U.S. domination to strong Saudi influence. The hospital dress code also reflects the tension between U.S. and Saudi culture. All male physicians at the hospital, including Saudis, wear western suits and lab coats; while at the Saudi university medical schools, male Saudi physicians wear *gutras* (head coverings) and *thobes* (long robes) of traditional Saudi male dress. Women physicians at KFSHRC wear the *hijab* if they are Muslim, meaning that they cover their hair and also may cover their faces. When examining a patient, they leave their eyes exposed. They do not, however, wear the *abayah*, the long black robe worn by all women in public in KSA. The *abayah* would be the appropriate dress in such a public place as a hospital, and it is worn by women visitors to the hospital. Women physicians and nurses, however, wear pants or long skirts and lab coats instead of the *abayah*. Lab coats have become an acceptable alternative to *abayahs* for women physicians, nurses, and other medical specialists.

The response to this dress policy indicates the tension between the two cultures in this hybrid. Some Muslim women enjoy the greater freedom by

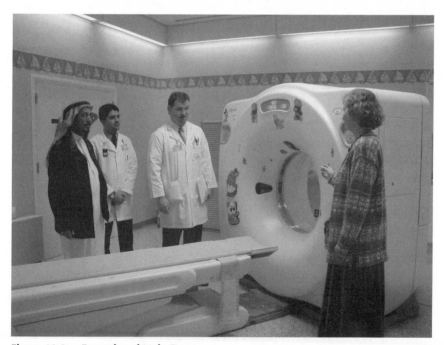

Figure 10.2.   Examples of Male Dress

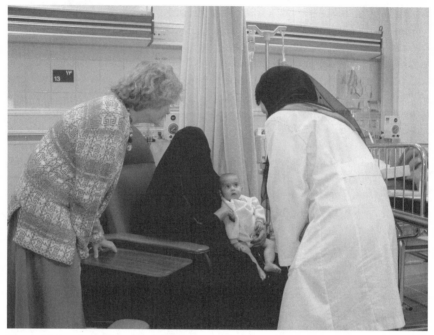

Figure 10.3.   Examples of Female Dress

leaving their hair uncovered with just a scarf in easy reach around their neck. Traditional Saudis at the hospital complained, however, about the indecent dress of women in the hospital. In a further flap about dress, some Saudis believe that female nurses in scrubs should wear scrub uniforms with long sleeves, so that their arms will not be exposed, and that they should veil.

Westerners, however, rationalized issues of dress as issues of sanitation. A woman in a veil or a man in a *gutra* (head covering), while putting in an IV or dressing a wound, could endanger the patient by allowing the veil or *gutra* to touch the sterile field. The same argument is made about long-sleeved scrubs for women. The sleeves could touch sterile fields. Western dress is seen as more sanitary (no mention is made of the danger of western neckties touching a sterile field.) When examining a patient, however, it is perfectly acceptable for a female physician to wear *hijab*, including covering her face, with the exception of her eyes. Female patients are typically covered, including their eyes. The most difficult area for a male physician to get permission to examine on a female patient is her face.

Without question, this is a hybrid culture in tension. As is the case in any national culture, the Saudis on the hospital staff are not of one mind regarding the propriety of hospital rules and regulations. Some Saudi staff are strict

Wahhabi traditionalists who see the hybrid hospital culture as containing many elements that are forbidden in Islam and who are disgusted by the allowing of what, to them, is immoral behavior. Other Saudis find the rules acceptable and enjoy the freedom the hospital environment gives them.

As for the other nationalities working in the hospital, their opinions and comfort levels with the rules and behaviors in the hospitals are as varied as the nationalities and diversity in their own countries. Some westerners, for example, think the Saudi rules inside the hospital, and certainly those outside it in Saudi public space, are silly and backward, while other westerners take a more culturally-relative position. Some of the hospital staff cope with the tensions by sticking to procedure during the work day and isolating themselves "with their own kind" after hours. Others make an effort to socialize with staff from a variety of cultural backgrounds.

None of the staff interviewed for this research disputed the value of the American "bones" of the hospital. They agreed that all procedures in the hospital must be up to the most exacting of international standards. The disputes, rather, were over issues of behavioral rules— for example, who sits where in the cafeteria or which days the swimming pool is open for men and which for women. Of course, time and again, behavioral rules affect western hospital standards, such as the dispute over whether Saudi dress endangered the sterile field when cleaning a wound.

The hybridity of the hospital culture is always in flux, the pieces of the puzzle always in movement, as if no one is satisfied with how they mesh together and everyone is always looking for a better fit. This is a characteristic of hybrid cultures. They inherently contain tension. Despite the tension, however, the hospital functions at an extremely high level. It seems that everyone acknowledges the vast cultural differences and, simply put, work gets done.

The External Environment and KFSHRC

Like other global businesses with multiple transnational partnerships, KFSHRC is affected by the geopolitical economy. Understanding this effect is essential to understanding transnational partnerships generally, as well as those in KSA specifically. The September 11 terrorist attack in the U.S. is an example of an external event that had serious and long-reaching effects on KFSHRC. An important reaction was the reluctance of westerners to come to the Kingdom and of Saudis to go to the west. KFSHRC has been dependent on the west for nurses, for example. Prior to 9/11, some 25 percent of the nurses were from the Philippines, 25 percent from Canada, and 12 percent from the U.S. Since 9/11, the numbers from Europe, the U.S., and Canada have dropped. The percentage from the U.S. dropped to five percent. The shortage of nurses is critical worldwide, and the Kingdom's rulers are especially concerned that their loss of nurses is due to perceived terror links in Saudi Arabia. KFSHRC is scrambling to solve its critical nursing shortage. No nurses were being trained at the time of this field research, though that is beginning now.

Another post 9/11 problem is caused by the new U.S. rules about mail. The hospital sends many tests to the Mayo Clinic and other U.S. hospitals for analyses. Some of these tests can only be done in the U.S. or Canada; the U.S., however, is reluctant to accept specimens from the Middle East. Packages are irradiated by the U.S. mail service and the specimens are live cells; thus the cells are killed. The hospital labels such packages clearly, "Please do not irradiate. These are live cells." Of course, with concern about biological warfare, live cells are exactly the kind of material the U.S. irradiation system is meant to kill. Consequently KFSHRC has had difficulty getting samples through to U.S. laboratories.

Thus world events are significant to the success of the hospital. Transnational partnerships are part of an open system that includes political and economic forces on the world stage. Environment is a critical factor in the success of transnational partnerships. There is great concern in the KSA government over the effect of world politics on its transnational partnerships. Government leaders see transnational partnerships as essential to the Kingdom's continued success, and anything that threatens them potentially limits that success.

KFSHRC TODAY

KFSHRC's success is the result of transnational partnerships that have succeeded against all odds. Meschi (1997) has commented that individuals often have a hard time articulating their own culture since it is the nature of culture that one is unaware of one's own. At KFSHRC, cultural differences were so stark there was no way to be unaware of them. The U.S. culture and the Saudi culture could not be further apart. They appear to be polar opposites. These differences may have worked to help traverse the cultural minefields successfully. In all transnational partnerships, culture is an issue, but it is sometimes ignored. At KFSHRC, no one could ignore the fact that culture was an issue. Yet despite these extreme differences and despite the presence of staff from over sixty countries, the partnerships have been a success. The goal of achieving a world-class, tertiary-care facility in the Middle East has been achieved, and the continuing transnational context of medicine practiced at the hospital is an effort to continue this world-class quality.

CONCLUSION

The strategy of (1) entering into transnational partnerships, (2) setting up training mechanisms for Saudis, (3) training Saudis in the desired knowledge, (4) replacing the foreign partners with Saudis (Saudi-ization), and (5) dissolving the partnership has been a primary factor in modernization in the Kingdom. While this chapter has focused on medicine, the same change-process has been used in other fields—for example, in the oil business and in education. In all fields, however, these partnerships were not always smooth—in fact, they were rarely smooth; yet they worked. One wonders how, when the cultures of the west and of Wahhabi Islamic Saudi Arabia are so drastically different, they managed to succeed at all.

Lessons Learned

Below are some lessons that were learned from the successes:

1. Be realistic about the problems from the outset.
   No one ever expected a rose garden. It was obvious from the outset that there would be culture clashes. All participants would have to make cultural adaptations in order to allow the partnerships to succeed. In situations where it is obvious that clashes will occur, parties are more realistic going in, and this is actually an asset. They are not blindsided by the cultural problems as partners are in partnerships where the cultures are more similar. In this case, problems were expected, and thus, while causing plenty of strife, did not cause the partnerships to fail.
2. Be aware of the external environment.
   The external environment is often a wild card that can wreck the most successful partnership. In this case, international politics affects the partnerships directly as well as the transfer of knowledge. Some environmental effects are not predictable, as in the example of 9/11, but others are predictable and should be expected.
3. Keep your eyes on the prize.
   The goal was clear: Transfer the knowledge and technology necessary to create a first-rate, modern system in Saudi Arabia, whether in the oil business, education, or medicine. The goal was more important than

the problems, and only by keeping the goal in mind could the problems be overcome. Ultimately cooperating to get the job done overcame the obstacles.

Literature Contribution

This chapter contributes to the literature in several ways. First, most of the literature on transnational partnerships concerns equity joint ventures, and this study increases our knowledge of nonequity joint ventures. Second, most studies of IJVs find that they fail and that cultural difference is a primary reason for the failure. This study provides an example where cultural difference is extreme but does not cause the ventures to fail. Furthermore the literature distinguishes between the success of the partnership process and the success of the partnership outcome. While the partnership process might be deemed a failure at KFSHRC, its outcome is a success; and it is by focusing on successful outcomes that the individuals involved are able to manage the partnership process.

Thus the chapter contributes to our understanding of both process and outcome success and the relationship between the two. In so doing, it underscores the importance of propensity, not only in a company's decision to undertake a cooperative venture but also in its decision to continue working in a partnership even when the cultural divide is great. Also the KSA example adds to the literature a description of the dynamic and interactive process involved in day-to-day interaction and negotiation in a complex and layered multicultural environment, as well as the changes in that interactive process over time. Finally, it also underscores the importance of context. Factors in the external environment must be considered when studying any transnational partnership. Not only do these factors explain why the partnerships were undertaken in the first place, but ongoing external factors contribute to their ultimate success or failure.

NOTE

1. I wish to thank the King Faisal Specialist Hospital and Research Centre, as well as the King Faisal Centre for Research and Islamic Studies, Riyadh, Saudi Arabia, for their support of this reserach.

Section 4

LESSONS LEARNED

11

Learning from the Partnership Experience

Elizabeth K. Briody, Tracy L. Meerwarth,
and Robert T. Trotter, II

INTRODUCTION

The purpose of this volume has been to explore and understand the cultural patterns surrounding the partnership experience.[1] Examining the ways in which culture permeates these collaborative arrangements makes it possible to place collaboration and partnerships in context, to learn from experiences, and to move into the future with an improved understanding of partnering and organizational effectiveness.

This chapter summarizes the lessons learned from our collective research. It emphasizes both a structural and dynamic perspective, while following the broad definitions provided in chapter 1. The diversity of cases widened the angle of our lens and put more information within our field of view, which allowed us to see the commonalities and the divergences in the various cases. Limiting the cases to specific types of partnerships (e.g., voluntary, private-sector, long-term), would not have allowed us to profit from the insights revealed through the sharp contrasts and striking similarities that we observed.

Some of our findings confirm past work, and others extend those findings into new realms. We anticipated that our cultural-models framework would enable us to explore the inner-partnership workings and their relation to the wider environmental context more holistically, and also that the metaphors selected to represent each case would have the potential to provide us with new information. This chapter provides a summary of the lessons learned from the composite findings in the various cases. It continues our cultural-models framework and draws out the cultural themes that are common to the ethnographic cases. It is supplemented by an analysis of the metaphors symbolizing those cases. At the end of the chapter, we conclude with a discussion of a metaphor for partnering activity that illustrates what we have learned about partnerships.

LEARNING FROM A CULTURAL-MODELS APPROACH

Our cultural-models approach has proven to be valuable in the identification and explanation of lessons learned. Much of the GM Collaborative Research Labs (CRL) relationship and reciprocity dynamics—the foundation model in chapter 2 (Trotter et al.)—are confirmed and extended by the ethnographic findings from the partnership cases in the book. The cases also extend the depth of our understanding of partnerships by exploring additional culture-theory aspects of partnerships in all four culture-theory areas we discussed (i.e., evolutionary theory, cognitive, theory, structural theory, and symbolic theory), expanding the lessons learned from this approach. As a result, we are able to move beyond simple dichotomies of partnerships—such as ideal and less-than-ideal—to a solid empirical model derived from the perspective of partnership participants. Our cultural-theory approach addresses Selsky and Parker's (2005, 866) critical question, "How can researchers capture the messiness of partnership practice in more complex models?" Our answer is to provide a clear framework for turning the messiness into complexity that displays definable patterns rather than chaos.

LEARNING FROM PARTNERSHIP FOCUS

The lessons learned in the cases include a better understanding of definitional variations of partnership terms, identification of structural and relational boundaries in partnerships, and partnership engagement and perspective. These lessons tend to emphasize the cognitive aspects of culture theory because the researchers are providing definitions of important categories of culture and are describing critical cultural domains to provide a clear and rich description of partnership culture.

Partnership Definition

All the partnerships documented in this book reflect our broad definition: "Collaborative arrangements, in which participants enter into relationships, combine their resources, time, and expertise through the various roles they play, and work toward the creation of new knowledge, products, and services." The cases range from a two-sided partnership involving many people in the Kingdom of Saudi Arabia and the Hospital Corporation of America (Jordan), to three-way partnering arrangements (Beauregard), to multiway (Eaton and Brandenburg) endeavors, to a web or network structure at Microsoft in which individuals are complexly connected to others, both within and beyond specific unit boundaries through various intermediaries (Lovejoy and Steele).

These cases reveal a structural diversity that extends beyond the common notion of a simple two-way partnership found frequently in the literature. This definition supports partnership forms that are highly complex in terms of relationships, viewpoints, roles, and boundaries. Maintaining an inclusive definition allows us to incorporate more diversity in the ways that individuals and organizations are connected to each other for a common purpose and to produce more lessons.

Lesson Learned

Expanding the definition of partnerships to focus on the underlying cultural dynamics of partnerships enhances our understanding of those cultural dynamics and increases the pool of potential insights that can then lead to generalizations.

Multiplicity of Relationships within a Partnership

The cases clearly demonstrate that any partnership involves a multiplicity of relationships even when there are only two partners. These muliplex relationships (in social-network research terms) result from the fact that people take on multiple roles, and those roles produce complex, rather than simple, relationship dynamics. While many researchers view partnership activities from a macro, or 30,000-foot perspective, all of the cases in this book focus significant attention on aspects of partnership functioning (e.g., interactions between groups, explanations for a particular behavior) and, at the same time, provide an orientation to the broader cultural environment.

An example is the Saudi and American explanation for hospital-staff dress code. The ethnographic data reveals the flap about dress as each ethnic group works to justify its own behavior and is unable to examine its own beliefs and values objectively. This example is then linked to the concept of the hospital's hybrid culture and its place within the wider Saudi society (Jordan). The cases also reveal how the individual (or organizational) partners may shift over time so that the partnership structure of today is often different from the structure of the past. Continuing the Jordan case, the composition of the hospital staff has been changing. Retrospective interviews and on-site observation led Jordan to use the term "Saudi-ization" to describe the changing partnering relationships between the "foreigner experts" and Saudi experts. The hospital culture increasingly reflects Saudi influence, which in turn has led to changes in how the staff members relate to one another.

Lesson Learned

vague

Partnering relationships must evolve over time in response to changes in the cultural environment if they are to increase the likelihood of success. Static relationships often result in partnership failure.

Multiplicity of Partnerships

A related finding is that some partnership participants are successfully engaged in multiple partnerships simultaneously. In the GM CRL data set, a few of the GM researchers were involved in two or more CRLs (Trotter et al.), but this pattern is far more noticeable in three of the cases in this book where individuals initiate and manage their own partnerships (Wasson; Beauregard; Lovejoy and Steele) and it is emerging as a pattern in the disaster-preparedness agencies (Eaton and Brandenburg). The pattern of multiple (and sometimes exclusive) partnerships connected by individuals or organizations reflects the added complexity of messy reality over simplicity. But since overlapping cultural groups (e.g., family, friendship groups, work ties) coexist in most people's lives, the cases provide solid examples of how culture theory explains this pattern.

Lesson Learned

Partnership participants operate within a layered cultural environment in which they are managing multiple partnership activities simultaneously. Because partnerships exhibit structural characteristics that are complex and layered, viewing them as simple models is a mistake that leads to conflict, loss of trust, and eventual partnership problems.

Multiplicity of Allegiances

In five of the cases, the partners are engaged in other work-related activities that are independent of the work of their particular partnerships. The partners include university professors who teach, conduct research, and engage in community service (Wasson; Gluesing et al.; Miller et al.). Partners also include municipal, county, or state employees (Eaton and Brandenburg) and owners of consulting businesses (Johnsrud et al.). The primary affiliation of these partners is to an institution, organization, or agency; the perspectives and behaviors that they display in their partnership roles reflect this primary allegiance. The partnerships are a way for them to engage in activities that complement and supplement their day jobs. This process can produce cultural conflicts that need to be resolved.

For example, the partners on both sides of the Ford Motor Company-Wayne State University case were not willing to compromise their core values. Negotiation has become a key strategy for maintaining the partners' autonomy while reaching, and later amending, agreements on managing the partnership (Gluesing et al.). The emergency-response agencies are described as "highly individualistic" in that they "traditionally work separately from other agencies during emergencies." Their unique procedures for communication during a disaster-preparedness exercise are not conducive to cross-agency information sharing and decision making (Eaton and Brandenburg). Allegiance is also central to the case involving the consulting partnership. The three partners decided against naming their partnership and creating a Website for it. Instead they have opted to keep their "individual corporate identities in the marketplace" with the individual contact information for each partner on all of their materials (Johnsrud et al.).

Lesson Learned

Competing allegiances threaten partnership stability and progress. Many successful partnerships create a successful hybrid culture that allows for multiple allegiances and reduces conflict. Negotiating common expectations and rules about competing allegiances also helps manage partnership dynamics.

Case Researchers' Perspectives

All of our cases combine the insider, or emic, perspective (from the standpoint of the partnership participants) with the ethnographic-outsider, or etic, view (from the perspective of a social science researcher). By contrast, most of the partnership literature has been written by outsiders who, because they do not capture emic perspectives, are unable to fully describe and explain the cultural beliefs, values, assumptions, and behaviors at play. The emic-etic combination is routine in ethnographic field research so that the ethnographic work is as complete and as accurate as possible, and comparable with the results of other studies. Our set of cases is unusual because the majority of the researchers are participants in the partnerships they are studying. Three of the cases have been written from a first-person standpoint (Beauregard; Johnsrud et al.; Lovejoy and Steele), while three others (Wasson; Gluesing et al.; Miller et al.) reflect the more neutral third person. Because the authors of these six cases have the added advantage of immediate access to the cultural processes associated with their partnerships, they are positioned to understand the nuances quickly and effectively. Moreover the richness of detail they provide is an important asset in understanding partnerships from the inside out.

Lesson Learned

Combining emic insider and etic (i.e., ethnographic outsider) perspectives has the potential to provide balance in interpretation and emphasis.

LEARNING FROM PARTNERSHIP ROLES

Roles, the meanings and behaviors associated with specific positions in cultural groups, are a mechanism for structuring social interactions, organizing expectations, and performing various kinds of activities. Role analysis, a part of structural theory, is an integral dimension of culture that helps explain how and why cultural groups organize behavior in specific ways. There are a variety of key roles within a partnership context that depend on such factors as partnership size, composition, nature and scope of the collaboration, and longevity. Key players are a set of partnership participants that hold the most critical, and often the most visible, partnership roles by facilitating relationships, planning, making decisions, boundary spanning, and sharing information, among others. Other partnership roles are often performed by those with particular technical expertise, administrative capabilities, and artfulness—or social and political savvy.

Key Players

All the cases document the role of key players—central figures who enhance the effectiveness of partnering relationships. The importance of key players in partnership work is evident in the GM CRL data set (Trotter et al.). There we see that key players function to hold the partnership network together through their ability to connect with and influence others. Such individuals often hold formally designated roles, though they may serve solely as an informal leader (e.g., mentor, technical expert, facilitator). Key players may act as champions for the collaboration to the public, gatekeepers who enable the partnership work to continue unencumbered, or as gurus/elders whose knowledge and experience is key to project success, among others.

Key players in a partnership exhibit multiple skills necessary for moving the work of the partnership forward and for keeping partnership participants connected. The three consulting partners routinely seek new business opportunities that would be compatible with the goals of their partnership (Johnsrud et al.). The faculty in the Ford Motor Co.-Wayne State University partnership worked at several critical junctures to mediate and resolve issues so that the partnership could progress (Gluesing et al.).

Lesson Learned

Individuals can make important contributions to partnership functioning when the appropriate role structure and responsibilities are in place.

Entrepreneurs

One of the key roles in any partnership is the entrepreneur whose behavior provides the energy behind the partnership's initiation and innovative developments. The role of partnership entrepreneurs encompasses such tasks as connecting with potential partnership participants, taking the lead in organizing partnership strategy and goals, securing necessary resources, and acting as a (or the) key leader to get the collaborative activity underway. Entrepreneurs have a vested interest in the partnership's creation, functioning, and outcomes. A can-do spirit, packaged into partnership entrepreneurs, emerges from all the cases.

The (organizational) entrepreneurs associated with modernizing Saudi Arabia (Jordan) and protecting the U.S. from terrorist attacks (Eaton and Brandenburg) had particular politico-economic goals in mind that had the potential to be achieved through partnerships. Individual entrepreneurs, such as those depicted in the Wayne State University-Technische Universität München partnership (Miller et al.) and the partnerships formed to provide cross-cultural training (Beauregard), exhibit imagination, competency, perseverance, and goal-directed behavior that has kept those partnerships flourishing despite the difficulties encountered.

Lesson Learned

Partnerships need entrepreneurial energy and charisma to furnish the partnership vison, to spearhead the initiative, and to help manage problems.

Role Changes

The roles that partnership participants play change over time. At an aggregate level, the number of partnership participants fluctuates as new members join and others leave and as roles have to be added or replaced. The Wayne State University-Technische Universität München partnership (Miller et al.) lost three of their five German faculty over the course of their partnership experience, which necessitated a steep learning curve for the new faculty and which added to the challenges of the American faculty of providing needed assistance (e.g., with classroom logistics, communication, content). In the GM

CRL case, the sociometric measure of fragmentation captures the amount of dislocation of individual connections in the network caused by the removal of key players and their connections to others (Trotter et al.).

Lesson Learned

Partnership sustainability is dependent upon the ability of participants to learn new roles or replace key players. Succession issues are critical in any partnership if the intent is to extend its longevity.

LEARNING FROM THE PARTNERSHIP LIFE CYCLE

Partnerships change in predictable ways and in predictable stages. The literature is replete with examples of the various phases associated with the partnership functioning. Typically the early stages focus on developing a partnership strategy and on selecting a particular partner, while the later stages involve the execution and evaluation of the work.

Partnership Stages

While some of our cases explicitly confirm the finding that partnership cycles consist of distinct intervals or phases, these cases also go beyond it by specifying the relational elements of those intervals—particularly the distinction between relationship development and maintenance. Relationship development at Microsoft occurs primarily during one of the four partnership stages, and relationship maintenance occurs during much of the remaining three stages (Lovejoy and Steele). By contrast, in the six-stage GM CRL cycle, the first three stages are associated with relationship development, the fourth and fifth stages with relationship maintenance, and the sixth stage with either relationship maintenance, development, or dissolution depending on the particular transition (i.e., partnership continuation, modification, splitting, termination) (Trotter et al.).

Lesson Learned

When a partnership is conceptualized in terms of relationship development and maintenance, it conveys an element of predictability that enables participants to anticipate the likely activities, events, and processes necessary to ensure effectiveness.

Partnership Life Spans and Activity Cycles

Partnerships should be viewed as renewable resources. The partnership stage, or life-cycle perspective, needs to be expanded into a life-span perspective. Some partnerships become dormant in the transition stage, then are revitalized and become active again. The GM CRL data indicates that some partnerships can go through several life-stage sequences in a single life span. One partnership cycle can be part of a much longer-term association, in which a revitalized partnership agreement follows from some earlier association (Trotter et al.). Other cases in our book illustrate this activity-and-dormancy cycle several times. The duration of the activity cycle varies from the GM CRL partnerships now designed to last for five-year cycles, to the three years necessary to complete the Engineering Management Masters Program (Gluesing et al.), to a one-semester rotation (Miller et al.; Wasson), to partnerships that may last just a few months (Beauregard; Johnsrud et al.). In each of these cases, the potential for the sequence to recur defines the cultural life span of the partnership far more clearly than a simple life-stage approach.

Lesson Learned

Partnership investigations need to take into account the possibility of a life-span (both activity and dormancy) time frame for partnership investigations. This life-span perspective allows us to learn lessons across multiple (longitudinal) cycles of partnership activities and to provide a more accurate evolutionary perspective of partnership dynamics.

Periodicity of Contact

One dimension of partnering that deserves more attention than is provided in the literature is the intermittent nature of some partnering relationships. One assumption in the literature is that partnership contact is constant and consistent (short, regularly spaced periodicity between interactions). Our cultural view of partnership time demonstrates that appropriate periodicity varies based on the expectations of the partners and that interaction can be spaced by fairly long periods, can be sporadic, or can be suspended (i.e., cultural time-out that doesn't count against the relationship). The varying periodicity can be due to factors both internal and external to the partnership.

Intermittent contact is a noticeable pattern in four of the cases and it reflects the nature of the work in which the participants are involved. In these cases, partnering arrangements are a function of the perceived necessity of demand-based contact with individuals playing particular roles.

For example, MCB Associates International actively seeks trainers who can bring the appropriate expertise and workshop skills to firms interested in developing cross-cultural competencies within their workforce. Once the training session(s) have been conducted, the contact between MCB Associates International and the trainer is likely to lapse until a new training opportunity emerges (Beauregard). The Lovejoy and Steele case illustrates a similar pattern—one that is largely tied to Microsoft's product-development cycle. The Eaton and Brandenburg case illustrates a lag in complying with the new disaster-preparedness mandates issued by the U.S. Department of Homeland Security in 2002. Emergency-preparedness agencies are just now getting to the point of having intermittent contact among themselves. As more disaster-preparedness exercises are scheduled, cross-agency contact is expected to become more frequent and regular, but the fact that the partnerships are targeted at unforeseeable events requires the ability of the partnership to survive periods of very low levels of interaction. The latter is a design requirement that has not been sufficiently explored, even though it replicates the basic problem of cohesion for any extended family.

Lesson Learned

The periodicity of partnership interactions needs to be understood and accommodated. Partnership design needs to accommodate irregular periodicity of partnering interactions and activities. They do not need to translate into a failed or terminated partnership, unless they are ignored.

Process and Product Outcomes

Successful partnerships involve simultaneous attention to both the process and performance aspects of partnerships. Process issues generally include managing the relationship and reaching agreement on the goals, while performance involves taking actions to fulfill a set of requirements or to accomplish a set of goals. An interesting question pertaining to the partnership cycle is whether process outcomes always precede product outcomes. Many of the cases in this book suggest that strong, healthy partnering relationships are a necessary condition for the completion of some final partnership product (Johnsrud et al.; Beauregard; Gluesing et al.; Lovejoy and Steele). Yet the data in some of the other cases suggests that product outcomes may be achieved with a less-than-ideal partnering relationship.

For example, the Wayne State University-Technische Universität München partnership continues to function well and result in impressive student evaluations despite the lack of institutional support (Miller et al.). Members of the Ridgemont disaster-preparedness agencies considered the Blackout of 2003 exercise to be successful despite insufficient cross-agency connections and processes (Eaton and Brandenburg). Both the British facilities firm and the Hospital Corporation of America realized their goals of constructing the King Faisal Specialist Hospital and Research Centre and establishing its working procedures under the directive of the government of Saudi Arabia with likely little concern for the importance of partnering relationships within the hospital (Jordan).

As a whole, the cases in this volume depict successfully performing partnerships with successful outcomes (from the perspective of the partners). They enhance student learning (Gluesing et al.; Miller et al.; Wasson), professional development and business opportunities (Beauregard; Johnsrud et al.), delivery of medical services (Jordan), product value (Lovejoy and Steele), and community safety (Eaton and Brandenburg). The participants in these partnerships use a combination of knowledge, skills, resources, and cooperative work practices to meet or exceed existing conditions or standards. While there may be selected weaknesses associated with the performance (e.g., Eaton and Brandenburg) and sustainability (e.g., Miller et al.) of some of these partnerships, all continue to function and set new performance goals.

Lesson Learned

The process emphasis in the partnership literature can be the basis for designing and managing successful partnerships, but the addition of the performance evaluation is also critical (as demonstrated in the relationship-dynamics model in chapter 2) to partnership success—at least for the partnerships that are concretely outcome or product oriented.

Partnership Transitions

Partnerships experience transitions that can be depicted structurally—as illustrated in the social-network diagrams of the GM CRLs (Trotter et al.)—and described in terms of behavioral change and a change in relationship dynamics at the end of a specific partnership cycle. Researchers have written about partnership transitions largely from the perspective of a failed partnership. The implicit assumption, and sometimes explicit point, is that a failure occurs unless the partnership continues.

One of the lessons we see in the case studies is that successful terminations may also be an indicator of partnership success. A potential benefit of a successful termination is that opportunities for follow-up work may arise because the relationship, whether at the individual or organizational level, has a history. Positive relationships can persist even when the organizational structure is terminated. Moreover the learning curve in collaborating with a former partner would likely be lower.

There are several examples among the cases where a partnership transition occurs because the collaborative work has been completed successfully. The Saudi Arabian partnerships are reported to end only when the goals have been accomplished (Jordan). The partnerships created to deliver cross-cultural training endure until the training has been completed and until evaluations and debriefing with the client firm have occurred (Beauregard). Successful partnership termination is also implicit in the Wasson and Lovejoy and Steele cases.

Lesson Learned

The nature of any partnership transition is culturally defined, and the definition of successful transitions needs to be expanded to include termination due to success, not just termination due to failure. In some cases, failure to terminate a partnership may actually be more of a failure of the partnership than its termination would be, especially where continuing negative relationships would produce continuing damage to both sides of the partnership.

Other transition options include those identified in the GM CRLs (e.g., continuation, modification, splitting) (Trotter et al.). Most of the cases in the book involve either the continuation or modification options. The Ford Motor Co.-Wayne State University partnership has undergone a few transitions. Several years after the partnership was initiated, Ford spun off Visteon Corporation, its internal manufacturer of component parts. For one year, the partnership continued in its initial form, splitting in 2001 when Visteon and Wayne State created their own partnership. A new transition is underway now in which Wayne State will partner with a number of universities to develop a master's program for automotive suppliers (Gluesing et al.). The Wayne State University-Technische Universität München partnership reflects a different set of circumstances. It has been successful from the perspective of the student participants and the faculty partners—especially Wayne State faculty members. Indeed, for those reasons, it has continued to be an active partnership. There is the potential, however, for this partnership to be discontinued or even permanently severed if new teaching faculty members opt not to participate and the current faculty partners pursue other unrelated projects (Miller et al.).

Lesson Learned

Partnership transitions can and should be managed to preserve strong relationships and maximize future potential.

LEARNING FROM RELATIONSHIP DEVELOPMENT AND MAINTENANCE

While partnerships require a level of commitment to the goals and tasks of the collaborative work, partnering activities occur in a sociocultural context. Participants interact with each other in a variety of ways to achieve those goals and complete those tasks. Interactions entail relationship development; strong, healthy interactions lead to relationship maintenance. The lessons learned from the construction and management of relationships generally can be associated with the cognitive (e.g., definitions, mental maps, domain organization) and symbolic (e.g., development and communication of meanings and ideals) dimensions of culture theory, as illustrated in the cases.

Systems of Exchange (The Cultural Meaning of Relationships)

Many of the partnerships in this book reflect a blended exchange system. Market exchange and reciprocity exchange are active and intertwined throughout the partnership life cycle. None of the partnerships operate under the rules of a pure market-exchange system; if money changes hands between partnering individuals or organizations (i.e., fee for service rendered), it complements, and sometimes is subordinate to, reciprocity exchange. For example, conscious efforts are made by MCB Associates International to build trust with the firms and cross-cultural trainers both prior to and following any monetary payments (Beauregard).

A similar pattern occurs at the start of two of the partnerships involving universities (Gluesing et al.; Miller et al.). Significant discussion and negotiation took place before those partnerships were formalized; much of the time spent planning those endeavors involved creating strong, working relationships. Moreover the lines of communication have remained open over the partnerships' history, though in the Miller et al. case, one of the key players (the Wayne State University associate dean) seems to have withdrawn from the partnership. At the University of North Texas, faculty members have indicated that reciprocity exchange is the basis for all of their partnering relationships—including those with the private sector that would likely involve market exchange (Wasson).

Lesson Learned

It is important to go beyond the baseline assumptions embedded in a market-based partnership framework and include both the symbolic dimensions of partnerships and relationships, as well as the organizational (cognitive) models for those partnerships.

Quality of Partnering Interaction

We found that trust and cooperation are valued components of the GM-CRL partnerships. They typically also co-exist with tension and conflict that must be addressed (Trotter et al.). We derived a number of lessons from the various cases, based on evaluating the discussions of the quality-of-interaction elements of our model.

Trust

A striking pattern is that the presence of trust varies across the cases. In five of the cases, trust is an integral part of partnership functioning. Indeed there is an implicit, if not explicit, assumption that trust contributes significantly to so-called "win-win" outcomes that benefit all partners. For example, the consulting partners refer to their "high level of trust as a point of pride" (Johnsrud et al.). Referring to one of its cross-cultural trainers, MCB Associates International comments that "Getting to know and trust each other more, we developed a strong working relationship that spilled over into other areas of collaboration for about six years." On the other hand, a lack of trust is portrayed among the emergency-preparedness agencies in Ridgemont primarily because of their different roles and because of the lack of cross-agency integration in the community (Eaton and Brandenburg). Such patterns produce an appropriate test of concept, since the lack of trust is also associated with a lack of performance in the partnership. On the other hand, the concept of trust is not apparent in the Miller et al. and Jordan cases. There are neither specific mentions of the term trust, nor examples to convey it. This pattern suggests that the emphasis on trust is strongly embedded in American culture. Trust is necessary for an American cultural model of partnerships, but it should not be assumed to be a dominant cultural theme in at least some cross-cultural partnerships.

Lesson Learned

As with all culture-specific models, the details of any model must be tested and assessed in both a single-culture and a cross-cultural context in order to allow the model to address the specific needs of either single-culture or multiple-culture partnerships.

Cooperation

A different pattern is evident for the component of cooperation. Cooperative behavior is associated with every case. For example, the consulting partners in the Johnsrud et al. case discuss their ability to "cooperate on decisions," while those in the Miller et al. case mention that "an agreement was struck to cooperate on developing a simulation." Similarly, in the Jordan case, we read that for the Saudis, "Cooperating to get the job done overcame the obstacles." In these examples, the term "cooperation" implies a readiness to work toward a shared goal and a resolve to accomplish that goal. That sense of willingness also appears in this statement from the Eaton and Brandenburg case in which the agencies engaged in a "cooperative, but not coordinated, effort to organize and carry out new federal mandates for emergency response." Interestingly the nature of this statement implies that cooperation probably is a necessary condition for success—perhaps a minimum standard of sorts.

Lesson Learned

Cooperation is important across all of the cultural variation and boundaries in the cases.

Conflict

Conflict is evident in the majority of case studies—as might be expected given the organizational and cultural differences typically associated with partnering behavior. The Eaton and Brandenburg case specifically refers to the "culture clash" among the Ridgemont agencies as a "major inhibitor . . . of organizational cooperation and partnering." Similarly, the Jordan case emphasizes a "hybrid culture in tension." A few of the other cases stress the "challenges" and "difficulties" of their partnering arrangements, but provide counterweight concepts such as "negotiations" "solutions," or "resolutions" to indicate that partnerships can and do address partnering issues (Gluesing et al., Miller et al., Beauregard).

In three of the cases, conflict, if discussed, is quite subtle. In the University of North Texas case, the overwhelming emphasis is on structural considerations and not on partnering interactions—which may explain why there is no discussion of conflict (Wasson). In the other two cases, there seems to be a conscious effort to manage partnering relationships as carefully as possible.

That drive may have tempered the "significant differences and needs" reported among the partners in the Johnsrud et al. case so that any tension would abate quickly. By contrast, the Lovejoy and Steele case is presented largely as an ideal in which conflict is not explicitly articulated.

Lesson Learned

A balanced approach—looking for the positive and negative dimensions of these cultural themes of trust, cooperation, and conflict—is probably the best approach for understanding the nature of partnerships.

Quality of Partnering Interaction Implications

Different cultures vary in their emphasis on the different parts of the model, and, as a consequence, there is a need to look at the interactions among the quality of interaction variables. There are some indications from our small sample of cases that trust is not necessarily as critical to partnership functioning in some cultures as it is in American culture. This may be due in part to the balance of power exhibited by one side of the partnership over the other. The three cases in which trust was not mentioned, or was reported to be lacking entirely, exhibit some imbalance in the directive forces in the partnerships.

The King Faisal partnership is a directed partnership; that is, many of its participants probably had little choice but to participate (Jordan). Adapting to Western practices and procedures that were often at odds with Saudi beliefs and values was required to achieve the goal of modernization. Under such circumstances, trust is not necessary, although compliance is. "Forced partnerships" is the label given to the mandated cross-agency interactions expected by the U.S. Department of Homeland Security (Eaton and Brandenburg). From the perspective of the agencies, trust would not be particularly likely under these circumstances—at least not in the early stages of agency intermingling. Finally, while students in the Miller et al. case certainly opt to participate in the simulation by signing up for the class, they have no control over the course content or requirements. Hence trust is not likely to be a key element in this kind of partnership either.

Lesson Learned

The presence of a power or directive imbalance in any partnership has an effect on the importance of any of the components in our collaborative partnership model. This imbalance must be assessed accordingly.

Turning to the elements of cooperation and conflict, we see that cooperation is essential in all the cases (even the highly-directive ones that probably experience more resistance than the nondirective partnerships), and that conflict is a commonly occurring element of partnership dynamics. Without cooperation, opportunities to build relationships are few in number, the collaborative work has little chance of being accomplished, and the likelihood of a long-term partnering arrangement is extremely limited. Cooperative partnering behavior can exist alongside tensions and disagreements and can do much to mitigate any potential negative effect. The presence of conflict, as reported in the cases, is a call for partner awareness and discussion and is an opportunity to try to reach agreement or reconciliation. A cooperative orientation can help to bridge that "cultural divide" (Miller et al.) so that the work of the partnership can proceed, and, if possible, trust can be built.

Lesson Learned

Cooperative partnering behavior may serve as a foundation for the development of trust and as a way to mitigate conflict.

Balance

Balance, with respect to both relationships and collaborative work, emerges as a key theme in the cases. When there is balance, the interacting or contrasting forces result in stability or equilibrium. Status and power differences among the partners are a potential source of opposition that can affect partnership functioning. Such differentials are notable among the emergency-preparedness agencies that now must comply with U.S. Department of Homeland Security and state regulations (Eaton and Brandenburg). Four of the agencies self-identify as first responders, but their status may be detrimental to partnership functioning if they appear to be an exclusionary group and neglect to establish working relations with other agencies.

A different form of balance involves managing periods of intense work, thereby nurturing the partnering relationship. In the Johnsrud case, the three partners take into account the work loads of their individual firms when making decisions about their time and commitment to the partnership work. The intent is that these work-sharing accommodations equalize over time.

Lesson Learned

Paying attention to the cultural meaning of relationships can have widespread, beneficial effects on partnering functioning and outcomes. In some cases, the meanings need to be negotiated, and in others they need to be understood.

Adaptability

Accommodation and flexibility are key themes in several of the cases. An ability to adapt to changing circumstances and conditions—both internal and external to the partnership—is essential for addressing and reconciling the inevitable issues that arise. In the Ford Motor Co.-Wayne State University, the emphasis on adaptability is unambiguous. Indeed, the authors emphasize a "negotiated culture of collaboration and 'win-win.'" Throughout this fourteen-year partnership, discussion, negotiation, and compromise have led to curricular, administrative, and staffing changes, among others, thereby enabling both partnership revitalization and expansion. Both partners value quality education, and that has motivated them to be actively engaged in identifying issues and proposing and implementing solutions (Gluesing et al.).

The theme of adaptability is also evident in the Wayne State University-Technische Universität München partnership (Miller et al.). Despite the lack of institutional support from Wayne State, the partnership ambles along. The faculty members have found ways to manage the situation without involving the administration. While they recognize that their partnering structure has significant resource weaknesses, there is still enough energy in the cultural system to keep the partnership going—at least for the short term.

Lesson Learned

Partnership relationships change through time. The flexibility to adapt to external as well as to internal conditions is necessary, but it has to be balanced by common goals and by the will to improve performance and succeed.

LEARNING FROM THE CASE METAPHORS

Chapter 1 provides a rationale for presenting each of the cases in a common format and for using a primary metaphor to help readers understand each case.

Symbols of Ideal Conditions

One condition that is apparent in the various metaphors is that they commonly symbolize ideal qualities to which partnerships could or do aspire. For example, in one, raw electricity is transformed into safe and usable power (Beauregard), and in another we know that the partnership is complete when the appropriate 3-D puzzle is finally assembled (Jordan). The metaphor of the ecological guild symbolizes an ideal state in which there is balance, harmony, and sustainability. It also symbolizes strategies that need to be put in place in order to improve communication and to reduce the information silo-ing and competition that those partnerships currently experience (Eaton and Brandenburg). In sum, each of the metaphors provides a symbolic reinforcement of the lessons to be learned in the chapters. We also found that an analysis of the collective set of metaphors provided additional lessons learned.

Lesson Learned

When partnership metaphors depict an ideal state of partnership culture, they can help guide participants in their achievement of partnership process outcomes (e.g., cooperative relationships) as well as product outcomes.

Cross-Cutting Symbols and Cultural Themes in the Metaphors

Three cultural themes (or symbolic characteristics) cross cut the case study metaphors: integration, transformation, and resolution. Partnering involves the process of integration, which is the interaction of people, resources, and knowledge within a coherent structure or model. Partnerships entail transformation, which is the process of converting energy, effort, and knowledge into some set of outcomes. Finally, partnerships must address issues and conflicts that have the potential to derail partnership performance through the process of resolution. These three processes are interconnected and can appear at any stage during the partnership cycle, which is a reason why the metaphors are powerful images and summary statements that relate to the holistic nature of the partnerships and that improve our understanding of them.

Integration

One way of visualizing the process of integration is by examining the structure of a composite material—an entity made up of distinct components in which two or more complementary substances combine to produce properties not present in any individual component. This combination achieves the greatest material capability. A partnership is like a composite in that the combination of efforts yields something stronger than independent efforts since each element makes up for deficiencies of the other.

Integration is symbolized by a variety of metaphors including elements of chemistry and energy (Beauregard; Miller et al.), human social organization

(Johsrud et al.; Gluesing et al.; Lovejoy and Steele), and physical puzzles or objects (Wasson; Eaton and Brandenburg; Jordan). In some metaphors, a new whole is created by joining and fitting things together in complex ways. For example, the use of a 3-D puzzle is made of interlocking, oddly shaped, seemingly incompatible pieces that reflect the integrated aspect of a hybrid culture (Wasson). Energy transformers convey momentum and power that help sustain partnerships (Beauregard; Miller et al.). Radial and weblike structures convey the possibility of extension and expansion in partnering activity (Wasson; Lovejoy and Steele). Other metaphors suggest a relatively harmonious partnering experience; the drivers on a road trip reflected through mirrors (Johnsrud et al.) and the competition-free ecological guild (Eaton and Brandenburg). High-performance racing teams convey a high level of cooperation that is highly beneficial to partnership functioning (Gluesing et al.).

Lesson Learned

Integration processes are key symbolic (and practical) elements in partnerships. They must be present throughout all partnership stages in order to provide strength and durability and to help partnership participants succeed. If the partnership is not integrated, it will not be effective.

Transformation

The second cross-cutting metaphorical theme is the idea of transformation. All of the metaphors have some element or characteristic that represents the need for change through time. Some metaphors symbolize the process of transformation directly (Johnsrud et al.; Gluesing et al.; Lovejoy and Steele; Jordan). The car-mirror metaphor transforms the experience of the three drivers by reflecting a composite account of their collective efforts in partnership (Johnsrud et al.). Similarly a driver's experience on the automotive test track is transformed by such factors as changing weather conditions or the behavior of other drivers on the track (Gluesing et al.); these obstacles symbolize the inevitable partnership difficulties that arise and that have to be managed, such as the need to widen the track in order to accommodate more lanes and drivers and to construct new test tracks. Other metaphors portray a physical outcome of the transformation process (Beauregard; Miller et al.; Wasson). The electrical transformer converts raw electricity, considered to be unstable and dangerous, into energy that can be distributed for use by communities. The transformer symbolizes the lead partner, MCB Associates International, whose role is to coordinate partnership activity. The distribution of electrical power can be compared to the customized cross-cultural training programs and the training materials. As with any kind of transformation, there is a chance that a power failure could occur in which the partnership suffers from some kind of short circuiting (Beauregard).

Lesson Learned

The theme of transformations identifies both the positive outcomes that partnerships enjoy and the obstacles that they encounter (i.e., the complexities inherent in partnership culture during transformation). Successful partnerships exhibit the transformation of relationships, ideas, and products.

Resolution

The third symbolic theme embedded in the metaphors is the idea of resolving conflict or tension. A partnership may become unstable or collapse if proper steps are not taken to resolve threats to its stability or progress. The Uranium-236 metaphor succinctly represents the jeopardy to the system if there is insufficient mass to continue a successful chain reaction. Without an inflow of new resources to the partnership, the energy that has been created will eventually abate; in that sense, the partnership is unstable (Miller et al.). The metaphor of the family and its relationships can be at risk if contact is interrupted, limited, or severed. The family-like partnerships within Microsoft are strained by intermittent contact and personnel turnover (Lovejoy and Steele). The metaphor of the dreamcatcher can have an element of fragility or vulnerability if the interconnected strings become frayed or broken (Wasson).

The metaphor of the automotive test track is extended to focus on partnership problem solving and resolution, which occurs in the pit. The pit is the place where teams can repair the vehicle; that is, develop and implement solutions to partnership problems. It is in this space where team members create "work arounds" or ways to adapt and change in order to ensure the drivers are prepared to go back into the race. The partners from Ford Motor Co. and Wayne State University are the team members who are brainstorming and trying out their solutions to the issues their partnership faces (Gluesing et al.). Partnering, like working in the pit, is a very active, and not passive, process.

Lesson Learned

Partnerships require ongoing interactions in order to keep partnering relationships strong and healthy enough to handle tension and conflict quickly and effectively and to propel the partnership forward with an increasing positive momentum.

THE QUILT AS A PARTNERSHIP METAPHOR

The cross-cutting elements of the eight partnership metaphors gave us an appreciation of the metaphor's power and applicability to the nature of partnership culture. It led us to identify a meta-metaphor for partnership activity that could symbolize what we learned in an analysis of the cases. Our meta-metaphor is a quilt in which different materials, designs, structural components, and symbols are stitched together using such techniques as piecework, appliqué, and embroidery. The diversity of materials and techniques maps well onto the variety of lessons learned from our partnership cases and model.

Quilt Layers: The Four Cultural Processes

Our partnership quilt is composed of four layers that represent the four culture theory elements used throughout the book (see figure 11.1). (1) The bottom layer, or quilt backing, corresponds to the structural elements of culture that establish the size and shape of the quilt. It is often made from a single piece of fabric, or pieces of the same fabric, that form a whole by serving as the quilt's foundation. (2) The insulating middle layer characterizes the evolutionary aspects of culture as reflected in the changes in filler material. The middle layer in antique quilts would have been made of wool or cotton. Newer quilts are filled with a sheet of material called batting, which provides sufficient warmth but is lightweight. (3) The top of the quilt, which includes enough blocks or panels to cover the top of a bed, signifies the cognitive elements of culture. It reflects the ideas, forms, and rules that quilters use in creating their decorative pattern. (4) Finally, the motifs or appliqués sewn onto the blocks embody the symbolic dimensions of culture. Each appliqué conveys a particular meaning for either the quilter or the recipient. The ultimate goal is for the meaning to be conveyed in depth and congruently for all parties involved.

Quilt Sashing: Partnership Integration and Resolution

Each square block in our quilt is surrounded by sashing or strips of cloth on all four sides so that when the quilt is completed, the sashing traverses above, below, and on each side. The sashing not only makes the quilt larger, but it also enables the viewer to focus on the individual block motifs. The sashing

Figure 11.1.　A Partnership Quilt

represents two of the three cross-cutting processes identified in our analysis of the eight partnership metaphors. The horizontal sashing represents the process of integration while the vertical sashing represents the process of resolution.

Quilt Motifs: Visual Images of the Case Metaphors

Each motif is appliquéd onto one of eight blocks; the middle block of the nine-block design is left blank for a special handwritten message characteristic of signature quilts. The eight motifs represent the visual images of the eight case-metaphors. The four motifs related to developing relationships are sewn onto the first column of vertical blocks on the left-hand side of the quilt, along with the bottom center block, while the four motifs pertaining to sustaining relationships are appliquéd onto the remaining blocks. As such, the motifs are arranged in a quasi-circular, clockwise pattern intended to convey the changes in relationships as the partnership ages. All eight metaphorical images have both overlapping and separate meanings so that collectively they illustrate the common and unique features of the partnership experience.

Quilting: Partnership Process

Quilting is the process of stitching the layers of the quilt together using thin quilting needles and a heavy-gauge quilting thread. The stitching follows a particular pattern—often in and around the motifs and other design features that compose the decorative top. The quilter's expertise is evident in the quality and regularity of the individual stitches, as well as in the amount of quilting. Quilting is often done as a communal activity such as a quilting bee, where members of a community work together to complete the stitching. The quilting process compares well with the partnership process. The quilting pattern serves as a guide to the quilters' stitching, just as the partnership goals help participants follow a particular course of action. The final product reflects the relational and technical skills of the quilting partners in completing the work they set out to do.

Quilts as a Reflection of Cultural Transformation

Once quilted, the binding along the outer edges of the quilt is added. By securing the whole piece, it brings to a close the process of transformation in which the quilters have been bound together. The quilters and the quilts they produce are a reflection of the local environment in which the quilting community operates, and they are tied to the wider cultural environment as well. The materials used in vintage quilts reveal as much about the quilt's function (i.e., for display versus daily use) as they do about the quilter's social status (i.e., silks and velvets versus calico).

Quilts made 150 years ago differ somewhat from the quilts of today in form, design, uses, and meanings. They provide a glimpse into a particular era and the conditions associated with it, just as partnerships do. This volume has tried to document some of that evolution and the explanations for it. The diversity and complexity of partnering arrangements today contrast with the formally crafted joint-venture arrangements thirty to forty years ago. Also changed is the burgeoning emphasis on cooperation—with partnerships as the vehicle—as a way to compete more efficiently and to secure resources more effectively. The cultural environment is changing how people work together. Many more partners are arriving at quilting bees these days hoping to contribute to the collaborative endeavor, accomplish the goals before them, and if they are lucky, create a sense of community, as well as provide a strong cultural model that will help participants accomplish collaborative goals.

NOTE

1. We appreciate the assistance we received in fine-tuning some of the key concepts used in this chapter. Marjorie Briody helped clarify distinctions between metaphors and other figures of speech, along with specific attributes of metaphors. Andrew Robinson contributed his artistic, graphics, and computer skills to design our partnership quilt. Chris Polakowski helped design and enhance the metaphorical motifs. Rita Solkin reviewed and clarified our description of quilts and quilt making so that we could reveal the partnership patterns. Rose Edward also made useful points about quilting that strengthened our partnership metaphor.

References

Adler, Nancy J. 1997. *International Dimensions of Organizational Behavior*. 3rd ed. Cincinnati, OH: South-Western College Publishing.

Adler, Nancy J., and Susan Bartholomew. 1992. Academic and Professional Communities of Discourse: Generating Knowledge on Transnational Human Resource Management. *Journal of International Business Studies* 23:551–570.

Ahuja, Gautaum. 2000. Collaboration Networks, Structural Holes, and Innovation: A Longitudinal Study. *Administrative Science Quarterly* 45:425–455.

Anderson, James C., Hakan Hakansson, and Jan Johanson. 1994. Dyadic Business Relationships within a Business Network Context. *Journal of Marketing* 58:1–15.

Andreosso-O'Callaghan, Bernadette, and Wei Qian. 1999. Technology Transfer: A Mode of Collaboration Between the European Union and China. *Europe-Asia Studies* 51:123–142.

Argyris, Chris. 1999. *On Organizational Learning*. 2nd ed. Oxford: Blackwell Publishing.

Auf der Heide, Erik. 1989. *Disaster Response: Principles of Preparation and Coordination*. Personal copyright. http://orgmail2.coe-dmha.org/dr/flash.htm.

Austin, J.E. 2000. Strategic Collaboration Between Nonprofits and Businesses. *Nonprofit and Voluntary Sector Quarterly* 29 (1):69–97.

Axelrod, Robert. 1984. *The Evolution of Cooperation*. New York: Basic Books.

Baba, Marietta L. 1999. Dangerous Liaisons: Trust, Distrust, and Information Technology in American Work Organizations. *Human Organization* 58 (3):331–346.

———. 1988. Two Sides to Every Story: An Ethnohistorical Approach to Organizational Partnerships. *City and Society* 2 (2):71–104.

Bachmann, Reinhard. 2001. Trust, Power and Control in Trans-Organizational Relations. *Organization Studies* 22 (2): 337–365.

Barkema, Harry, John H.J. Bell, and Johannes M. Pennings. 1996. Foreign Entry, Cultural Barriers, and Learning. *Strategic Management Journal* 17 (2):151–166.

221

Bartlett, Christopher A., and Sumantra Ghoshal. 1989. *Managing Across Borders: The Transnational Solution*. 2nd ed. Boston, MA: Harvard Business School Publishing.

Batorski, Martha, and William Hughes. 2002. Beyond Process-centering: Emerging Capability and Alliance-based Business Models. *The Outlook Point of View*. Accenture, New York.

Beer, Michael, Sven C. Voelpel, Marius Leibold, and Eden B. Tekie. 2005. Strategic Management as Organizational Learning: Developing Fit and Alignment Through a Disciplined Process. *Long Range Planning* 38:445–465.

Befu, Harumi. 1977. Social Exchange. *Annual Review of Anthropology* 6:255–281.

Bernard, H. Russell, ed. 1998. *Handbook of Methods in Cultural Anthropology*. Walnut Creek, CA: Altamira Press.

Bernard, H. Russell. 2005. *Research Methods in Anthropology: Qualitative and Quantitative Approaches*. 4th ed. Menlo Park, CA: Altamira Press.

Blankenship, Ralph L. 1977. *Colleagues in Organization: The Social Construction of Professional Work*. New York: John Wiley and Sons.

Bloedon, R.V., and D.R. Stokes. 1994. Making University/Industry Collaborative Research Succeed. *Research-Technology Management* 37 (2):44–48.

Borgatti, Stephen P. 2003. The Key Player Problem, Dynamic Social Network Modeling and Analysis: Workshop Summary and Papers. *The National Academy of Sciences*: 241–252.

——. 2002a. KeyPlayer 1.1 User's Guide. Analytic Technologies, Natick, MA.

——. 2002b. Key Player. Analytic Technologies. Natick, MA.

——. 2002c. NETDRAW. Analytic Technologies. Natick, MA.

Borgatti, Stephen P., Martin G. Everett, and L.C. Freeman. 1999. *UCINET V for Windows: Software for Social Network Analysis*. Natick, MA: Analytic Technologies.

Boster, James. 1986. Can Individuals Recapitulate the Evolutionary Development of Color Lexicons? *Ethnology* 25 (1):61–74.

Bourdieu, Pierre. 1966. The Work of Time, In *The Gift: An Interdisciplinary Perspective*. 135–147. Amsterdam: Amsterdam University Press.

Boydell, Katherine, and Tiziana Volpe. 2004. A Qualitative Examination of the Implementation of a Community-Academic Coalition. *Journal of Community Psychology* 32 (4):357–374.

Brannen, Mary Yoko. 1998. Negotiated Culture in Binational Contexts: A Model of Culture Change Based on a Japanese/American Organizational Experience. *Anthropology of Work Review* 28 (2–3):6–17.

Brannen, Mary Yoko, and Jane E. Salk. 2000. Partnering Across Borders: Negotiating Organizational Culture in a German-Japanese Joint Venture. *Human Relations* 53 (4) (April):451–487.

Brinkerhoff, Jennifer M. 2002a. Government-Nonprofit Partnership: A Defining Framework. *Public Administration and Development* 22:19–30.

——. 2002b. *Partnerships for International Development: Rhetoric or Results?* Boulder, CO: Lynne Rienner Publishers.

Briody, Elizabeth K., S. Tamer Cavusgil, and Stewart R. Miller. 2004. Turning Three Sides into a Delta at General Motors: Enhancing Partnership Integration on Corporate Ventures, *Long Range Planning* 37:421–434.

Brown, John Seeley, Allan Collins, and Paul Duguid. 1989. *Situated Cognition and the Culture of Learning*. Champaign, Ill.: University of Illinois at Urbana-Champaign.

Bruce, Margaret, Fiona Leverick, Dale Littler, and Dominic Wilson. 1995. Success Factors for Collaborative Product Development: A Study of Suppliers of Information and Communication Technology. *R&D Management* 25 (1):33–44.

Bruno, T.J. c. 2004. Non-Zero-Sum Collaboration, Reciprocity, and the Preference for Similarity: Developing an Adaptive Model of Close Relational Functioning, *Personal Relationships* 11 (2):135–161.

Büchel, Bettina and Peter Killing. 2002. Interfirm Cooperation Throughout the Joint Venture Life Cycle: Impact on Joint Venture Performance. In *Cooperative Strategies and Alliances*, 751–777, Amsterdam: Pergamon.

Burnes, Bernard. 2004. Kurt Lewin and the Planned Approach to Change: A Reappraisal. *Journal of Management Studies* 41 (6):977–1002.

Burt, Ronald S. 2002. The Social Capital of Structural Holes. In *The New Economic Sociology: Developments in an Emerging Field*. 148–190, New York: Russell Sage Foundation.

———. 1992. *Structural Holes: The Social Structure of Competition*. Cambridge: Harvard University Press.

Callan, Victor J., and Peta Ashworth. 2004. *Working Together: Industry and VET Provider Training Partnerships*. Adelaide, Australia: National Centre for Vocational Education Research.

Carleton, J. Robert, and Claude S. Lineberry. 2004. *Achieving Post-Merger Success: A Stakeholder's Guide to Cultural Due Diligence, Assessment, and Integration*. San Francisco, CA: Pfeiffer.

Cheadle, Allen, Sandra Senter, Loel Solomon, William L. Beery, and Pamela M. Schwartz. 2005. A Qualitative Exploration of Alternative Strategies for Building Community Health Partnerships: Collaboration Versus Issue-Oriented Approaches. *Journal of Urban Health: Bulletin of the New York Academy of Medicine* 82 (4):638–652.

Chelst, Kenneth, John Sidelko, Alex Przebienda, Jeffrey Lockledge, and Dimitrios Mihailidis. 2001. Rightsizing and Management of Prototype Vehicle Testing at Ford Motor Company. *Interfaces* 31 (1):91–107.

Child, John, and David Faulkner. 1998. *Strategies of Cooperation: Managing Alliances, Networks, and Joint Ventures*. Oxford: Oxford University Press.

Cobb, P. Denise, and Beth A. Rubin. 2006. Contradictory Interests, Tangled Power, and Disorganized Organization. *Administration and Society* 38 (1) (March):79–112.

Coleman, James S. 1988. Social Capital in the Creation of Human Capital. *American Journal of Sociology* 94:S95–S120.

Collins, James C., and Jerry I. Porras. 1997. *Built to Last: Successful Habits of Visionary Companies*. Harper Business: New York.

Cornelissen, Joel P. 2005. Beyond Compare: Metaphor in Organization Theory. *Academy of Management Review* 30 (4):751–764.

Cravens, David W., and Shannon H. Shipp. 1993. Analysis of Co-operative Interorganizational Relationships, Strategic Alliance Formation, and Strategic Alliance Effectiveness. *Journal of Strategic Marketing* 1:55–70.

Dacin, M. Tina, and Michael A. Hitt. 1997. Selecting Partners for Successful International Alliances: Examination of U.S. and Korean Firms. *Journal of World Business* 32 (1) (Spring):3–17.

D'Andrade, Roy G. 1995. *The Development of Cognitive Anthropology*. Cambridge: Cambridge University Press.

D'Andrade, Roy G., and Claudia Strauss, eds. 1992. *Human Motives and Cultural Models*. Cambridge: Cambridge University Press.

Das, T.K., and Bing-Sheng Teng. 1998. Between Trust and Control: Developing Confidence in Partner Cooperation in Alliances. *Academy of Management Review* 23 (3) (July):491–512.

Denscombe, Martyn. 2003. *The Good Research Guide for Small-Scale Social Research Projects*. 2nd ed. Maidenhead, Berkshire, England: Open University Press.

Dent, Christopher M. 2003. Transnational Capital, the State and Foreign Economic Policy: Singapore, South Korea and Taiwan. *Review of International Political Economy* 10: 246–277.

Dick, Butch. Visual Artists & Carvers. http://www.songheesnation.com/html/artists/artists-butch.htm (accessed June 7, 2004).

Dowling, Bernard, Martin Powell, and Caroline Glendinning. 2004. Conceptualising Successful Partnerships. *Health and Social Care in the Community* 12 (4):309–317.

Doz, Yves L. 1996. Evolution of Cooperation in Strategic Alliances: Initial Conditions or Learning Processes? *Strategic Management Journal* 17 (Summer):55–83. Special Issue: Evolutionary Perspectives on Strategy.

Doz, Yves L., and Gary Hamel. 1998. *Alliance Advantage: The Art of Creating Value Through Partnering*. Boston, MA: Harvard Business School Press.

Doz, Y.L., P. Olk, and P. S. Ring. 2000. Formation Processes of R&D Consortia: Which Path to Take? Where Does It Lead? *Strategic Management Journal* 21:239–266.

Drabek, Thomas E., and David A. McEntire. 2002. Emergent Phenomena and Multiorganizational Coordination in Disasters: Lessons from the Research Literature. *International Journal of Mass Emergencies and Disasters* 20 (2):197–224.

Duysters, Gerard, Geert Kok, and Maaike Vaandrager. 1999. Crafting Successful Strategic Technology Partnerships. *R&D Management* 29 (4):343–351.

Dwyer, Robert F., Paul H. Schurr, and Sejo Oh. 1987. Developing Buyer-Seller Relationships. *Journal of Marketing* 51 (2):11–27.

Dynes, Russell R., and Kathleen J. Tierney, eds. 1994. *Disasters, Collective Behavior, and Social Organization*. Newark, DE: University of Delaware Press.

Ellis, Carolyn, and Arthur Bochner, eds. 1996. *Composing Ethnography: Alternative Forms of Qualitative Writing*. Walnut Creek, CA: AltaMira Press.

Fixman, Carol S. 1990. The Foreign Language Needs of U.S. Based Corporations. *Annals of the American Academy of Political and Social Science*. Foreign Language in the Workplace 511 (September):25–46.

Foster, George. 1965. Peasant Society and the Image of Limited Good. *American Anthropologist* 67 (2) (April):293–315.

Foster, Mary K., and Agnes G. Meinhard. 2002. A Regression Model Explaining Predisposition to Collaborate. *Nonprofit and Voluntary Sector Quarterly* 31 (4):549–564.

Freeman, Robert E. 1993. Collaboration, Global Perspectives, and Teacher Education. *Theory into Practice* 32 (1) (Winter):33–39.

Gannon, Martin J., and Associates. 1994. *Understanding Global Cultures: Metaphorical Journeys Through 17 Countries.* Thousand Oaks, CA: Sage Publications.

Gannon, Martin J., ed. 2001. *Cultural Metaphors: Readings, Research Translations, and Commentary.* Thousand Oaks, CA: Sage Publications.

Geertz, Clifford. 1973. *The Interpretation of Cultures: Selected Essays.* New York: Basic Books.

Geppert, Mike, and Ed Clark. 2003. Knowledge and Learning in Transitional Ventures: An Actor-Centered Approach. *Management Decision* 41 (5/6):433–455.

Gill, Jas, and Richard J. Butler. 2003. Managing Instability in Cross-Cultural Alliances. *Long Range Planning* 36 (6):543–563.

Glaister, Keith W., and Peter J. Buckley. 1997. Task-Related and Partner-Related Selection Criteria in UK International Joint Ventures. *British Journal of Management* 8:199–222.

Glucksberg, Sam. 2003. The Psycholinguistics of Metaphor. *Trends in Cognitive Science* 7 (2) (February):92–96.

Gluesing, Julia C. 1998. Building Connections and Balancing Power in Global Teams: Toward a Reconceptualization of Culture as Composite. *Anthropology of Work Review* 18 (2):18–30.

Gluesing, Julia C., Tara Alcordo, Marietta L. Baba, David Britt, Kimberly H. Wagner, Willie McKether, Leslie Monplaisir, Hilary Ratner, and Kenneth R. Riopelle. 2003. The Development of Global Virtual Teams. In *Virtual Teams That Work: Creating Conditions for Virtual Team Effectiveness,* 353–380. San Francisco, CA: Jossey-Bass.

Goldman, Marcio. 2001. An Ethnographic Theory of Democracy. Politics from the Viewpoint of Ilhéus's Black Movement. *Ethos* 66 (2):157–180.

Granovetter, Mark S. 1974. *Getting a Job: A Study of Contacts and Careers.* Cambridge, MA: Harvard University Press.

———. 1983. The Strength of Weak Ties: A Network Theory Revisited. *Sociological Theory* 1:201–233.

Gray, Barbara. 2004. Strong Opposition: Frame-Based Resistance to Collaboration. *Journal of Community and Applied Social Psychology* 14 :166–176.

Gudykunst, William B. 1994. *Bridging Differences: Effective Intergroup Communication.* 2nd ed. Thousand Oaks, CA: Sage Publications.

Gulati, Ranjay, Tarun Khanna, and Nitin Nohria. 1994. Unilateral Commitments and the Importance of Process in Alliances. *Sloan Management Review* (Spring):61–69.

Haddow, George D., and Jane A. Bullock. 2003. *Introduction to Emergency Management.* Burlington, MA.: Butterworth Heinemann.

Hagedoorn, John. 1993. Understanding the Rationale of Strategic Technology Partnering: Interorganizational Modes of Cooperation and Sectoral Differences. *Strategic Management Journal* 14:371–385.

Hall, Edward T. 1980. *The Silent Language.* Garden City, NY: Doubleday and Co., Inc.

———. 1966. *The Hidden Dimension.* Garden City, NY: Doubleday and Co., Inc.

————. 1983. *The Dance of Life: The Other Dimension of Time.* Garden City, NY: Doubleday and Co., Inc.

————. 1976. *Beyond Culture.* Garden City, NY: Doubleday.

Hall, Edward.T., and Mildred Reed Hall. 1989. *Understanding Cultural Differences: Germans, French and Americans.* Yarmouth, ME: Intercultural Press.

Ham, Rose Marie, and David C. Mowery. 1998. Improving the Effectiveness of Public-Private R&D Collaboration: Case Studies at a US Weapons Laboratory. *Research Policy* 26 (6) (February):661–675.

Harrigan, Kathryn Rudie, and William H. Newman. 1990. Bases of Interorganization Co-Operation: Propensity, Power, Persistence. *Journal of Management Studies* 27 (4):417–434.

Harris, Marvin. 1968. *The Rise of Anthropological Theory: A History of Theories of Culture.* New York: Thomas Y. Crowell.

't Hart, Paul, Liesbet Heyse, and Arjen Boin. 2001. Guest Editorial Introduction New Trends in Crisis Management Practice and Crisis Management Research: Setting the Agenda. *Journal of Contingencies and Crisis Management* 9 (4):181–188.

Harvey, Jerry B. 1988. *The Abilene Paradox and Other Meditations on Management.* San Francisco: New Lexington Press.

Hoffman, Susanna M., and Anthony Oliver-Smith, eds. 2002. *Catastrophe & Culture: The Anthropology of Disaster.* Santa Fe, New Mexico: School of American Research Press.

Holland, Dorothy, and Naomi Quinn, eds. 1987. *Cultural Models of Language and Thought.* New York: Cambridge University Press.

Hord, Shirley M. 1986. A Synthesis on Research on Organizational Collaboration. *Educational Leadership* 43 (5):22–27.

Huber, George P. 1991. Organizational Learning: The Contributing Processes and the Literatures. *Organization Science* 2 (1) (February):88–115.

Hutt, Michael D., E.R. Stafford, B.A. Walker, and P.H. Reingen. 2000. Defining the Social Network of a Strategic Alliance. In *Sloan Management Review*, 51–62.

Ikkink, Karen Klein, and Theo Van Tilburg. 1999. Broken Ties: Reciprocity and Other Factors Affecting the Termination of Older Adults' Relationships. *Social Networks* 21 (2):131–146.

Iles, Paul, and Maurice Yolles. 2002. International Joint Ventures, HRM and Viable Knowledge Migration. *International Journal of Human Resource Management* 13 (4) (June):624–641.

Inkpen, Andrew C., and Steven C. Currall. 1998. Trust, Control and Learning in Joint Ventures: A Theoretical Framework. *Journal of International Management* 4:1–20.

Iyer, Karthik N.S. 2002. Learning in Strategic Alliances: An Evolutionary Perspective. *Academy of Marketing Science Review [Online]*10. http//www.amsreview.org/articles/iyer10-2002.pdf.

Johnson, Hazel, and Gordon Wilson. 2006. North-South/South-North Partnerships: Closing the Mutuality Gap. *Public Administration and Development* 26:71–80.

Johnsrud, Cristy S. 2002. Business Incubation: Emerging Trends for Profitability and Economic Development in the U.S., Central Asia and the Middle East. Washington, D.C.: *U.S. Department of Commerce, Technology Administration.*

——. 1994. Industry, University and Government Perspectives on Technology Transfer: Market Pull, Technology Push and Organizational Heterarchies. In *Management of Technology IV*. 341–348. Norcross, GA: Industrial Engineering and Management Press, Institute of Industrial Engineers.

Kanter, Rosabeth Moss. 1994. Collaborative Advantage: The Art of Alliances. *Harvard Business Review* 72 (4):96–108.

——. 1999. Change Is Everyone's Job: Managing the Extended Enterprise as a Globally Connected World. *Organisational Dynamics* 28 (1):7–23.

Kelley, Colleen, and Joyce Meyers. 1995. *The Cross-Cultural Adaptability Inventory*. Minneapolis, MN: National Computer Systems, 1995.

Kelly, James G., L. Sean Azelton, Cecile Lardon, Lynne O. Mock, S. Darius Tandon, and Mamie Thomas. 2004. On Community Leadership: Stories about Collaboration in Action Research. *American Journal of Community Psychology* 33 (3–4):205–216.

King Faisal Specialist Hospital and Research Centre Healthcare System. 2003. *Facts and Stats*. Riyadh: King Faisal Specialist Hospital and Research Centre Healthcare System.

Kirk, Jerome, and Marc L. Miller. 1986. *Reliability and Validity in Qualitative Research*. Beverly Hills, CA: Sage Publications.

Kleinman, Arthur. 1980. *Patients and Healers in the Context of Culture: An Exploration of the Borderland Between Anthropology, Medicine, and Psychiatry*. Berkley, CA: University of California Press.

Koehler, Gus A. 1995. What Disaster Response Management Can Learn from Chaos Theory. Conference Proceedings. California Research Bureau, California State Library, Sacramento, CA., May 18–19.

Kogut, Bruce. 1988. A Study of the Life Cycle of Joint Ventures. In *Cooperative Strategies in International Business*. 169–185, Lexington, MA: Lexington Books.

Kolb, David A. 1984. *Experiential Learning: Experience as the Source of Learning and Development*. New Jersey: Prentice Hall.

Lambert, Douglas M., Margaret A. Emmelhainz, and John T. Gardner. 1999. Building Successful Logistics Partnerships. *Journal of Business Logistics* 20 (1):165–181.

Lampl, Linda L., Cristy S. Johnsrud, and Susan Squires. 2004. Using Ethnographic Methods to Capture Tacit Knowledge Workshop. NCRADA-NAVAIR ORLANDO TSD, Orlando.

Landis, Dan, and Janet M. Bennett, and Milton J. Bennett, eds. 2004. *Handbook of Intercultural Training*. 3rd ed. Thousand Oaks, CA: Sage Publications.

Laszlo, Alexander L. 2001. Systems Research and Behavioral Science. *The Epistemological Foundations of Evolutionary Systems Design* 8 (4) (July):307–321.

Learned, Kevin E. 1992. What Happened Before the Organization? A Model of Organization Formation, *Entrepreneurship: Theory and Practice* 17 (1):39–49.

Lee, Y.S. 1996. Technology Transfer and the Research University: A Search for the Boundaries of University-Industry Collaboration. *Research Policy* 25:843–863.

Lévi-Strauss, Claude. 1971. *The Elementary Structures of Kinship*. Revised ed. London: Eyre and Spottis-woode.

Lewin, Kurt. 1947. Frontiers in Group Dynamics: II. Channels of Group Life; Social Planning and Action Research. *Human Relations* 1 (2):143–153.

Lieberman, Ann. 1986. Collaborative Research: Working With, Not Working On . . . *Educational Leadership* 43 (5):4–9.

Lorange, Peter, Johan Roos, and Peggy Simcic Brønn. 1992. Building Successful Strategic Alliances. *Long Range Planning* 25 (6):10–17.

Lowndes, Vivian, and Chris Skelcher. 1998. The Dynamics of Multi-Organizational Partnerships: An Analysis of Changing Modes of Governance. *Public Administration* 76 (2) (Summer):313–334.

Lui, Steven S., and Hang-yue Ngo. 2004. The Role of Trust and Contractual Safeguards on Cooperation in Non-equity Alliances. *Journal of Management* 30 (4):471–485.

MacCormack, Terry. 2001. Let's Get Personal: Exploring the Professional Persona in Healthcare. *The Qualitative Report*, 6 (3) (September).

Machado, Kit G. 1989–1990. Japanese Transnational Corporations in Malaysia's State Sponsored Heavy Industrialization Drive: The HICOM Automobile and Steel Projects. *Pacific Affairs* 62:504–531.

Macneil, Ian R. 1974. The Many Futures of Contract. *Southern California Law Review* 47:691–816.

Madhavan, Ravindranath, Balaji R. Koka, and John E. Prescott. 1998. Networks in Transition: How Industry Events (re)Shape Interfirm Relationships. *Strategic Management Journal* 19(5):439–460.

Malinowski, Bronislaw. 1988. The Group and the Individual in Functional Analysis. In *High Points in Anthropology*. New York: A.A. Knopf, 272–293.

Marrow, Alfred J. 1947. In Memoriam: Kurt Lewin, 1890–1947. *Sociometry* 10 (2):211–212.

Mauss, Marcel. 1990 [1923; 1925; 1954]. *Essai sur le don.* (English translation) *The Gift: Forms and Functions of Exchange in Archaic Societies*. London: Routledge.

McGivergan, D.A. Jr. 1995. Balanced Reciprocity and Peer Polity Interaction in the Late Prehistoric Southeastern United States. In *Native American Interactions: Multiscalar Analyses and Interpretations in the Eastern Woodlands*, 229–246. Knoxville, TN: University of Tennessee Press.

McLaurin, Shamla. 2003. Homophobia: An Autoethnographic Story. *The Qualitative Report* 8 (3) (September):481–486.

Meerwarth, Tracy L. 2004. Fueling and Driving Partnership Continuation: The Researchers' Role as Advocate, Society for Applied Anthropology Meetings, Dallas, TX.

Meerwarth, Tracy L., Elizabeth K. Briody, and DevadattaM. Kulkarni. 2005. Discovering the Rules: Folk Knowledge for Improving Partnerships. *Human Organization* 64 (3):286–302.

Meschi, P. 1997. Longevity and Cultural Differences of International Joint Ventures: Towards Time-Based Cultural Management. *Human Relations* 50 (2):211–228.

Mowery, David C., ed. 1998. Collaborative R&D: How Effective Is It? *Issues in Science and Technology* 15 (1) (Fall): 37–45.

Mowery, David C., ed. 1988. *International Collaborative Ventures in U.S. Manufacturing*. Cambridge, MA: Ballinger.

Murray, Vic. 1998. Interorganizational Collaboration in the Nonprofit Sector. In *International Encyclopedia of Public Policy and Administration*. 1192–1196 (2). Boulder, CO: Westview.

Myers, Randy. 1995. The Art of Partnering: How Silicon Graphics Grapples with more than a Dozen Strategic Alliances. *CFO*. Pp. 31–34, December: 26–27, 29, 31–34.

Nardi, Bonnie, Steve Whittaker, and Heinrich Schwarz. 2000. It's Not What You Know, It's Who You Know: Work in the Information Age. *First Monday* 5, no. 5.http// firstmonday.org/issues/issue5_5/nardi/index.html (accessed January 28, 2007).

Nettle, Daniel D., and Robin I.M. Dunbar. 1997. Social Markers and the Evolution of Reciprocal Exchange. *Current Anthropology* 38 (1):93–100.

Nordin, Fredrik. 2006. Identifying Intraorganisational and Interorganisational Alliance Conflicts—A Longitudinal Study of an Alliance Pilot Project in the High Technology Industry. *Industrial Marketing Management* 35:116–127.

Olie, René. 1994. Shades of Culture and Institutions in International Mergers. *Organization Studies* 15 (3):381–405.

Oliver-Smith, Anthony. 1996. Anthropological Research on Hazards and Disasters. *Annual Review of Anthropology* 25:303–328.

Ortony, Andrew. 1975. Why Metaphors Are Necessary and Not Just Nice. *Educational Theory* 25 (1):45–53.

Ouchi, William G. 1984. *The M-Form Society: How American Teamwork Can Capture the Competitive Edge*. Reading, MA: Addison-Wesley.

Park, Seung Ho, and Michael V. Russo. 1996. When Competition Eclipses Cooperation: An Event History Analysis of Joint Venture Failure. *Management Science* 42 (16) (June):875–891.

Parkhe, Arvind. 1993. 'Messy' Research, Methodological Predispositions, and Theory Development in International Joint Ventures. *Academy of Management Review* 18 (2):227–269.

———. 1991. Interfirm Diversity, Organizational Learning, and Longevity in Global Strategic Alliances. *Journal of International Business Studies* 22 (4):579–601.

Parker, B. and J.W. Selsky. 2004. Interface Dynamics in Cause-Based Partnerships: An Exploration of Emergent Culture. *Nonprofit and Voluntary Sector Quarterly* 33 (3):458–488.

Pike, Kenneth L. 1966. Emic and Etic Standpoints for the Description of Behavior. In *Communication and Culture*, 52–163. New York: Holt, Reinhart and Winston.

Polanyi, Karl. 1944. *The Great Transformation: The Political and Economic Origins of Our Time*. Boston, MA: Rinehart and Company.

Powell, Walter W., and Elisabeth S. Clemens. 1998. Introduction, in *Private Action and the Public Good*. 13–19. New Haven: Yale University Press.

Priess, Kenneth, Steven L. Goldman, and Roger N. Nagel. 1996. *Cooperate to Compete: Building Agile Business Relationships*. New York: Van Nostrand Reinhold.

Quarantelli, Enrico L. 1966. Organizations Under Stress. In *Symposium on Emergency Operations*, 3–19. Santa Monica, CA: Systems Development Corporation.

———. 1983. *Delivery of Emergency Medical Services in Disasters: Assumptions and Realities*. New York: Irvington Publishers, Inc.

Radcliffe-Brown, A. R. 1940. *Structure and Function in Primitive Society.* New York: The Free Press.

Reed-Danahay, Deborah. 1997. *Auto/Ethnography: Rewriting the Self and the Social.* Oxford and NY: Berg.

Ring, Peter Smith, and Andrew H. Van de Ven. 1994. Developmental Processes of Cooperative Interorganizational Relationships, *Academy of Management Review* 19 (1):90–118.

Ramsay, John. 2004. Trope Control: The Costs and Benefits of Metaphor Unreliability in the Description of Empirical Phenomena. *British Journal of Management* 15:143–155.

Romney, A. K., Susan C. Weller., and W. H. Batchelder. 1986. Culture and Consensus: A Theory of Culture and Informant Accuracy, *American Anthropologist* 88:313–351.

Rugh, William A. 2002. Education in Saudi Arabia: Choices and Constraints, *Middle East Policy* 9:40–55.

Sahlins, Marshall D. 1966. On the Sociology of Primitive Exchange. In *The Gift: An Interdisciplinary Perspective.* 26–38. Amsterdam: Amsterdam University Press.

———. 1972. Stone Age Economics. Berlin: Aldine de Gruyter.

Sastry, M. Anjali. 1997. Problems and Paradoxes in a Model of Punctuated Organizational Change. *Administrative Science Quarterly* 42 (2):237–275.

Schensul, Jean J., and Margaret D. LeCompte. 1999. *Designing and Conducting Ethnographic Research.* Vol. 1. Walnut Creek, CA: Altamira Press.

Schön, Donald A. 1983. *The Reflective Practitioner: How Professionals Think in Action.* New York: Basic Books.

Schrage, Michael. 1990. *Shared Minds: The New Technologies of Collaboration.* New York: Random House.

Schuler, Randall S. 2001. Human Resource Issues and Activities in International Joint Ventures. *International Journal of Human Resource Management* 12 (1)(February):1–52.

Selsky, John W., and Barbara Parker. 2005. Cross-Sector Partnerships to Address Social Issues: Challenges to Theory and Practice. *Journal of Management* 31 (6) (December):849–873.

Senge, Peter M. 1990. *The Fifth Discipline: The Art and Practice of the Learning Organization.* New York: Currency.

Sengir, Gülcin H., Robert T. Trotter, II, Elizabeth K. Briody, Devadatta M. Kulkarni, Linda B. Catlin, and Tracy L. Meerwarth. 2004. Modeling Relationship Dynamics in GM's Research-Institution Partnerships. *Journal of Manufacturing Technology Management* 15 (7):541–559.

Shortell, Stephen M., Ann Zukoski, Jeffrey A. Alexander, Gloria J. Bazzoli, Douglas A. Conrad, Romana Hasnain-Wynia, Shoshanna Sofaer, Benjamin Y. Chan, Elizabeth Casey, and Frances S. Margolin. 2002. Evaluating Partnerships for Community Health Improvements: Tracking the Footprints, *Journal of Health Politics, Policy and Law* 27 (1) (February):49–91.

Shupe, Jim. A Three-Part FAQ on Dream Catchers. July 26, 1995 submission to the Soc.culture.native Newsgroup. http://www.nativetech.org/dreamcat/dreamfaq.html (accessed March 18, 2005).

Simberloff, Daniel, and Tamar Dayan. 1991. The Guild Concept and the Structure of Ecological Communities. *Annual Review of Ecology and Systematics* 22:115–143.

Smith, Mike, and Mike Beazley. 2000. Progressive Regimes, Partnerships and the Involvement of Local Communities: A Framework for Evaluation. *Public Administration* 78 (4) (Winter):855–879.

Squires, Susan E., and Sarah C. Uhl. 1993. What About Collaboration? Conference paper presented at the American Anthropological Association Conference, Washington, D.C..

Squires, Susan E., Cynthia J. Smith, Lorna McDougal, and William R. Yeack. 2003. Inside Arthur Andersen: Shifting Values, Unexpected Consequences. *New Jersey: Financial Times Prentice Hall.*

Stake, Robert E. 1995. *The Art of Case Study Research.* Thousand Oaks, CA: Sage Publications.

Steward, Julian H. 1972. *Theory of Cultural Change: The Methodology of Multilinear Evolution.* Champaign, IL: University of Illinois Press.

Stone, C.N. 1993. Urban Regimes and the Capacity to Govern: A Political Economy Approach. *Journal of Urban Affairs,* 15 (1):1–28.

Storck, John, and Patricia A. Hill. 2000. Knowledge Diffusion Through 'Strategic Communities'. *Sloan Management Review*: 63–74.

Strauss, Anselm L., and Juliet Corbin. 1990. *Basics of Qualitative Research: Grounded Theory Procedures and Techniques.* Newbury Park, CA: Sage Publications.

Stuart, F. Ian. 1997. Supplier Alliance Success and Failure: A Longitudinal Dyadic Perspective. *International Journal of Operations and Production Management* 17 (5/6):539–558.

Swan, William W., and Janet L. Morgan. 1992. *Collaborating for Comprehensive Services for Young Children and Their Families: The Local Interagency Coordinating Council.* Baltimore: Paul H. Brookes.

Takahashi, Lois M., and Gayla Smutny. 2002. Collaborative Windows and Organizational Governance: Exploring the Formation and Demise of Social Service Partnerships. *Nonprofit and Voluntary Sector Quarterly* 31 (2):165–185.

Tenni, Colleen, Anne Smyth, and Carlene Boucher. 2003. The Researcher as Autobiographer: Analysing Data Written About Oneself. *The Qualitative Report* 8 (1) (March).

Tierney, Kathleen J., Michael K. Lindell, and Ronald W. Perry, eds. 2001. *Facing the Unexpected: Disaster Preparedness and Response in the United States.* Washington, D.C.: Joseph Henry Press.

Tocqueville, Alexis de. 1990. *[1840] Democracy in America.* Vol. II. New York, NY: Random House, Inc.

Tomlinson, Frances. 2005. Idealistic and Pragmatic Versions of the Discourse of Partnership. *Organization Studies* 26 (8):1169–1188.

Trotter, Robert T., II. 1997. Anthropological Midrange Theories in Mental Health Research: Selected Theories, Methods, and Systematic Approaches to At-Risk Populations. *Ethos* 25 (2):259–274.

Trotter, Robert T., II, and Elizabeth K. Briody. 2006. *"It's All About Relationships" Not Buying and Selling Ideas: Improving Partnering Success Through Reciprocity* 10540. Warren, MI: GM Research Publication, June 14.

Trotter, Robert T., II, Elizabeth K. Briody, Linda B. Catlin, Tracy L. Meerwarth, and Gülcin H. Sengir. 2004. *The Evolving Nature of GM R&D's Collaborative Research Labs: Learning From Stages and Roles*, 9907. Warren, MI: GM R&D Center Publication.

Trotter, Robert T., II, and Jean J. Schensul. 1998. Methods in Applied Anthropology, In *Handbook of Methods in Cultural Anthropology*, 691–736. Walnut Creek, CA: Altimira Press.

Tsang, Eric W. K. 1999. A Preliminary Typology of Learning in International Strategic Alliances. *Journal of World Business* 34 (3):211–229.

Tuckman, Bruce W. 1965. Developmental Sequence in Small Groups. *Psychological Bulletin* 63 (June):384–399.

Tuckman, Bruce W., and Mary Ann C. Jensen. 1977. Stages of Small Group Development Revisited. *Group and Organization Management* 2 (4):419–427.

Turpin, Tim. 1999. Managing the Boundaries of Collaborative Research: A Contribution from Cultural Theory. *International Journal of Technology Management* 18 (3–4):232–245.

University of New Hampshire Infrastructure Institute. http://www.ni2ciel.org. Center for Infrastructure Expertise, Critical Infrastructure Library, Glossary (accessed December 20, 2007).

Vaara, Eero. 2002. On the Discursive Construction of Success/Failure in Narratives of Post-Merger Integration. *Organization Studies* 23 (2):211–250.

Van Maanen, John, and Stephen R. Barley. 1984. Occupational Communities: Culture and Control in Organizations. *Research in Organizational Behavior* 6:287–365.

Vangen, Siv, and Chris Huxham. 2003. Enacting Leadership for Collaborative Advantage: Dilemmas of Ideology and Pragmatism in the Activities of Partnership Managers. *British Journal of Management* 14:S61–S76.

Vereecke, Ann, and Steve Muylle. 2006. Performance Improvement Through Supply Chain Collaboration in Europe. *International Journal of Operations and Production Management* 26 (11):1176–1198.

Wasserman, Stanley, and Katherine Faust. 1994. *Social Network Analysis: Methods and Applications*. Cambridge: Cambridge University Press.

Weber, Edward P., Nicholas P. Lovrich, and Michael Gaffney. 2005. Collaboration, Enforcement, and Endangered Species: A Framework for Assessing Collaborative Problem-Solving Capacity. *Society and Natural Resources* 18:677–698.

Weimann, Gabriel. 1980. Conversation Networks as Communication Networks, Abstract of PhD dissertation, University of Haifa, Israel.

Weismantel, Mary. 1995. Making Kin: Kinship Theory and Zumbagua Adoptions, *American Ethnologist* 22 (4):685–704.

Weller, Susan C. 1998. Structured Interviewing and Questionnaire Construction. In *Handbook of Methods in Cultural Anthropology*, 365–409. Walnut Creek, CA: AltaMira Press.

Weller, Susan C., and A. Kimball Romney. 1988. *Systematic Data Collection*. Beverly Hills, CA: Sage Publications.

Wenger, Etienne. 2003. Communities of Practice: Learning as a Social System. *Systems Thinker* WordNet ® 2.0, Princeton University. http://www.co-i-l.com/coil/knowledge-garden/cop/lss.shtml (accessed June, 1998).

Wenger, Etienne, Richard A. McDermott, and William M. Snyder. 2002. *Cultivating Communities of Practice: A Guide to Managing Knowledge*. Boston: Harvard Business School Press.

Wenzel, George W. 1995. Ningiqtuq: Resource Sharing and Generalized Reciprocity in Clyde River, Nunavut. *Arctic Anthropology* 32 (2):43–60.

Wilson, David T. 1995. An Integrated Model of Buyer-Seller Relationships. *Journal of the Academy of Marketing Science* 23 (4):335–345.

Wong, Alfred, Dean Tjosvold, and Pengzhu Zhang. 2005. Developing Relationships in Strategic Alliances: Commitment to Quality and Cooperative Independence. *Industrial Marketing Management* 34:722–731.

Yan, Aimin, and Ming Zeng. 1999. International Joint Venture Instability: A Critique of Previous Research, A Reconceptualization, and Directions for Future Research. *Journal of International Business Studies* 30 (2):395–413.

Yang, Xiaohua, and Marilyn Taylor. 1999. Assessing the Effects of Structural and Project Characteristics on R&D Strategic Alliances. *Journal of High Technology Management Research* 10 (1):105–122.

Yin, Robert K. 2003. Case Study Research: Design and Methods. *Applied Social Research Methods Series,* 3rd ed. Thousand Oaks, CA: Sage Publications. 5.

Index

joint work, 7, 9–11, 19–28, 32–34, 37–38, 41, 48, 50–53

key players, 9, 21–22, 25, 27, 29–32, 35, 50, 200, 202, 207. *See also* partnership role
KFSHRC. *See* King Faisal Specialist Hospital and Research Centre
kinship, 44–46, 143, 146–47, 151
knowledge and technology transfer, 177, 180–82, 191
KSA. *See* Saudi Arabia, Kingdom of

lessons learned, 3, 42, 87–88, 103–6, 110–11, 116–22, 140–41, 155–57, 175–76, 191–92, 195–216. *See also* best practices
longitudinal studies, 6, 78, 125, 149, 203

market exchange, 5, 15, 45–46, 48, 51–52, 59, 128, 207–8
MCB. *See* MCB Associates International
MCB Associates International, 75–83, 88, 204, 207–8, 214
meaning or meanings: cultural, 5, 46, 117, 138, 169, 171, 180, 200, 207, 216, 218; of the exchange, 46, 48–50; of the term partnership, 7, 76; of a metaphor, 12; of partnerships, 9, 15, 20, 32, 69, 105–6, 110, 176, 207, 211
metaphors, 6, 11–12, 44, 53, 77, 80, 94, 108, 126, 128, 139, 146–147, 150, 159–60, 168–169, 174, 178–79, 195, 212–18 (*see also* partnership symbols); car mirror, 108–9, 121, 214; dreamcatcher, 57–58, 60–62, 71–72, 215; ecological guild, 94–95, 99–100, 102, 104, 106, 213, 214; electrical transformer, 77–78, 81, 85, 213; high–performance automotive race track, 126–33, 135–41, 214–15; quilts and quilting, 216–18;

spiderweb, 143, 145, 147–48, 196 (*see also* web of relationships); three–dimensional puzzle, 177–78, 183, 185–87, 189, 212, 214; Uranium–236, 159–60, 174, 176
Microsoft Corporation, 66, 143, 146–49, 152–57, 196, 202, 215
Middle East, 184, 190
midrange theory, 4–5
mixed exchange systems, 51
model or models, 4, 59–62, 76, 133, 135, 143, 145, 162, 171, 213; cultural model of partnerships, 7, 10–11, 13, 15–54, 195–96, 205, 208–10, 216 (*see also* cultural models theory); evolutionary, 78, 81 (*see also* partnership evolution); experiential learning (*see* experiential learning); kinship, 146–147; of cultural interactions and reciprocity, 48–49; of relationship effectiveness. *See* relationship effectiveness
modeling. *See* systems dynamics modeling
modernization, 177, 179, 183, 185, 191, 210
multilevel cultural context, 170
multiplicity: of allegiances, 198; of partnerships, 198; of relationships, 197
mutual: agreement, 93, 101, 113, 125; benefit, 9, 81, 83 (*see also* win–win outcomes); understanding, 117, 179

Native Americans, 57, 69
NAVAIR TSD. *See* Naval Air Systems Command, Training Systems Division
Naval Air Systems Command, Training Systems Division, 115, 121
Navy, US., 114–16, 118, 120–21
negotiated working culture, 125–26, 135, 138
negotiation, 17, 22, 51–52, 70, 117, 126–127, 130, 132, 136, 139–41,

164, 167–68, 173, 177, 180, 192, 199, 207, 209, 212

network theory. *See* social network theory

nonprofit sector, 7, 59–60, 62, 71–72, 128

nuclear family. *See* family

Ojibwe, 57

organizational fitness, 13

organizational and cultural differences, 8, 52, 92, 209. *See also* culture differences

partner autonomy or independence, 6, 71, 73, 91–106, 111, 120, 125, 178, 198–99

partnering. *See* partnership

Partnership: across sectors, 7; challenges, tensions, or difficulties of, 9, 21, 37, 47, 52, 69–70, 76, 80–81, 83, 85, 105, 119, 121, 125, 130, 139, 145, 161, 167, 175, 177, 189, 201, 209, 211, 214; complexity of, 5–6, 21, 26, 30, 35, 57, 70, 174, 198, 218; continuation, 27, 78, 88, 102, 115–116, 125, 133, 139–41, 154, 173, 175, 176n1, 180, 184–85, 190, 192, 202, 205–6, 215; cultural model of, 4, 6, 10–11, 15, 17, 20, 32, 37, 39, 44, 47, 49, 50, 208 (*see also* cultural models theory); culture, 4, 8–10, 12–13, 20, 23, 75, 92, 111, 113, 116, 118, 127, 134–35, 138, 141, 144, 157, 185–86, 196, 213, 215–16 (*see also* negotiated working culture; *see also* hybrid culture); cycle of (*see* partnership life cycle); definition of, 6–7, 32, 46–48, 50, 63–64, 76, 102, 126, 144, 162, 178–79, 195–97, 206–7; difficulties (*see* partnership challenges); dissolution (*see* partnership termination); dynamics, ix, 4–6, 8–12, 15, 17–19, 26, 28, 32–33,

35–38, 46–50, 52, 154, 196–97, 199, 203, 205, 211; evolution, 19–21, 28, 31, 38–39, 50, 78, 80–81, 83, 88, 129, 203, 216, 218 (*see also* evolutionary theory); failure of, 8, 51, 72, 82, 85, 114, 192, 198, 205–6, 215; fitness, 13; functioning, ix, 3, 16, 25, 81, 95, 97, 99–101, 189, 197, 200–2, 205, 208, 210–1, 214; goals, 3, 6–10, 14, 16, 22, 25, 33, 35, 51–52, 57–59, 61, 64–66, 68, 73, 76–83, 86–88, 92–93, 96, 99, 101–2, 117, 119–20, 125–27, 135, 139, 143–45, 147–49, 153, 157, 161, 178–179, 182, 190–92, 200–1, 204–7, 209–10, 212, 216, 218–19 (*see also* partnership motivation); issues of (*see* partnership challenges); learning. (*see* lessons learned; *see* best practices); life cycle of, 3, 5, 9, 15–16, 18, 20–21, 24, 27–30, 32, 37–38, 41, 50–52, 58, 146, 149, 153, 157, 166, 202–5, 207, 213; life spans of, 203; maintenance, xi, 3, 9, 13, 15, 18–19, 21, 24–25, 28, 33, 42–43, 45–48, 50–52, 59, 64, 77–78, 83, 88, 95, 109–11, 113, 118, 120–122, 125, 129, 132, 136, 139–41, 143, 145–46, 156, 160, 167, 169, 174–75, 185, 199, 202, 205, 207, 213–14, 217–18 (*see also* relationship maintenance); modification, 3, 9–10, 13, 24, 27, 43, 47, 52, 119, 202, 206; motivation of, ix, 3, 7–8, 58–59, 61–62, 92–93, 110, 121, 136–38, 159, 181–82 (*see also* partnership goals); outcomes (*see* partnership performance); performance, 4, 10–11, 72, 94, 100, 104, 108, 114, 117–18, 120–21, 126–27, 129–133, 135, 139, 165, 175, 204–5, 208, 212–14 (*see also* partnership success; *see also* win–win outcomes); phases (*see* stages); power, 5, 9, 52, 70, 80–81,

About the Authors

Elizabeth K. Briody
Elizabeth Briody is a technical fellow and cultural anthropologist at General Motors Research and Development where she has been employed since 1985. Her area of expertise is organizational culture. Her recent ethnographic research projects have focused on perceptions of an ideal plant culture, examining stakeholders perspectives on Integrated Health, and improving the effectiveness of research partnerships, and cultural issues pertaining to global product programs. She received the French *Baccalauréat* in *philosophie et lettres*, and BA, MA, and PhD degrees in anthropology. She is an adjunct professor at Michigan State, Northern Arizona, and Wayne State universities. She is also past president of the National Association for the Practice of Anthropology, a section of the American Anthropological Association. She enjoys spending time with her husband and children, gardening, making crafts, and collecting nativity sets from around the world.

Robert T. Trotter, II
Bob Trotter is a Regent's professor of anthropology at Northern Arizona University. His primary research interests are in business anthropology (collaboration designs, cultural models for work process improvements, and health issues) and medical anthropology (HIV-AIDS, substance abuse, traditional healing, disabilities, and cross-cultural health care delivery programs). His research includes work on community and organizational collaborations for the World Health Organization, the U.S. Centers for Disease Control and Prevention (CDC), the National Institutes of Health, and General Motors Corporation. He has also focused on the applied uses of anthropological theory (cognitive anthropology, cultural models, social network analysis, and culture-change theory) and the application of ethnographic methods in applied research. His publications include several

books and more than 125 articles in scientific journals, plus an as-yet unpublished cook book entitled *The Hungry Husband's Survival Guide*. Recipes are available upon request.

Patricia Sachs

Patricia Sachs is the founder and CEO of Social Solutions, Inc., a business that builds sustainable organizations. SSI's global team works in partnership with organizations that focus on understanding the wicked problems encountered in global work and leveraging the value of diverse global perspectives to develop a strategic innovative edge. Dr. Sachs holds master's, PhD, and post-doctoral degrees from the City University of New York in economic anthropology and cognitive-developmental psychology. She is coinventor on two patents for visualizing and modeling work. The work of Social Solutions has been highlighted in publications including *Strategy and Business*, *Marketing News*, *Computer World*, *Scientific American*, *Fast Company*, *Business Week*, *Wired*, the *Washington Post*, *Social Science Monthly Review*, and *Communications of the ACM*. www.social-solutions.com.

Cristy S. Johnsrud

Cris Johnsrud is president of Pathfinder Research, Inc., a firm providing research, consulting, and management-support services in the area of technology-based economic development. Cris holds PhD, MA, and BA degrees in cultural anthropology and works with engineers, program managers, and business executives to transform ideas, discoveries, and inventions into commercial products and new business enterprises. She partners with others to consult and to produce training workshops in technology transfer, knowledge management, and transition management for entrepreneurs. Publications include an international review of business incubation, a comprehensive report on Florida's innovation economy, an exploration of storytelling in organizations, and more than fifty papers and reports on organizational linkages, corporate culture, and organizational dynamics. She is a past board member, program chair, and corresponding section editor of the National Association for the Practice of Anthropology, a section of the American Anthropological Association, and a fellow of the Society for Applied Anthropology and of the International Association for Management of Technology. Crus and her husband raise champion Australian Shepherd dogs, one of which is also a therapy dog at nursing homes.

Mary Beauregard

Mary Beauregard is president of MCB Associates International, an intercultural training firm that designs and delivers cultural-training workshops for corporations conducting global business. She has developed training programs on countries in Asia, Europe, Latin America, and the Middle East and has recently designed a program for real estate professionals seeking a better understanding of cultural differences in order to service their international customers. Her client base spans many industries, including automotive, apparel, media promotion, and the U.S. government. Mary and her team developed a model for applying cultural theory to the practical needs of their corporate clients, and they continue to work with new clients and trainers to create customized cultural workshops for specific business practices. She has recently written a series of Cultural Insights for an international communications firm in the Midwest. Seven beautiful grandchildren are the joy and focus of her spare time.

Linda L. Lampl

Linda Lampl, PhD, is a principal and cofounder of Lampl Herbert Consultants (LHC), a woman-owned small business co-founded with partner Thomas A. Herbert, PhD, in Tallahassee, Florida, in 1978. Lampl serves as working CEO and president of the corporation and as a consultant in each of LHC's core service areas: organizations and business management, public policy, the environment, and new technologies. LHC's clients include federal, state, and local governments; U.S. military research and development organizations; and private industry. Lampl is past treasurer of the National Association for the Practice of Anthropology, a section of the American Anthropological Association. She received her BA and MS degrees in anthropology and a PhD in communication research from Florida State University; her doctoral work included an ethnography of the creation of public-water policy in Florida. She recently contributed to the *Harmful Algal Research and Response: A Human Dimensions Strategy*, edited by Marybeth Bauer, and coedited *Letters from the Future, Linking Students and Teaching with the DIVERSITY of Everyday Life* with Deborah A. Brunson and Brenda Jarmon (2006). Lampl's life theme is partnerships; she practices in a range of settings that include her daily family life, the work environment, and communities.

Susan E. Squires

Susan Squires, PhD, was trained as a traditional cultural anthropologist. She earned her PhD from Boston University in 1990. Since that time, she has designed and conducted ethnographic studies for a range of business and corporate clients from manufacturers to high-tech companies such as Yahoo, Sprint, *San Jose Mercury News*, Laerdal, SC Johnson, and the American Heart Association. Her book, *Creating Breakthrough Ideas* (2002), co-edited with Bryan Byrne, documents her research theory and methodology and chronicles the application of these methods as used by other anthropologists in business and design.

Christina Wasson

Christina Wasson is an associate professor in the Department of Anthropology at the University of North Texas. She is a linguistic anthropologist whose work explores the intersections of communication, organizations, and technology. Her findings are based on extensive linguistic and ethnographic research in corporations. Christina Wasson received her PhD from Yale University. She is a fellow at both the Texas Center for Digital Knowledge and the Center for Collaborative Organizations at UNT. She has published articles and book chapters in the fields of anthropology, organization studies, and discourse studies on topics such as language use in organizations, team decision-making, and virtual group-work. She has also been a manager in several consulting firms. Her efforts to bring insights from linguistic anthropology into dialogue with organizational phenomena have led to her being selected for roles such as keynote speaker at the First International and Interdisciplinary Symposium on Communication within Organizations; invited speaker at the Human Resources Institute; and invited speaker at the International Conference on Language in Organizational Change and Transformation. She is on the advisory board of the Ethnographic Praxis in Industry Conference.

Julia C. Gluesing

Julia Gluesing is a business and organizational anthropologist and research professor in Industrial and Manufacturing Engineering at Wayne State University. Julia also serves as the associate director of the Institute for Information Technology and Culture (IITC) and is an adjunct professor of anthropology. In her current assignment in engineering, she is responsible for the development of a global engineering management master's program for working engineers. She is working with Tsinghua University and Tongji University in Beijing and Shanghai, China, on the delivery of degree and non-degree programs. Julia teaches the management of technology change and virtual teaming in global organizations and serves as a leadership project advisor in the Ford and Visteon Engineering Management Masters Program (EMMP). In her research, she is the principal investigator on a National Science Foundation grant, the "Digital Diffusion Dashboard," to study the diffusion of innovation across the global enterprise by tapping into an organization's information-technology infrastructure. Julia has been a principal investigator or coprincipal investigator on five previous National Science Foundation research grants. She has published professionally, most recently as a contributing author in *Virtual Teams that Work: Creating Conditions for Virtual Team Effectiveness* (Jossey-Bass 2003), *Handbook of Managing Global Complexity* (Blackwell 2003), and *Crossing Cultures: Lessons from Master Teachers* (Routledge 2004).

Kenneth R. Riopelle

Ken Riopelle is a co-founder and principal of Cultural Connections. He received a PhD in adult education from the University of Michigan, an MA from Eastern Michigan University in educational leadership, and a BA in communication from Michigan State University. He is a faculty member and leadership project adviser in the Ford Motor Company and Wayne State University Engineering Management master's program, where he teaches the management of technology change in the global enterprise. His professional experience spans over twenty-five years using qualitative and quantitative research designs and methods to help companies develop and target their products and services and to evaluate their performance with customers.

Kenneth R. Chelst

Kenneth Chelst received a BA from Yeshiva College, an MS in operations research from New York University, and a PhD in operations research from MIT. He is currently chair of the Department of Industrial and Manufacturing Engineering of Wayne State University. His research interests include structured decision making in engineering management and the effect of globalization on the engineering and manufacturing management functions. Dr. Chelst has received a dozen teaching awards with many of them coming from Ford Motor Company for his teaching of structured decision making. Dr. Chelst played a lead role in the development of the Engineering Management Masters Program, which has achieved national recognition. This program emphasizes team projects and providing the corporate sponsor with immediate return on educational-investment dollars. He also consults with Urban Science Applications Inc., a worldwide leader in the planning of new car dealership networks. Dr. Chelst is a member of INFORMS (Institute for Operations Research and the Management Sciences) and is directing an ongoing project to develop operations-research activities for use in the high school math classroom.

Alan R. Woodliff

Alan Woodliff is the retired director of Advanced Business Development for Visteon Corporation, where he was responsible for the strategic direction of the company's global advanced-product development, including oversight of the advanced development of a range of automotive products and technologies designed to help automakers deliver exceptional consumer value. Dr. Woodliff also served as the codirector of the University Relations Committee and the Wayne State University/Visteon EMMP program. Dr. Woodliff's automotive career spans thirty years with a variety of global experiences, including engineering and manufacturing, sales, planning, program management, and quality. Dr. Woodliff's career began as a product engineer in 1970 with General Electric's Aircraft Engine Group in Ohio. From 1971 to 1973, he served in the U.S. Navy and then was hired by Ford Motor Company in Dearborn, Michigan in 1973. Dr. Woodliff worked for Ford until 2000, holding a series of engineering design and management positions, including advanced-product engineer, program manager in the United Kingdom, quality manager, manufacturing-engineering manager, and automotive-components manager for the Lincoln LS and Jaguar programs. From 2000 to 2006 at Visteon, Dr. Woodliff has held the positions of director of Climate Sales, director of the Lincoln Customer Business Unit, and director of Advanced Business Development. Born in Wyandotte, Michigan, Dr. Woodliff holds a bachelor's degree in aerospace engineering, a master's degree, and a doctorate in mechanical engineering, and a master's degree in business administration, all from the University of Michigan. He is a member of the board of trustees of Children's Hospital of Michigan and the executive advisory board of the Mechanical Engineering Department of the University of Michigan. Dr. Woodliff lives in Dearborn, Michigan, with his wife and children.

Tracey Lovejoy
Tracey Lovejoy is an ethnographer and user-experience strategist who has worked at Microsoft Corporation since 2001. Her ethnographic projects have been wide in range, and she has worked with demographics such as baby boomers and people who work in large organizations or live in locations such as North America, Europe, Asia, and South America. Most of Ms. Lovejoy's projects consider how various technologies, such as the mobile phone or personal computer, integrate into people's daily lives. She then integrates the behaviors, practices, needs, and issues that emerge during fieldwork into the design and implementation of products. In addition, Tracey is the cofounder of the Ethnographic Praxis in Industry Conference, a conference that brings together people who consider the theoretical and methodological development of ethnography in industry practice. She received her BA in international relations from UCLA and her MA in social science from the University of Chicago, where she focused on anthropology and ethnographic methods. In her free time, she enjoys traveling to new places, frequenting the dog park, reading, and spending time with friends and family.

Christine Z. Miller

Christine Miller is a PhD candidate in anthropology and management at Wayne State University. Her dissertation research incorporates an ethnographic study of the role of culture in mediating the relationship between formalization and innovation in product development at a Tier One automotive supplier. An interest in exploring how sociality and culture influence the design and development of new products is reflected in Christine's research and teaching. She has conducted field research and analysis for Motorola Labs and currently teaches in the graduate program in design management at the Savannah College of Art and Design.

Amy Goldmacher

Amy Goldmacher is a PhD candidate in the department of Anthropology at Wayne State University in Detroit, Michigan. She received her MA in anthropology from Wayne State and her BA in anthropology with honors from Grinnell College in Iowa. Prior to attending graduate school, Amy spent six years in the publishing industry, working in the editorial, marketing, and sales divisions of a college textbook publisher. Currently, Amy is a teaching and research assistant in the department of Industrial and Manufacturing Engineering at Wayne State. Some recent automotive industry projects include an assessment of cost-reduction processes and an implementation strategy for a new engineering process. In addition to conducting research on the relationship of technology and culture and diffusion of innovations, she is improving how anthropology students receive training to enable them to find jobs in industry after graduation.

Dr. Jörg Siebert

Dr. Jörg Siebert is a consultant at Siemens Management Consulting, the internal strategic consultancy of Siemens. He received his doctorate degree in business administration and management from the Technische Universität in Munich, Germany. His dissertation discussed stability and change aspects in connection with leadership systems and was based on a two-year Benchmarking study with forty global players. Jörg taught in the business school at the Technische Universität in Munich.

Tara A. Eaton

Tara Eaton is the research manager of the Institute for Information Technology and Culture and a PhD candidate in business and organizational anthropology at Wayne State University in Detroit, Michigan. Her dissertation research focuses on the role of culture in global information technology offshoring and outsourcing partnerships. Her other research interests include

U.S.-Asia business relationships, the diffusion of technology, organizational and work culture, and the practice of ethnography in industry. She has an MA in anthropology and a BA in both English and anthropology.

Dale C. Brandenburg

Dale Brandenburg is director of the Institute for Learning and Performance Improvement at Wayne State University in Detroit, Michigan. He specializes in needs assessment, evaluation, and organizational learning. His primary publications are concerned with training evaluation and the implementation of workplace-performance models. He received his PhD degree in educational measurement and statistics from the University of Iowa.

Ann T. Jordan

Ann T. Jordan is associate dean and professor of anthropology in the College of Public Affairs and Community Service at the University of North Texas in Denton, Texas. She holds a BA degree in religion as well as MA and PhD degrees in anthropology. Her research interests include organizational anthropology, especially organizational culture, work-group and work-process analysis, and transnational business; Middle East studies, especially globalization and transnational business in Saudi Arabia; and North American Indian studies, especially traditional religion and change, and urban Indian communities. Her most recent books are *The Creek Indian Medicine Way* (2002), co-authored with David Lewis, Jr., and *Business Anthropology* (2003). She is currently writing a book on modernization and globalization in Saudi Arabia.

Tracy L. Meerwarth

Tracy Meerwarth is a cultural anthropologist who has worked as a contract researcher for General Motors Research and Development since 2001. She holds an MA in anthropology from Northern Arizona University in Flagstaff. Her professional interests include cognitive anthropology, cultural modeling, and the intersection of space and culture. Tracy's research at GM R&D examines the complex dynamics of partnerships and informal rule-making behavior as GM partners with private-sector suppliers. She and her colleagues hold a U.S. patent on modeling collaborative relationships. She also has helped build a cognitive cultural model of ideal automotive-plant culture in order to increase relationship effectiveness and collaboration. Tracy has published several scholarly papers and has presented at the Society for Applied Anthropology and American Anthropological Association annual meetings. She is a competitive golfer and triathlete.

Linda M. Miller

Linda Miller recently retired as the director of manufacturing for Ford Motor Company's Powertrain Operations. In that capacity, she was responsible for nine plants in Canada, the United States, and Mexico. Ms. Miller holds a BS degree from Truman State University in mathematics, an MA degree in mathematics from the University of Kansas, and an MBA from the University of Detroit Mercy. During her more than thirty years at Ford Motor Company, Ms. Miller held a variety of positions in manufacturing, strategic planning, and supplier quality. She was the first woman at Ford to run a manufacturing plant and is recognized as a pioneer woman in the industry. She is the recipient of numerous awards including the 1997 Magnificent Seven Award from the Business and Professional Women's Club/USA for pioneering in the automotive industry; the 2000 and 2005 Automotive News 100 Leading Women Award, and in 2004, the Spirit of Leadership Award from Women's Automotive Association International. She is presently the chairperson of the University of Detroit Mercy Business School Advisory Board and the president of the Truman State University Foundation Board of Directors.

Gülcin H. Sengir

Gülcin Sengir is a computer scientist with General Motors Research and Development. Her research interests include knowledge systems, serious games, and visual analytics. Her recent projects focus on understanding and modeling interactions on the plant floor and in GM's research partnerships. She holds a bachelor's degree in chemistry and a master's in computer science.

Nelle Steele

Nelle Steele is an ethnographer working in product development at Microsoft Corporation. As part of the User Experience team in the Windows Mobile and Tailored Platforms Division, her work spans understanding people and their mobility and technology-adoption behaviors in a variety of contexts, and then driving those findings into product design. Before coming to Microsoft in 2000, Nelle earned master's degrees in both cultural anthropology and industrial relations from the University of Wisconsin Madison.